insult to
intelligence

Also by Frank Smith

The Genesis of Language
(edited, with George A. Miller)
Understanding Reading
(three editions)
Psycholinguistics and Reading
Comprehension and Learning
Reading Without Nonsense
(published under the title *Reading* in the U.K.)
Writing and the Writer
Essays into Literacy
Awakening to Literacy
(edited, with Hillel Goelman and Antoinette A. Oberg)
Joining the Literacy Club

insult to
intelligence
the bureaucratic invasion of our classrooms
frank smith

HEINEMANN
Portsmouth, NH

Heinemann Educational Books, Inc.
70 Court Street Portsmouth, N.H. 03801
Offices and agents throughout the world

Copyright © 1986 by Frank Smith
First paperback edition 1988
This edition published by arrangement
with William Morrow & Co., Inc.

Library of Congress Cataloging-in-Publication Data
Smith, Frank, 1928—
  Insult to intelligence : the bureaucratic invasion of our
classrooms / Frank Smith. — 1st softcover ed.
      p. cm.
  Reprint. Originally published: New York : Arbor House, c1986.
  Bibliography: p.
  Includes index.
  ISBN 0-435-08478-X (soft)
  1. Teaching. 2. Instructional systems—United States.
3. Learning, Psychology of. 4. Education—Aims and objectives.
I. Title.
LB1025.2.S59 1988   88-8082
371.1' 02—dc19   CIP

Cover designed by Wladislaw Finne

Printed in the United States of America
10 9 8 7 6 5 4 3 2

CONTENTS

PREFACE

For nearly twenty years I have studied two conflicting realities. One is the reality of the human brain, and especially of how children and adults learn. Children learn constantly, and so do adults—when they have not become persuaded that they can't learn. The time bomb in every classroom is that students learn exactly what they are taught. They may not learn what their teachers think they are teaching them, but their teachers are probably not teaching what they think they teach. To see what students learn in school, look at how they leave school. If they leave thinking that reading and writing are difficult and pointless, that mathematics is confusing, that history is irrelevant, and that art is a bore, then that is what they have been taught. People learn what is demonstrated to them, and this reality will not change to suit the convenience of politicians and educational administrators.

The contrasting reality I have studied is that of how schools and other educational institutions teach, and especially of how the prepackaged instructional programs and tests, which are supposed to promote learning, work. Educational systems are quite a different reality from that of the human brain. And the two realities are in conflict.

Despite romantic notions to the contrary, schools and universities are not good places for learning. North America leads the world in the destruction of its educational institutions. The natural intelligence of children and adults is ignored and insulted. The dedication and expertise of teachers is undermined and circumvented. And the devastation is caused by politicians, administrators, and educators blinded by a bureaucratic myth.

The myth is that learning can be guaranteed if instruction is delivered systematically, one small piece at a time, with frequent tests to ensure that students and teachers stay on task. Elaborate instructional programs and systems are produced, glossily packaged and extravagantly advertised, claiming impossible levels of effectiveness and playing continuously on parental guilt. Detailed "objectives" are specified for the particular module of instruction that teachers should be engaged in at any particular time, and equally detailed tests are imposed to ensure conformity to the chosen path, no matter how much confusion, frustration, and despair result.

There is an alternative, but it is everywhere under attack. Sensitive and imaginative teachers inspire learning of lasting depth and complexity—a love of learning itself—in students with all kinds of interests and abilities. But success like this is achieved only when teacher and student have the mutual respect and trust that is the basis of all effective learning. Establishing such respect is difficult enough under the widespread constraints of overcrowded classrooms, limited budgets, inadequate teacher training, and grudging recognition and remuneration. The respect is impossible when classroom activities are controlled by outside "authorities" who destroy the sensitivity and imagination of teachers, who know little of the way worthwhile learning occurs and nothing of the individuals supposed to be doing the learning.

Trivialized and coercive programmatic instruction is expected to produce "quality education." The myth is founded upon a misguided and irrelevant theory of learning and the awesome presumption that experts outside the classroom can make better decisions about helping students learn than teachers who can actually see and talk with the students. The result is the ritualistic teaching of nonsense, educational junk food, instruction with no significant intellectual content. The issue is essentially political, a question of who will control how students are taught: teachers or programmers.

The struggle for the control of education is so pervasive and insidious that most teachers, parents, and students are unaware that it is taking place. Programmatic instruction has become entrenched in countless textbooks, course outlines, and curriculums, from kindergarten to college. To many people, programmatic instruction—learning one specified thing at a time—*is* education. Programs are credited with any learning that students and teachers are able to achieve, and students and teachers are blamed for the failures of programs.

The struggle has been in progress for thirty years—and it will be decided in the next few years by the way in which computers are used in education.

The computer is the ultimate weapon of instructional programmers, and in many people's minds at least, it is a device to take the place of teachers. Anyone who believes that students learn best from systematic instruction and tests can say goodbye to teachers. For dispensing programmatic instruction, computers are cheaper and more efficient than humans.

In *Insult to Intelligence* I will catalog stupidities committed by ignorant though often well-intentioned people who impose meaningless tasks and demeaning tests on students in the expectation that worthwhile learning will occur. But I will also demonstrate the fluent way in which all children—and older students—are naturally capable of learning. And I will show how teachers and parents can protect students from programmatic instruction, ensuring that they are free to reach for far higher levels of accomplishment than programs and tests ever aim.

Above all, I want to provide ammunition for the political battle that teachers and parents must wage if education is not to fall totally into the hands of the outsiders who harness and constrain the brains of students. I became involved in this battle when my own children first went to school, and I saw eager minds dulled and diverted by the meaningless classroom rituals and materials that had already begun to insinuate themselves into instruction. I spent three years with leading international researchers at Harvard University's Center for Cognitive Studies, exploring the incredible intellectual achievements of all young children, starting at birth, as they effortlessly learn what no one deliberately tries to teach them about their language, their culture, and the world. And for the next two years I worked with large federally-funded educational research and development projects in which well-meaning experts prepared tests and instructional programs based on theories that were the exact opposite of how I had discovered people actually learn. I saw the beginning of the massive endeavors to employ irrelevant space age technology in the reduction of education to fragmented and decontextualized trivialities. I discovered the brutally simple motivation behind the development and imposition of all systematic instructional programs and tests—a lack of trust that teachers can teach and that children can learn.

Most teachers are under intense and relentless pressure to

follow prescribed instructional procedures, regulated and supervised by state and federal authorities rather than by local school boards and parent-teacher associations. Bureaucrats have taken over. The management of schools was traditionally the domain of the communities in which they were situated. Now the content of the curriculum, how the curriculum is to be taught, and even the selection of classroom materials, is largely determined by distant government employees. The deadening influence starts at the top, and the decline in standards and expectations seeps inexorably down.

For the past fifteen years I have been privileged to see the other side of the picture. I have worked in schools and in colleges of education with thousands of classroom teachers and with their students of all ages, in North and South America, in Europe, and in Australasia. Everywhere, I have seen it demonstrated that students know how to learn and that teachers can be trusted to teach, even while the students and teachers were struggling under prescribed instructional regimes of unrelieved tedium and irrelevance.

Insult to Intelligence is a reflection of everything I have learned from children, students, and teachers. Their situation is critical and urgent. Our schools should not remain places where the enormous potential of the human brain is systematically eroded, and possibly destroyed. The invasion of education by instructional programmers must be turned back now.

My thanks to Mary-Theresa Smith,
who contributed
many educational and editorial insights.

CHAPTER 1

Meet the R-bbit

Meet the enemy, as I met it at the 1983 convention of the International Reading Association, held appropriately enough in the heart of Mickey Mouse land at Anaheim, California. Its name was R-bbit (which I pronounce "are-bit").

The reading convention is the largest educational conference in the world, attended annually by nearly 15,000 teachers, researchers, and educational administrators, all looking for something new to put into classrooms. The sale of instructional materials is much bigger business for publishers than the sale of fiction and other general trade books, and the reading convention regularly attracts over 500 exhibitors. The exhibitors range from lone entrepreneurs promoting their bright ideas or hopes for fortune to the largest international communications conglomerates. In recent years the number of displays of computer-based instructional programs and materials at educational conferences has grown almost to equal that of old-fashioned "printware." But the prescriptions and the hucksterism remain the same.

I encountered the r-bbit when I investigated why crowds of

1

teachers were consistently gathering in one area of the exhibition hall. The teachers were, I found, observing a demonstration of a computerized reading lesson. They were gazing at a cartoon representation of a desert scene on the screen of a small desktop computer. There was a bright blue sky above, a yellow landscape below, a few cacti, and in the center of it all a rabbit with large floppy years and a mischievous look. In large print on the side of the screen were the letters r-bbit. A flashing message at the bottom of the screen was appealing: "Please tell me your name." (And if the appropriate accessories are purchased, the computer will speak its remarks aloud.)

The demonstrator was trying to persuade someone to oblige this friendly computer. Eventually a teacher typed "Cynthia" on the keyboard, and the computer immediately responded, "Can you fill in the missing letter in r-bbit, Cynthia?"

The demonstrator urged the teacher to give the wrong answer. (Promoters of educational programs are always anxious to demonstrate the remarkable things their systems do when mistakes are made.) "Type K," said the demonstrator helpfully. Cynthia typed K.

Bells rang, lights flashed, the rabbit's ears drooped, and the computer announced, "Too bad, Cynthia. K is not the right answer. Would you like to try again?"

"Type the right answer this time," suggested the demonstrator. "Type A." The teacher typed A.

Once again bells rang and lights flashed, but now the rabbit's ears perked up and it began munching on a carrot that magically appeared from off-screen.

"Well done, Cynthia," said the computer. "A is the correct answer. Your score so far today is 50 percent. Your score last time was 0 percent. That is a 50 percent improvement. Congratulations. Would you like to try another one?"

I looked around. The entire audience of professional educators was entranced, though no one more than the demonstrator, who must have seen the r-bbit scores of times before.

I have not selected r-bbit as a particularly ridiculous component in an inept and improbable program. The r-bbit was selected by the demonstrator, who presumably knew from experience how to appeal to teachers and school administrators. The r-bbit was just part of one instructional disk. All of the major educational publishers today—and many manufacturers of computer systems and of the "software" that determines what computers do—produce instructional software in glossily packaged sets. These packages may include scores of computer disks and supporting materials and cost $2,000 or more per child. But the packages claim to provide everything a child requires during years of schooling to learn to read and to write, to learn math, history, geography, science, and any other subject. They can look like bargains. There are over 10,000 educational software programs on the market today. I have chosen the r-bbit as the symbol of the programmatic approach to instruction which believes that children learn by practicing one systematic thing after another—"Fill in the blank and find out whether you're right or wrong." Millions of r-bbits can be found in the workbooks, activity sheets, and computerized lessons that claim to teach the facts and skills of language, arithmetic, science, social studies, art, and every other subject under the academic sun. Fill-in-the-blank (or indicate the right one-word answer, which is the same thing) is by far the most common form of instruction in schools today.

The theory behind the r-bbit and behind all of its short-right-answer relations is that if learners are presented with one item after another and tested to ensure that each item is learned before they can move on to the next step, then sufficient learning will accumulate to teach a skill. In advertising, in formal discussions, and even in the professional literature of educational psychology, the technique of the r-bbit is known as "teach and test." More bluntly, program developers themselves often refer to the system as "drill and test." To teachers who have become aware of its consequences, the method is known as "drill and kill."

The R-bbit at work

Every child in regular classrooms in the Montebello Unified School District near Los Angeles from kindergarten through fourth grade works through eighteen "levels" of the Macmillan primary grade "Series R" reading program. So do hundreds of thousands of children in other American classrooms, because Macmillan's is the most popular reading program in the United States. In the intermediate grades the Montebello children move on to another series, produced by Houghton Mifflin, although the Macmillan program continues through to the eighth grade in junior high (up to a forty-eighth "level").

The complete package of Macmillan primary grade materials for Montebello students making their way up the eighteen levels from kindergarten to the end of fourth grade consists of ten student texts, seven workbooks, nine practice books, ten sets of practice masters, seven sets of "comprehension and writing masters," three readiness tests, seven initial placement inventories, ten assessment tests (each in alternative A and B forms), four testing/management resource books, and three achievement tests plus sets of student profile cards and class profile cards at each level. Supplementary material across the eighteen levels includes seven skill development charts, four vocabulary development charts, ten solo books, and ten "Extras! For Reinforcement," three sets of ABC cards, five sets of phonic picture cards, five sets of word cards, three sets of story cards, three packs of games, seven records or cassettes, and five tutorial programs.

Not surprisingly, there is also a total of ten "teacher's editions" to help teachers make their way through the thickets of materials and to keep track of everybody's progress. There are even ten sets of letters for teachers to send to parents. The emphasis on isolated skills and continual testing is made clear in the "instructional strategy that ensures skill mastery" outlined to teachers at the beginning of their editions: "INTRODUCE—Every skill is given a thorough introduction at its appropriate level. REVIEW—Every skill is thoroughly reviewed soon after it is introduced. REVIEW —Key skills are again reviewed after a short time. TEST—Priority skills are tested for the first time, but never at the level in which they have been introduced. MAINTAIN—Priority skills are maintained after the first test to assure skills retention. RETEST—Priority skills are retested at succeeding grades to provide a continuous check on student progress."

What are all these "priority skills" that are so insistently reviewed and retested throughout the program? In phonics, children are introduced, one letter at a time, to initial consonants and (optionally) short vowels, starting at the beginning of kindergarten. They move on to final consonants at the "preprimer" level, to long vowels at the "primer" level, and then to medial consonants in first grade. Diphthongs and initial clusters of consonants (like *ch* and *str*) are withheld until children are on the brink of second grade, when they also begin to be exposed to "variant spellings" and the most common sound in the English language, the "neutral vowel" *schwa* (a word that most adults are unfamiliar with and a sound that can be represented in English by *a, e, i, o,* or *u*—met*a*l, s*e*rve, li*o*n, circle, c*u*rve.) In comprehension, "scope and sequence" charts maneuver the children through such abstractions as "main ideas," paraphrases, facts, opinions, and themes.

Thousands of questions are provided for teachers to ask, with right answers provided so that teachers can properly evaluate the response. For one very short story called "Rico and the Red Pony," intended to introduce students to the color red, there are seven "literal comprehension" questions ("Where was Rico's flower shop?"), five "interpretive thinking" questions ("Why did Rico yell when he saw a car or a bus?"), five "critical thinking" questions ("Why do you think Rico had the pony if he didn't like it?"), and three "creative thinking" questions ("Where would you like to pretend to be if you were on the red pony?"). A page of the workbook and a page of the skills practice book are devoted to further exercises on such questions, with further material for children who get confused. There are more questions than there are sentences in the story, more paragraphs of guidance for teachers than there are pages in the story, and the ritual is repeated day after day, week after week, year after year. Children are expected to identify characters, recall details, specify behavior, relate setting to characterization, recall details, state motives, discuss character traits, infer causes and/or effects, draw conclusions, predict outcomes, locate words printed in bold type, identify words containing particular sounds or letters, analyze illustrations, identify "main ideas," identify details, identify nouns, recognize the characteristics of nouns, suggest titles for paragraphs, paraphrase sentences, and underline individual words and letters.

The r-bbit is well represented in these exercises. Here is a selection:

> Choose the same letter, *d, t* or *r,* to go at the beginning and end of the following pairs of words: __ish, ba__; __ake, ja__; __ail, si__.
>
> Insert *windows, winter, woman, work, walk* or *water* into "I _____ to school every day. It is cold in the _____. Mother goes to _____ in the morning."
>
> Fill in the correct alternative: "The water was very _____ (deep, dip);" "The _____ will soon be a flower (sad, seed);" "Nicky thinks he does not _____ a sister (nod, need)."

A correct answer is always provided for the teacher so that the child can be promptly marked right or wrong (even though other answers might be quite appropriate in some circumstances).

A typical *Testing and Management Resource Book* for one grade of the Macmillan program includes a readiness test teacher's manual, a readiness test, an assessment test teacher's manual, assessment test forms, and reinforcement masters. There are pages of instructions for the teacher before each test and subtest that tell the teacher what to say when asking questions and in responding to various answers. Each manual serves as a script that the teacher can follow, like an actor, who cannot improvise, while the children put their fingers on the right spot, produce the right sound, circle the right picture, underline the right letter, complete the blank. For any errors children make, teachers are directed to the pages in the workbook to which the child must return. If the specific skill not mastered is circling initial *str,* then further drill can be found on pages 224 and 262 of the particular teacher's edition, page 84B of the workbook, and page 39 of the skills practice book. Evaluation charts and student profiles are completed after every test to show at a glance when students have mastered given skills and specific levels.

There is nothing in the real world that is like any of this pedagogical treadmill. Nobody learns anything, or teaches anything, by being submitted to such a regime of disjointed, purposeless, repetitive, confusing, and tedious activities. Teachers burn out, pupils fall by the wayside, and parents and administrators worry about the lack of student "progress" or interest. Yet the examples I have given are from a *popular* program, a best-seller, a model for teachers and administrators. These are activities that everyone takes seriously, because they promise so much, take up so much time, and generate so many scores and comparisons.

And the computer is coming along fast. Milliken Publishing Company of St. Louis claims to be *the* leader in electronic publishing. It advertises computerized "learning system" packages covering eight grade levels of mathematics instruction, eight of language arts, five of writing skills, seven of grammar, five of spelling, and nine of reading comprehension. "Each package includes a teacher's guide with easy-to-follow instructions." But in any case, "little direct supervision is required." As an additional inducement to teachers who want to hand over all their responsibilities to the publishers, "Every Milliken courseware diskette comes with a comprehensive management program that will allow you [the teacher] to make individualized or group assignments, identify student problem areas [i.e., spot students who can't do what the program demands], generate performance print-outs, and more. . . . All achievement records are automatically maintained."

A Milliken spelling drill features a multicolor hen on a nest with twelve eggs, one of which hatches into a chicken every time a scrambled word is typed correctly. (Unscrambling jumbled words does not help children to spell and drives many of them to despair, but it is a very easy instructional activity to devise). A Milliken sentence-combining exercise gives the example: "I have a dog. She is friendly. I have a friendly dog." (illustrated by a friendly cartoon dog, of course), along with the mysterious explanation "That's how we use describing words such as: red green fat thin quiet." In "Math sequences" there is a bold "Well done Chuck!" for a student who has typed out the correct working of a long-division problem. An "Edufun! learning game" uses a screen full of fish, underwater weeds, and a chest of treasure to illustrate $2 + ? = 3$. And there is the inevitable r-bbit—"The magicians _____ their audiences with their magic.   (a) astounded (b) injured (c) worried (d) warmed"—plus the option of hitting a key to get clues. I have not selected these examples because they are particularly ridiculous. The examples have been boldly advertised across facing color pages in educational journals and magazines like *Learning,* embraced by a beaming teacher and seven smiling students. The examples were selected by Milliken Publishing Company, which has learned what is most likely to appeal to teachers or administrators who want to buy classroom software.

Why the R-bbit Is Rife

It is not difficult to see why computer-based instructional programs are attractive to many children, teachers, administrators, politicians, and parents, too. Children prefer the r-bbit because schoolwork is presented like the Saturday morning television cartoon show. If children must engage in totally meaningless activities, like filling in missing letters of random words, that is the way to do it. There are so many outrageous advertisements for educational software in teachers' journals that I do not keep precise notes on them all, but I remember one that boasted that its programs could teach anything that would be too boring to teach in any other way —like the seller of a food processor *bragging* that its machine can make nonnutritive products appetizing.

The r-bbit is attractive to teachers because it keeps children quiet and occupied. Despite its cute format, which like the flashy graphics of most printed classroom materials is often designed to appeal to teachers rather than to children, the entire approach has an *authority* that is difficult to resist. R-bbit programs present clearly defined tasks that can be dealt with one at a time. The programs "remember" how each child has "progressed" from day to day and can cope with wrong answers. There is little difficulty for the teacher in answering the child's question, "What should I do next?" (answer: "Ask the computer."), and there is little risk that the child will ever ask, "Why am I doing this?" As the advertisement for the "totally new" Ginn Reading Program tells teachers: "You'll find the actual instructions and directions you need to achieve the comprehension goals you want. Our Teacher's Edition has explicit instructions to teach, practice, extend, test, and review all the skills necessary for comprehension. Every skill is clearly defined for both you and your students. So there's never any guesswork about what you should do and why. . . . It's the sensible way to teach reading comprehension."

The r-bbit is attractive to administrators because it so generously provides *scores,* which can be used to support any decision and justify any action. Some degree of learning can always be demonstrated (unless it is convenient to demonstrate that certain children are not learning, in which case the program can provide evidence for that, too). When politicians press with the question "What are you doing to ensure quality education?" the administrators can say that they are using the latest r-bbit program. In fact, in many jurisdictions the program will be imposed upon schools and teachers, as the Macmillan and Houghton Mifflin programs are imposed in Montebello. All children have to have the same program because they are all expected to take the same examination, and no one must have an advantage or disadvantage. Besides, everyone knows that quality control can only be exercised through standardization. Programs, especially if they can be delivered by computer, are more reliable than teachers.

The claims are unbounded—that the programs will teach reading and writing (or anything else)—and the complexity of the materials is daunting. For reading there are self-contained segments or "modules" claiming to teach alphabet skills, acoustic skills, phonic skills, blending skills, sight recognition skills, comprehension skills, and reasoning skills, all accompanied by appropriate tests. The programs even claim to be based on extensive scientific research and to include the latest theoretical advances that will presumably make all of the competition out of date (just like next year's automobiles).

Parents are impressed. Parents are always concerned that their children should attend to what they think teachers believe is important. And the promotional material accompanying programs almost invariably adds a note for parents like, "Can you afford not to give your child the advantage of this opportunity?" The advertising is rarely ever qualified. There is no suggestion that some children might not learn with a particular method or set of materials (unless there is something wrong with the child). There are no advertising standards for the promotion of educational products, or surgeon-general's warnings that the product could be dangerous to mental health.

What's Wrong With the R-bbit

This entire book constitutes a detailed answer to the question of what is wrong with the r-bbit—and what parents and teachers can do about it. The objections to r-bbit programs apply to all areas of instruction, but I shall concentrate on examples involving literacy. Reading and writing are basic to every academic activity in school, not only as subjects to be taught but as the means of engaging in learning and of demonstrating learning. The way literacy instruction is delivered to children illustrates educational technology at its most intense. I shall also focus primarily on children because they are the most conspicuous victims of programs and tests, but again, the damage affects learners of all ages.

Objections to drill-and-test programs can be set out briefly under the following four headings:

(1) The programs do not reflect the way that anyone learns about language or about anything worthwhile. Programs control teachers and assume they are incapable of making educational decisions. Even in subjects like math, history, and science, where conventional wisdom says that facts, dates, and formulas may be usefully learned by rote, most teachers understand the difference between explaining something that makes sense and trying to cram apparently pointless information into confused and reluctant minds. With programs, someone outside the classroom determines what teacher and student must do next, even though the outsider does not know and

cannot see the student. The r-bbit assumes that students will not learn unless they are controlled, graded, and rewarded, and ignores what they learn by being engaged in meaningful activities. The r-bbit is misguided and manipulative.

(2) The language arts programs do not reflect normal reading, writing, or language generally. The r-bbit teaches children nothing about the way people employ spoken or written language. Filling in blanks is not the way anyone uses language, spoken or written. No one ever says to a child "Put on your _____ and we'll go to the game as soon as you guess the missing word." There are easier ways to learn the alphabet, and any other of the so-called "skills" of literacy, than the drills and tests dictated by instructional programs. Many children, and teachers and parents, too, think that reading and writing *are* the exercises done in the classroom. Children are learning that reading and writing are "school activities," punitive, pointless and boring, not to be engaged in unless teachers require them. The r-bbit is irrelevant and misleading.

(3) Programs are usually designed by people who know how to write instructional programs rather than by people experienced in teaching children. Every bit of rubbish in the activity kits and worksheets that have occupied so much of children's school and homework time is now being put into r-bbit software for computers. Computerized instructional programs are produced by computer experts, just as most of the arguments and visions for employing computer-based instruction in education are advanced by computer experts rather than by experienced educators. Even where "expert" consultants are involved in the production of educational software—and the list of credits is often liberally sprinkled with Ph.D.s—the general concern is still likely to be more with what the computer can do than with how children most effectively learn. The r-bbit is ignorant.

(4) The programs—whether in print or on computer screens—deny children opportunities to learn or to see any sense in what they are learning. Instead of reading and writing, the children fill in blanks.

The children who cannot do this very well spend even more time trying to fill in blanks and even less time reading and learning to read. Teachers have less time to teach reading and writing. Systematic instruction, presenting one item to be learned at a time, is the systematic deprivation of experience, like shutting infants up in a dark room and allowing them to see only one thing at a time. The r-bbit is dangerous.

Why the R-bbit Is a Threat

The r-bbit and all the other programs are a huge part of education, and their junk-learning influence is growing. Bureaucratic centralized authorities are demanding the tighter control of teachers in the names of "accountability" and "excellence." The control can only be maintained through the specification of what teachers should teach, and how and when they should teach it. And when the prescribed instructional programs fail, as they invariably do, teachers and students are blamed and the controls are tightened even more. There is enormous pressure for the expansion of computer-based instruction, and not just from the producers of computers and instructional software. Politicians, bureaucrats, administrators, and even parents will press for the expanded use of computers in education; they will continue to confuse economy with efficiency. Uncertain or lazy teachers who cannot think of more productive ways of using computers will open the classroom doors to the programs. They will admit the agent of their own destruction.

Computer-based instruction has come along just in time to tip the balance in a classroom struggle that has been waged for three decades. The struggle has been between autonomous teachers, able to make immediate classroom decisions about how best to help students to learn, and the designers and promoters of programmatic instruction, who want to have every classroom decision made in advance. Programmatic instruction has been failing. No one claims that students are academically any further advanced than they were thirty years ago, despite the proliferation of programs and tests. As I write these words another wave of books and reports has been published deploring the level of illiteracy in the United States—forty percent of the population by some counts—and asserting that even the ability to think is being drilled out of our children. But instead of blaming the inadequacy of tests and programs, educational planners and administrators attribute the failure to an insufficiency of programs and tests. Teachers and students have always succeeded in getting around programs, or ignoring them—so the argument goes.

But computers are the ideal devices for programmatic instruction. They are more attractive to children, more effective drillmasters than teachers, and more easily controlled by administrators. They are even cheaper than teachers, whose salaries are the largest and least tractable component in the spiraling costs of education. The world has entered the age of computers, and schools will not be able to resist them. Schools should not want to reject computers; the new technology has much to offer learners and teachers. But teachers must know how to handle computers; they should not allow computers to take their place.

However, teachers often have been so programmed in what passes for their own professional education that they have not learned how children learn. Teachers have been trained to believe that the materials and procedures they are expected to rely upon in the classroom are the best way to teach. I have been told by my own academic colleagues that teachers cannot be trusted with "theory"—they need to be told what they should do. What teachers have been taught is how to surrender their classroom autonomy to drill-and-kill instruction.

The situation is critical. It will not be easy for children to defend themselves against the r-bbit as they grow up in the computerized classroom, so parents and teachers must fight the battle for them. Unfortunately, parents and teachers are often unable to see classrooms for what they are. Adults may be inclined to take most of what is done in the classrooms for granted—if it's "education" then it must be good—especially since the materials that are used make such spectacular claims for what will be achieved. Adults may need completely fresh eyes with which to observe what is going on; the eyes of observers with no preconceptions. It may help to visualize how a classroom would look to unprejudiced explorers.

The Explorers' Point of View

Imagine that ripples from earth's television and radio broadcasts have revealed to the inquisitive inhabitants of a distant galaxy that something called literacy is a critical concern in many schools on our planet. They decide to send a mission to earth to investigate what literacy is. The exploratory mission warps through time and space to observe classrooms in the English-speaking world.

On the mission there are archeologists, whose task is to deduce what literacy is from the artifacts they find. What evidence do they discover in the classrooms? They observe many isolated letters of the alphabet, fragmented words, and a few bits of sentences, none of which seem to serve any purpose. Letters and words are festooned all over classroom walls, mostly in the form of lists—the days of the week, the months of the year, the names of birds, animals, and fish, and of children themselves. But none of this print seems to *say* anything; it has no purpose as far as the explorers can see. In fact every few weeks the teacher may change all of this writing, as if tired of looking at the same landscape day after day. The explorers conclude that all this writing is decoration, an alternative to wallpaper.

The archeologists also study all the paper artifacts they find in the desks and on the shelves around the classroom. Once again they find many lists of random letters and random words, but they also find many sentences, most of them with spaces in them. Entire workbooks and worksheets are made up of these honeycombed fragments of language, suggesting to the explorers that schools may be infested with insects that chew appetizing morsels out of words and sentences. They may also find a few things called *stories* in some of the classrooms, but most of these will be short and dull, and almost invariably accompanied by lists of questions designed to make a test out of the task.

The archeologists also meet the r-bbit, but cannot see how its antics have anything to do with literacy. What purposes of self-expression or communication could machines and cartoon characters have? Nothing the machines *say* makes any sense to them.

The explorers have long and anxious debates about what all

this evidence can mean. They come to the conclusion that the artifacts are related to an esoteric ritual. There is no point in looking for any *meaning* in the materials, any message in the media; their only apparent purpose is to be handled in the proper way for the mysterious ceremonies that take place in classrooms. Since the objects found in classrooms seem to provide few clues to any practical utility they might have (unlike most objects in the world outside), the archeologists have to hope that the other specialists on their mission have more success.

The mission's anthropologists examine the behavior of teachers and children. It quickly becomes obvious to the explorers that reading and writing are not things that teachers do themselves, at least not by preference, but rather are drills and exercises that they want the children to perform, presumably as some kind of uplifting moral discipline. Why else should anyone think it worthwhile to go through lists of forty words or more like "boots, army, watches, maps, inch . . . ," marking each one *s* or *p* according to whether it is singular or plural (and deducting two points for each error), as the Steck-Vaughn *Red Book of Language Exercises* demands? Why labor through lists like "noisy, track, looked, ladder, beat . . . ," drawing circles around all the vowel sounds, as Houghton Mifflin's *Troubleshooter Word Attack* drills require? The only things most teachers are seen reading for personal reasons in the classroom are memoranda, which they clearly would rather not read at all. Otherwise, teachers only read to copy things onto the chalkboard or to lead children in their catechisms. It is the same with writing. Apart from reluctantly composing occasional reports to parents and supervisors, the only kinds of writing teachers are seen to do is to copy material onto the chalkboard, make marks on what children have written, and record signs and numbers in registers. None of this activity has any utility, as far as the explorers can see.

The children in classrooms seem to have come to similar conclusions. They will only read and write if they are required to do so, and then reluctantly. Reading and writing make many children anxious. Usually they will only write if they are given a score for doing so, a reward that most teachers seem eager to provide, even though it may subsequently cause the recipients considerable distress.

The explorers are even more puzzled by computers. The machines distribute scores, but they don't seem to be scored themselves. They say things they do not mean (how can a machine have a conversation with a human?) and represent language in ways in which it is never normally used. Why should machines be engaged in these activities? The visitors conclude that the computer is an altar in an obscure ceremony that apparently all school inhabitants participate in but which serves no useful purpose except generating the peculiar classroom coinage of grades and scores.

Perhaps, in desperation, the literacy explorers will consult with other missions, which have gone into similar classrooms to find out what mathematics is, or science, or social studies. They will find the same evidence and the same conclusions: All of these activities are arcane rituals and ceremonies, the sole purpose of which is the manipulation of the marks, scores, and grades by which children are judged. The emphasis on scores seems inseparable from a preoccupation with errors. On the one hand, errors seem like something to be avoided. Teachers and parents are always alert to detect mistakes and to chastise children who commit them. On the other hand, the adults always seem to be striving to push children into situations where error is likely, avoiding anything that children might find easy or agreeable to do, and seeking activities that will be "challenging" for them.

What This Has to Do With Children

We must come back to our own side of the space-time warp. Every human child is an archeologist and anthropologist, an unprejudiced explorer from another galaxy. Children learn from the artifacts they find in their environment and from the behavior of the people around them. Their greatest insight about written language before they come to school is probably that written language is different from the pattern on the wallpaper—that signs and labels have a purpose, that they *do* something more than just decorate the landscape. Where do children learn that reading and writing are boring and difficult, that learning is tedious, that they are themselves dullards, that collaboration is cheating, and that nothing at school is worth doing without a score? Instead of thinking that the failings of students reflect what they have not learned, we should regard these failings as what they have been taught.

It is often difficult to persuade teachers of all this. Many teachers have come to believe that it is natural for children to be motivated by scores, to be secretive and competitive, to be apathetic to learning. To persuade teachers otherwise, it is sometimes necessary to go to the beginning, to remind them how children learn to talk and to understand spoken language.

CHAPTER 2

The Learners' Clubs

We underrate our brains and our intelligence. Formal education has become such a complicated, self-conscious and overregulated activity that learning is widely regarded as something difficult that the brain would rather not do. Teachers are often inclined to think that learning is an occasional event, requiring special incentives and rewards, not something that anyone would normally engage in given a choice. Such a belief is probably well-founded if the teachers are referring to their efforts to keep children moving through the instructional sequences that are prescribed as learning activities in school. But reluctance to learn cannot be attributed to the brain. Learning is the brain's primary function, its constant concern, and we become restless and frustrated if there is no learning to be done. We are all capable of huge and unsuspected learning accomplishments without effort.

The World of Speech

Learning to talk and to understand spoken language is a monumental intellectual achievement. Babies arrive in the world with no prior knowledge or expectations about language. They have no choice but to learn from the artifacts they find around them and from what they see people doing. They must behave like archeologists and anthropologists from another world. And they do so effortlessly and inconspicuously.

Children are so competent in learning that they are usually denied credit for their abilities and achievements. Myths protect adults from the true knowledge of how much children learn, not occasionally but all the time. Indeed, it can be astonishing to adults to discover how much children are learning.

Forget the condescending myth that children do not learn very much when they learn spoken language. All children except the most severely deprived or handicapped acquire a vocabulary of over ten thousand words during the first four or five years of their lives. At the age of four they are adding to their vocabulary at the rate of twenty new words a day. By seven this rate may have increased to nearly thirty words, every day of the year, including holidays, with no allowance for forgetting. By late adolescence the average vocabulary is at least fifty thousand words, perhaps over one hundred thousand, depending upon how the counting is done. How do children manage to learn twenty new words or more a day? Not from formal instruction. Not from flashcards or by filling in the blanks; not from the r-bbit.

Teachers have told me it is impossible for children to learn words at such a rate, whatever the research shows. I ask these teachers how they can be so sure. They tell me it takes them an hour to teach children ten words on a word list, they forget five by the next day, and by the end of the week they might remember only two. So how could they possibly be adding to their vocabulary at the rate of twenty words a day? I have to say it must be when the children are not working on the word lists.

Children not only learn words, they learn how to put words together into conventional phrases and sentences, so that they can understand and be understood. Every child learns a very specialized grammar. Children may not learn to talk the way their school teachers talk, but they do not see themselves as teachers. Children learn to talk like the people they see themselves as being. They learn to talk the way their friends talk. Children learn the vocabulary and grammar of the language spoken around them, its idioms and jargon, its distinctive patterns of intonation and gesture, and its complex rules of eye contact, body posture, and interruption. And children learn all this with exquisite precision—they learn to be *exactly* like their peers. A complete description of the complexities of language as it is actually used defies the lifetime efforts of professional linguists, yet infants learn the fundamentals in a few short and busy years, without anyone suspecting what they are doing.

Forget also the dismissive myth that language is a biological predisposition, that the way we talk is in our genes. Our language is not inherited from our parents. We talk the way our parents talk only if we grow up in the company of our parents. Our biological parents may be English-speaking, but if we are raised in a Chinese community then we will speak that community's dialect of Chinese, and we will have as much trouble later in life trying to learn English as our parents would trying to learn Chinese. Every aspect of language must be *learned*.

Babies are born capable of learning any dialect of any language in the world today. And no one would suggest that the 3,000 or more languages currently spoken on earth constitute a full set, that there are no alternative possibilities. There have been other languages in the past and there will be other languages in the future (at least if the human race survives). Infants are capable of learning languages that do not yet exist.

Forget the demeaning myth that children learn about language through imitation. A grain of truth underlies this view, but it is not that children learn by blindly mimicking the behavior of adults. Children no more parrot the noises and gestures of grown-ups than they walk around the room making sounds like the vacuum cleaner. They don't learn to do what the vacuum cleaner does; they learn to use the vacuum cleaner the way the people around them do. When children emulate the language of adults they do so for purposes of their own. If young children say they want to be taken for a walk, it is because they want to go for a walk, not because they have just heard an adult utter those words. They imitate when it is useful to do so, to achieve a purpose of their own. Indeed, when infants don't know the appropriate way to say something they want to say they invent a way. Children learn in the course of accomplishing their own ends. They are selective and discriminating, and they learn far more about language than they ever could if they blindly imitated the sounds they heard adults making.

Forget finally the misleading myth that children learn to talk because adults deliberately set out to teach them language. Parents, like other family members and friends, may indeed be *teachers* of children, but this is because of what they *demonstrate* about spoken language, not because of any organized instruction that they provide. Children learn to be users of spoken language by observing and overhearing how other people use it, by becoming apprenticed to language users, and especially by being helped to say things and to understand things themselves. None of this is anything like the way children are expected to learn in school. In the broader world of learning, there is no systematic instruction, and there are no curriculum guides or lesson plans, no workbooks, exercises or drills, no tests or marks, no assignments, no grades, no specified objectives, no formal teacher accountability. There are no r-bbits.

The Revolution That Died in Schools

Theories, arguments, and research evidence to support the view of children's learning that I have just outlined can be inspected in a multitude of books and professional reports on child language development. But I am also writing from personal experience. Chance put me near the center of events at a time when the academic disciplines of linguistics and psychology were being shaken and re-formed by a radical new way of looking at language and learning and when the first books from this new point of view were being written, including one of my own. The new perspective on language and learning promised to produce dramatic changes in education, but when translated into instructional procedures it was distorted into a travesty of itself, and in the schools the revolution quickly faded and died.

Twenty years ago I was living in Australia, working as an editor on a newspaper in Perth and, like most parents of young children, observing with some trepidation the beginning of my children's formal education. I was also pursuing a writer's interest in language by studying a variety of subjects at the University of Western Australia. Even in that distant part of Australia, there was growing academic excitement in the mid-1960s because of the radical theories and trenchant arguments of a brash young American linguist at the Massachusetts Institute of Technology named Noam Chomsky.

Before Chomsky, the most influential linguistic theories tended to regard language as a relatively uncomplicated system involving words that had arbitrary but rather direct and obvious relationships to objects, feelings, or events, and rules of grammar which determined how these words should be put together into acceptable sentences. Children basically learned to talk by imitating adults and by being taught the rules of grammar.

The culmination of this simplistic approach to language from a psychological point of view was a massive volume entitled *Verbal Behavior,* published in 1957 by Professor B. F. Skinner, who was then and still is the dean of American behavioristic theory. Behaviorists believe that all behavior, human and animal, can be explained in terms of habits established when instinctive or accidental responses to environmental stimulation are "reinforced" by some kind of reward. They have no use for "mentalistic" terms like "mind," "thought," or "feelings," which they regard as unobservable and unscientific fictions. Skinner had demonstrated with rats and pigeons that quite complex behavior could be shaped through experimental manipulation, and in *Verbal Behavior*—which is behavioristic jargon for "language"—Skinner argued at great length that children learn to use language in precisely the same way that pigeons can be taught to peck at colored lights, by having appropriate responses reinforced. Skinner was also famous for contributions to the development of teaching machines and of systems of "programmed learning."

In the same year, 1957, the then unknown Chomsky published

a doctoral dissertation that argued abstractly that the traditional grammar taught in classrooms and employed by linguists was not an adequate representation of how language actually works. Grammar could not function as a prescribed set of rules that people are taught in order to produce conventional sentences, but rather must be a dynamic system of great complexity inside every language user's head which actually generates sentences and the understanding of sentences. The dissertation was short, technical, and published by a relatively obscure publishing house in Holland. It attracted little general attention.

But two years later, in 1959, Chomsky published an unexpected and scathing review of Skinner's *Verbal Behavior* in the academic journal *Language*. Chomsky ridiculed Skinner's belief that the laboratory study of animal behavior could cast any light on the nature of language or on how it is learned. Language, even the language of children, is too rich, too complex, to be regarded as "habit-learning." Detail by detail, Chomsky demolished all of Skinner's arguments, insistently asserting that the behavioristic approach trivialized both language and learning. The scholarly, reasoned, and merciless review was a unique academic hatchet job that left academic psychologists and linguists stunned—especially because, to many, it seemed absolutely irrefutable.

At a stroke, Chomsky established a new and revolutionary linguistic theory, which is still the most influential theory in formal linguistics today, and he devastated what had become the dominant theory in experimental psychology. Chomsky's theory literally turned conventional views of language upside down. Instead of regarding the production and understanding of sentences as something that proceeds linearly, from left to right so to speak, with words being organized through grammar into phrases and sentences which then convey meaning, the new view began with meaning. Sentences grow from entire meanings, from complete intentions, not one word at a time. The theory talked of the internal grammar metaphorically, in terms of "tree structures" with a meaningful sentence on the topmost branch, noun phrases and verb phrases proliferating in the branches below, and the roots embedded in sense and purpose.

The first prominent experimental psychologist to put

Chomsky's views to the test with actual human behavior was a former behaviorist, George A. Miller, who was then a professor at Harvard University. Miller and his collaborators conducted pioneering research studies that demonstrated that when children and adults put words together to make meaningful statements, they indeed use a generative internal grammar of the kind that Chomsky proposed. In a landmark article in the journal *American Psychologist* in 1962, Miller took his own indirect swipe at behaviorism by concluding that "mind is more than a four-letter Anglo-Saxon word."

In a long and influential collaboration, Chomsky and Miller were primarily responsible for the establishment of the brand new discipline of *psycholinguistics* in universities all over the world, spanning the traditional academic boundaries between psychology and linguistics. Their work brought into partnership linguists who were probing the exact nature of language which people learn and use universally, and psychologists who were striving to understand how this learning and use actually takes place.

Miller and his Harvard colleague Jerome Bruner, a world-renowned child psychologist and educator, also founded and directed a "Center for Cognitive Studies" in a converted old house on Kirkland Street in Cambridge, Massachusetts. At this center, outstanding researchers from Harvard, M.I.T., and other universities employed psycholinguistic theory in careful and ingenious studies of infants, with and without their mothers. The researchers were learning from children how even the youngest of babies could use and respond to the people around them in order to make intelligent sense of the world. The research demonstrated that children are not miniature and defective users of adult language, but that they work out language for themselves, learning when they are helped to say and understand what interests them, and inventing when they find it necessary.

With Chomsky playing an active role in its affairs, the center became a mecca for scholars, researchers, and a few fortunate graduate students, from all over the world. When I received an unexpected invitation to leave the newspaper world of Perth to enroll in a doctoral program at the Center for Cognitive Studies, I could not resist the opportunity. I expected to find myself learning more about language in the abstract, but instead spent three exhilarating years exploring the nature of learning, especially as it is exhibited by the fresh clear minds of infants.

A year after I arrived in Cambridge, the Cognitive Center was moved from the old house on Kirkland Street to the shining new tower of the William James Building, which had just been constructed further up the street to house all of the Harvard faculties of social science. The Cognitive Center was established on the eleventh floor, four stories above the floor where Professor B. F. Skinner had set up his office and his pigeon laboratories. I cannot remember ever seeing him on the eleventh floor.

I once asked Skinner if he had ever read Chomsky's review of his book. He said he had glanced at it but not read it through. He hadn't understood the language. The language Skinner did not understand was the "mentalistic" language that gave the credit for learning to individual intentions and intelligence rather than to outside manipulation.

I met many enthusiastic students at Harvard in those days who aspired to write dissertations "bridging the gap" between the seventh and eleventh floors of the William James building. They hoped to perform the crucial experiment that would determine once and for all who was right, Chomsky or Skinner, or they wanted to develop the new super-theory that would bring the psycholinguists and the behaviorists together. But the crucial experiment was never performed, and the convergent theory was never devised for the simple reason that the difference between the two sides was not one that evidence or argument could ever resolve. The difference was one of world view. The psycholinguists believed in observing and analyzing behavior in a natural setting, more like anthropologists than experimental psychologists, without artificial management of what the learner had to do. The behaviorists were convinced that learning should only be studied under conditions of rigorous laboratory control. The psycholinguists were striving to comprehend what went on in the mind when learning occurred. The behaviorists did not believe that anything existed that they could not directly observe and count, like the number of times a pellet of food has to be presented to a hungry pigeon before it learns to peck whenever a light of a certain color comes on, or how long a child has to be reinforced with praise or a piece of candy before saying "a" whenever the letter A is flashed on a screen.

During all this excitement in the academic world, the field of education itself was in ferment. In the year Skinner published his book on language and Chomsky's dissertation appeared in print, the Russians put a dog in a cramped satellite into orbit around the earth. One direct consequence of this and subsequent Soviet space achievements was that federal authorities in the United States government, led by President John F. Kennedy, decided to take some giant steps forward in raising the quality of education, particularly by eradicating illiteracy and improving math and science training. It was expected that all of this would be achieved through rigorous instructional control. In education, the behaviorists have so far had the last laugh.

As I shall explain, the view of language and learning that psycholinguistics promised was superficially examined by the educational planners and set aside as too vague. Notions that children learned best by being immersed in everyday experience did not fit well with the philosophy that believed in quality control and the delivery of instruction to children as if they were on a production line. In the new programmatic atmosphere of classroom control, Skinner's theories won out after all. R-bbits joined the rats, and the word "psycholinguistic" became devalued as an empty catchphrase in publishers' promotions of behavioristic instructional materials.

I soon began to see Chomskian linguistics distorted in the classroom. Psycholinguists had argued that there was no point in trying to drill grammar into children, especially the old formal "structuralist" grammar of nouns and verbs, which they claimed never helped anyone to say anything or understand anything. But instead of leaving grammar drills aside completely and concentrating instead on the actual use of real language for worthwhile purposes, educational programmers established objectives and produced programs that required children to study and parrot a perverted form of Chomskian grammar. Children began to receive instruction in a contrived system of tree structures, with combinatorial rules for noun phrases and verb phrases, popularized as the "New Grammar," but just as pointless and oppressive as the one it was supposed to replace. Chomsky and the psycholinguists pointed the way to discover how children learn, but their insights have still not penetrated many classrooms.

Learning About Language Incidentally

If children master spoken language without formal instruction, then how can such learning be best described? Many striking metaphors have been devised to capture the nature of the learning, characterizing children as "inventors" or "scientists," and defining learning as "experimentation" or "hypothesis-testing." George Miller once referred to children as "informavores"—they eat up new knowledge. My alternative is more down to earth. I call it the "Can I have another donut?" system of language learning. Every child learns to say, "Can I have another donut?" not in order to *say,* "Can I have another donut?" but in order to *get* another donut. The language learning is incidental, a by-product of the child's attempt to achieve some other end. The child wants to get another donut, and in the course of doing so learns how to ask for it. In fact, neither the child nor anyone else around is likely to be aware that language learning is taking place.

A British linguist, Michael Halliday, pointed out in 1973 that children do not learn to talk the way linguists learn language—as an abstract system that can later be used to fulfill a variety of purposes. Children learn language and its uses simultaneously. In fact, it is through its uses that language is learned. Children have difficulty in learning anything that to them seems to have no purpose. This is the reason why the r-bbit is a totally unnecessary and inadequate means of teaching children to talk, and why the drill-and-test type program is such a misguided means of trying to teach children to read and write. There is no point in filling in the second letter of r-bbit.

Learning is not the occasional and difficult thing it is often thought to be. That learning requires effort is another myth. The stress and strain comes from trying to learn and failing. When learning is successful, it is totally inconspicuous. Children learn all the time, but the only indication that learning has taken place usually, is the sudden demonstration that they know something they didn't know before. Parents are for ever saying, "Where did the child learn to say that?" And the situation is exactly the same with adults. We learn all the time without suspecting that we are doing so, and the main reason we are unaware of learning is because no effort is involved. We are painfully aware when we have failed at something we have deliberately set out to learn, yet we tend to blithely ignore the kind of learning we do every day.

Take some simple examples. Most people can tell you about the last movie they saw, or the program they watched on television the previous evening, or the last newspaper or magazine that they read, and they have almost total recall. They can tell you what they wore yesterday and the day before, what they ate, and what the weather was like. They can tell you whether many well-known people are alive or dead. And they learned all of this without trying, without being aware that they were in fact learning. We learn every time we make sense of something; we learn in the act of making sense of the world around us. Understanding takes care of learning. If you understand what you see in a movie, you will probably remember what you see, at least for as long as it is important for you to do so.

We *still* learn to talk in the way we learned as babies, and we continue to be completely unaware that this learning is taking place. In fact, we cannot help learning in this way. My Canadian friends are always telling me when I come back from some travels that I've picked up an American accent or that I'm speaking like a Londoner again. An American friend of mine named Donald Graves went to Scotland for a few months to study at the University of Edinburgh. When he came back he had a distinctly Scottish lilt in his voice which is still there two years after the visit. Don Graves did not go to Scotland to learn to speak like a Scot, he did not practice or take lessons, and at the time he was not aware of what he was learning. In fact, he would just as soon not have learned what he did. He tells me he is still *embahrrrrassed* by the way he talks.

The examples that I have just given are so commonplace that some people want to deny that this is "learning." They want to call it something else, like "memory." But remembering something in these everyday ways reflects exactly the same kind of learning that a child accomplishes in first making sense of spoken language. It is the kind of learning we are normally unaware of because it takes place continually and effortlessly, while we think we are doing something else (like enjoying a movie or reading a magazine). If learning does not take place in this way, then we are bored. We find it difficult to tolerate situations in which there is nothing new to be made sense of, nothing to learn. It is only when we deliberately try to learn (or teach) something that does not make sense that learning is difficult to accomplish. And what we are aware of then is not learning, or even the failure to learn, but the confusion of not being able to make sense of what we are engaged in. The struggle to learn is usually a struggle to comprehend. The moment of comprehension is the moment of learning. Learning is a smooth, continuous flow from one understanding to another, not a series of sporadic lurches from confusion to confusion.

Infants constantly find much that is new in the world to do and to understand. They learn whenever someone or something helps them to do something they want to do or to understand something they want to understand. And with spoken language they accomplish all of this enormous amount of learning by the simple device of joining a club, the club of people who use spoken language.

Joining the Spoken Language Club

The spoken language club is perhaps the first community that every infant joins. Its club members are the people whose life the infant will share, the group to which the infant belongs. There are no special requirements for admission to this club—no entry fees, no tests, no need of personal recommendations—infants join the spoken language club by a single act of mutual acceptance. The club members say in effect, "Welcome, you're one of us," and the infant's unspoken response is, "I'm just like you."

Advantages of membership in the spoken language club are identical with those in any other club—a tennis club, for example, or a dining club, or a debating club, any kind of association. The first advantage is that more experienced members show newcomers what activities are. Until you join a club you often do not know what its club members do. I once thought that the primary activity of members of sailing clubs would be sailing. Now I know that many members never go near the water. But I had to join a sailing club to find this out. In the spoken language club, other people show you what speech can be used for. The first thing an infant needs to learn is that talking does things; that the strange noises that people make are not meaningless sounds or the incidental creaking of the mechanism. Talking helps you do things.

The second advantage of any club is that more experienced members help newcomers to engage in whatever club activities the newcomers find interesting and useful. In the spoken language club, spoken language users help the newcomers to make use of speech. They don't *teach* them, they *help* them. More experienced speakers help the infant to say what the infant is trying to say and to understand what the infant is trying to understand. No one ever says, "Three out of ten again today, dummy. You'd better spend more time on your worksheets." There is no filling in the missing sound. The learning is always collaborative; people are engaged in mutual activities in which the more able and the less able can do things together.

The third advantage of any club is that there is no coercion. Members are not forced to engage in activities that do not interest them, nor are they denied participation in activities that attract them. In particular, no one is excluded on the basis of level of ability. No one in the golf club says, "Your swing hasn't improved enough during the past six weeks, we're going to throw you out." Differences in ability, and in experience and interests, are taken for granted. In the spoken language club especially, new members feel very secure. It is taken for granted that "You're one of us." And this acceptance is the most favorable circumstance for language learning, because it is through apprenticing oneself to more experienced club members that learning takes place.

It may be argued that teaching is going on in the club situation, but it is a kind of teaching that is (like the learning it produces) continual, unconscious, and effortless. It does not involve delivering instruction in a fragmentary and decontextualized way that someone else has decided is "systematic." An infant says, "Waw waw waw," and someone else says, "You mean, 'Please may I have another donut.' " Adults or older children say "Look at the big plane up there" and point so that the child knows what they are talking about. Adults give running commentaries on what they are doing with the child. Always, the instruction is relevant. Always, the learner can make sense of it. Anything that the infant cannot understand and that isn't clarified is ignored by learner and "teacher" alike. Infants learn from what they understand, and the other club members make language understandable to them, in the normal course of everyday activities.

The message the child constantly receives is, "You're one of us. We take it for granted that you will become just like us." And the child—or adult—learns to talk like a member of the club, without anyone suspecting that learning is taking place.

How Children Learn

In October 1982 I organized a symposium. I managed to persuade the University of Victoria, in British Columbia, where I was teaching at the time, to invite fourteen researchers from Europe and North and South America to spend five days on campus talking about preschool children. The researchers came from a variety of academic disciplines, including anthropology, sociology, linguistics, psychology, and education, and they had observed children in a variety of countries and cultures: in Alaska and Mexico City, Puerto Rico and Papua-New Guinea, Africa and Europe; in White, Black, Chinese, Mexican-American, Catholic, Jewish, and Protestant communities, some rich, some poor, in different parts of the United States. The children they had observed had only two things in common—they had all learned a great deal about reading and writing, and they had done so without the benefit of formal school instruction.

The researchers were concerned with what children are able to learn about how written language is used, without formal schooling, and how children learn what they know. (The practical issue here was not so much what children can do without school as what schools must respect if they are to ensure that every child has the opportunity to become literate.)

As at every academic conference there was a good deal of debate, of dispute even, about procedural and definitional matters, such as exactly what should be called "literacy." But on three points there was little disagreement at the Victoria symposium. The points of agreement were: (1) all children learn constantly, without the need for special incentives or reinforcement, (2) children learn what is done by the people around them, and (3) children learn what makes sense to them. More specifically, children learn about using written language from the people around them, from the way those people themselves use written language. The mass of evidence on which these conclusions were based is set out in detail in a book entitled *Awakening to Literacy,* from which I have drawn the following picture.

(1) All Children Learn Constantly

You have to look at the world through the eyes of children to find out how much children learn. If you look from the point of view of an experienced adult you will pay too much attention to those things that children do not yet know, rather than giving them credit for the intellectual feats they have already achieved. Take the elementary matter of working out that written language says things.

How do children get the idea that written language is worth paying attention to in the first place? How do they learn that there is a difference between print and the pattern on the wallpaper? Before children can learn anything specific about reading and writing, they have to work out that writing does things that decoration does not. Most three-year-old children can show where it tells you that the contents of the package is corn flakes. They point to the "words," not to the decoration. They may claim the words say, "Corn Flakes," when the word they are pointing to reads, "Cereal," and what they are showing is that they have learned the distinction between the print and the decoration.

I once asked Matthew, a three-and-a-half-year-old friend of mine in Toronto, to read a street sign for me. He said immediately that it read, "Roundwood Court." Actually the sign said, "Timberbank Boulevard." Why did Matthew say what he did? Because he lived on Roundwood Court. He obviously knew what street signs were for. Would Matthew have done any better by trying to "sound out" the word "Timberbank" one letter at a time? Learning to distinguish one word from another is trivial once you begin to understand how written language works, but pointless and confusing before you are able to comprehend what people are talking about.

Parents can see the development of insight into written language by just watching the changing way children use markers and paper. The first marks are likely to be balls of spaghetti, tangled scribbles and stab marks, whether they represent writing or pictures. But while the "drawings" tend to organize themselves into strokes and loops in the middle of the page, "writing" becomes unraveled into individual lines, horizontal or vertical depending on the conventions of the community in which the child lives. Soon the lines get breaks in them, as children discover the existence of words, and in due course individual words are broken up into "letters," even though the child may have to invent many of them. The young author may even ask you to read the story that has been written in these lines and squiggles. Meaning comes first—the process of understanding written language starts with understanding entire stories or statements and then goes on to understanding sentences, words, and finally letters, the reverse of the way most children are expected to learn to "read" in school.

Glenda Bissex, a teacher and researcher from the University of Vermont who attended the Victoria symposium, tells how her own son Paul discovered the excitement of being an author at the age of four and put a sign on his door saying, "Gnys at Wrk." She was so impressed with the young genius at work that she wrote a scholarly book about children and literacy with Paul's sign, in the original spelling, as the title.

Children are always striving to understand the form as well as the function of the world they are discovering. They constantly hypothesize—and where necessary change their minds—about the way written language works. Another participant in the Victoria Symposium, Emilia Ferreiro, has intensively studied what sense children in Mexico City make of the function of letters in words. Not unreasonably, many children speculate that the number of letters in a word reflects the size or importance of the object named. Isn't it reasonable that *elephant* should be a bigger word than *ant?* A few counterexamples will quickly persuade a child to try another hypothesis, but what is important is that the child keeps on testing and reflecting. Ferreiro tells of asking three- and four-year-old children how many letters they thought they had in their names, before they understood anything about the alphabet. Most children thought they deserved three. How many letters in your baby brother's name? the researcher asked. "Two?" How many in your big brother's name? "Four?" In your mother's? "Five?" How many letters in your father's name? "Thousands?"

In Victoria I have been following the progress of two-year-old Zachary who was given access to a computer for his own explorations. Zachary liked the fact that if he left his finger on a key on the computer keyboard he could get a whole sequence of identical letters on the screen. And another key would erase the letters he did not want. Ask him to write his name and for a while Zachary would produce Z, three times. He wrote his mother's name as MMMM. And for his father, Jim, Zachary spread a string of Js right across the screen.

Children not only learn the kinds of things that they see can be done with written language, as both reader and writer, but also explore how these particular things might be done. They are developing a world of literacy all the time. And the particular things they learn are the things they see being done by other people around them.

(2) Children Learn What Others Do

What exactly do preschool children learn about written language? If they come from a family where television guides and telephone directories are used, they know about television guides and telephone directories. If catalogs are consulted, they know about catalogs. If their friends send greetings cards, they know about greetings cards. If messages are left on refrigerator doors, they know about messages on refrigerator doors. Children almost invariably know something about what the written words that appear in television commercials say. ("It's new, it's blue, it's improved.") They know about the writing on cans and wrappers, on doors, and in stores.

Yetta Goodman, a teacher and education professor from the University of Arizona at Tucson, told the Victoria Symposium that in 5,000 attempts it had proved impossible to find a four-year-old child in the United States who could not read the word McDonalds. I believe that not one of the children thought the word was Muh-Cuh-Doh-Oh-Nuh-Ah-Luh-Duh-Suh, trying to "sound out" the individual letters, though many of them thought it said "hamburgers." But isn't that what the word means?

Suppose a child does not come from a literate background, some teachers will ask? The answer is that it then becomes even more important for the school to provide a literate environment for the child: more cards, notes, signs, and catalogs, and even less filling in the blanks and drilling in the sounds of letters. Besides, it is a myth, in North American cultures at least, that people in some socioeconomic groups use written language less than others.

Two social scientists from the University of California at San Diego, Alonzo Anderson and Shelley Stokes, told the Victoria Symposium how their research team had spent over 2,000 hours counting "literacy events" in the nearby homes of Black-American, Mexican-American, and Anglo-American children. A "literacy event" was any occasion when someone in the family used written language in daily living (shopping, for example), entertainment, school-related activities, religious observance, or work. Contrary to cultural stereotypes, there was no significant difference in the number of literacy events in the three groups—only in the nature of the events. Low-income minority preschool children spent more than eighty minutes every day in literacy activities, as much time as more "privileged" children. Asked why children from poor and ethnic

minorities tend to fall short of others in literacy and school achievement, Anderson and Stokes concluded that the impediments were
social and institutional rather than cultural, economic, or ethnic.
One should also look at the type of instruction such children are
likely to receive. It is a destructive fallacy that "disadvantaged"
children are especially in need of rigorous systematic reading and
writing instruction—with the inevitable exclusion of meaningful
literacy events.

Children learn how written language is used from the way
people in the community to which they belong use written language.

(3) Children Learn What Makes Sense to Them

Children may temporarily be wrong in some of their ideas
about what written language does and about how it works. They
learn by testing their own hypotheses about language, making sense
of it in their own terms. Preschool children's ideas about literacy
are never nonsensical. The ideas always make sense, to the child at
least; the ideas are always reasonable possibilities. It is not until they
get to school that children ever get the idea that reading and writing
might not make sense. And it is not until they get to school that they
are confronted with examples of written language and with reading
and writing activities that are sheer nonsense. Before children get
to school their natural tendency is to ignore nonsense. How can you
learn from something you do not understand? At school they are
often tested to find out what confuses them, and the instruction then
concentrates upon that.

Children learn what makes sense to them; they learn through
the sense of things they want to understand. Television guides
make sense, and so do telephone directories, catalogs, greetings
cards, and notes on the refrigerator door—if you are among people
who use those kinds of things. Stories make sense. Before learning
to write children must first solve the problem of finding out what
written language is *for,* what it does. Without this insight, no reading or writing instruction will ever make sense. Children solve the
problem by making sense of the way people around them use

written language. Children find out about reading and writing by joining the literacy club.

Joining the Literacy Club

The literacy club is, of course, a club of people who use written language. Children join the literacy club the way they join the spoken language club—with the implicit act of mutual acceptance: "You're one of us," "I want to be just like you." There are no special admission requirements, no entry fees.

The advantages of joining the literacy club are the same as those of joining the spoken language club or any other club. First, the activities of experienced club members are quickly revealed to new members. The newcomer is shown in the normal course of everyday activities what written language can be used for. This is no vague matter of "demonstrating the value of reading and writing" as abstract general abilities, but the much more direct and immediate experience of making use of signs to get to intended destinations, using books for the enjoyment of a story, or making a shopping list to ensure that nothing is forgotten. These are activities which need no justification or explanation in themselves. The activities happen quite naturally, almost incidentally, to involve reading and writing.

Advantages of membership continue in the literacy club. Newcomers are helped to engage in club activities on the occasions when it is most useful and interesting for them to do so. There is no coercion. They are helped to buy (or to make) birthday cards when they want to send birthday cards; they find assistance—with the story, the telephone directory, the recipe, the instruction manual, the note on the refrigerator door, the McDonalds sign—when the assistance is relevant. There is never a formal, tedious, and meaningless period of instruction; no one says, "Put away your books, it's time to practice 'Mc' words." And no one ever gives a struggling beginner a low score; differences in interest and ability are expected. In the words of George Miller (in the title of his book) children learn language by becoming the "Spontaneous Apprentices" of people who know how to do things with language, spoken or written.

The "teaching"—if it has to be given that name—is as inconspicuous as the learning. Someone tells a child, "We'll stop at that Texaco station up the road," as naturally as they might say, "Look at that horse in the field over there." Experience in reading gas station signs is provided in the same incidental way as opportunities to learn what horses look like. The novice never has to struggle to practice and learn something that does not make sense.

And once again, membership in the literacy club adds to the individual's sense of personal identity, of who he or she is. "Hi kid, you're one of us," say the members of the literacy club. From the beginning, the child is a *reader* or a *writer,* a member of the guild, who takes learning for granted and who will learn. These are the children who will attempt to read and to write beyond their "level of ability," who will challenge themselves constantly in written language activities for the simple reason that they see themselves as competent readers and writers.

Assistance Across Time and Space

There is an odd advantage to becoming a member of the literacy club—the more experienced club members who can help novices most need not be people who are physically present, as they usually are in the spoken language club. The people who help children most in reading and in writing may be thousands of miles away; they may even be dead. I am referring to authors, of course. One of the leaders in research on how children learn to read, Margaret [Meek] Spencer of London University, says that it is authors who teach children to read. Not just any authors, but the authors of the stories that children love to read, that children often know by heart before they begin to read the story. This prior knowledge or strong expectation of how the story will develop is the key to the learning to read, says Professor Spencer. The child already knows what the story will be, and the author shows the child how to read it. (Spencer comments that it is a tragedy that so much of the "reading instruction" that children receive in schools stands between the child and the author.)

Authors also show children how to write. How else than by reading, or being read to, could children, or anyone else, learn all the subtle conventions of plot, narrative, characterization, mood, style—or of spelling and punctuation for that matter? You have to read in a special way to learn about writing in this manner, you have to read like a writer, like a member of the club. But it is the only way to learn to write, as any experienced member of the club of writers knows. Exercises in writing sentences and paragraphs—or in filling in the blanks—never made anyone an author or even a secretary.

The fact that distant authors can and must teach so much about reading and writing does not mean that the people around you are not important. These are the people who initiate you into the club in the first place, who read stories to you when you cannot read them for yourself, and who write with you so that you can see yourself as a member of the writers' club.

Learning in Other Clubs

I am not just talking about children, nor just about language. I am describing how people of all ages learn everything. Children may perhaps seem to learn faster than adults, but that could be because they have more to learn and may be more open to learning —infants and most children have not decided that there is not much left for them to learn. But no one learns differently from the way I have described. We all learn in the clubs to which we belong.

Donald Graves, the inadvertent Scot I referred to a few pages ago, was once a grade school teacher and is now a successful and highly-regarded teacher of teachers at the University of New Hampshire. He once told me that he had sat down and listed all the major things he had learned in his life—not only obvious abilities like tying shoe laces and riding a bicycle, but more subtle matters like how to manage time and the value of money. Against each item he wrote the name of the person most responsible for teaching him what he had learned. And he was surprised to discover how little he had learned at school, only about twenty percent of over one hundred items on the list. He was hoping to put them all together in a book that would be called simply "Teachers," though few of the characters were teachers in the formal classroom sense.

"My mother and father recall very few of the episodes that I've written about them," Graves later wrote to me. "But they are as vivid as yesterday to me when I write them. Learning after college was the most exciting of all, when I could finally pursue my own curriculum. When I had a chance to set up my own teachers for learning my way, the learning/teaching events began to multiply still more rapidly. So much of my learning was by hanging around, then by setting up others to teach me in the way I learned best. That kind of learning obviously excludes much of school instruction as we know it."

From whom did Graves learn? He says an uncle taught him how time could be used and wasted; a golf pro taught him to teach by observing; a gardener taught him not to take himself too seriously; a friend in the Coast Guard taught him to expect the unexpected; a school janitor taught him about being a principal; and a more experienced member of the club of authors taught him to find his voice in writing. There were no r-bbits, no dreary drills and exercises, and no formal tests.

Many clubs occupy the attention of children during the first years of their lives. Infants not only learn to talk like the kind of people they see themselves as being; they also learn to walk like them, dress like them, groom and ornament themselves like them, eat and drink like them. They learn to perceive the world in the way the people around them perceive it, and to share their hopes and fears, their beliefs and expectations, their imperatives and values. They learn a culture.

Once again, none of this knowledge is inherited. Children do not become like their parents unless they grow up with their parents and share their parents' perceptions of the world. The cultures we learn and the social roles we acquire are those of the people with whom we identify, of the kind of person we see ourselves as being. Every baby is capable of making sense of any culture in the world today. I do not know how many cultures there are, but the total is surely more than the number of languages that there are. And once again, no one would suggest that there could be no other cultures and societies in the future. The world is changing every day. Every child has the awesome power of being able to make sense of cultures that do not yet exist.

CHAPTER 3

Why Learning Sometimes Fails

If the human brain learns so powerfully and consistently, why does it so often seem to let us down? The answer is that whether we learn—or rather what we learn—depends on the conditions under which we try to learn or are required to learn. We can't learn everything we put our minds to, but not because of built-in faults in our basic learning equipment. No one's brain is a lemon in the way that automobiles can be.

Learning Instead of Understanding

A simple cause of many failures to learn is trying to learn something that doesn't make sense. We can't memorize anything from a book that confuses us. What is there to memorize, except the confusion? We can't recall anything about a situation that bewilders us, except the bewilderment. The problem is not that we can't learn, but that we can't make sense of what we want to learn.

I have not learned much in my life about automobile engines, but not because I have never tried. Many people have tried to talk to me about automobile engines, often wanting to discuss my own in the most intimate detail. Over the years I have bought many textbooks on automobile mechanics that are now well thumbed through for the first twenty or thirty pages and untouched beyond. The reason I haven't learned from the people or the books is that the discussion has always been above my head. I don't think that my failure has anything to do with intellectual abilities—I've been able to learn other things. And I can't believe I lack certain critical neurological interconnections in the brain that are essential for understanding automobile engines. Nor can I blame lack of effort. I've made determined attempts to master the contents of the text-books. Rote memorization of facts about engines just hasn't helped. My need has been for someone knowledgeable and patient enough to take me on as an apprentice, preferably to work with me on my own car's engine in ways that I can follow.

Teachers are effective when they make themselves understandable to the learner, no matter how little the learner knows, not when they overwhelm the learner in the vain hope that understanding will eventually follow. It is the teacher's responsibility to be comprehensible, not the student's to comprehend.

Researchers into language and learning have recently shown great interest in what they term "prior knowledge": the fact that it is easier to understand what people say or write when there is an existing understanding of what they are talking about. Professor Richard Anderson, director of the federally-funded Center for the Study of Reading at the University of Illinois, has discovered that students categorized as "low achievers" in school usually have limitations in their prior knowledge rather than defective learning abilities. The students do not understand what is going on. How well a student succeeds in reading a passage or solving a problem in math depends less on specific skills of reading or mathematics than on familiarity with similar passages or math problems. The learning situation should be blamed, not the learner. Why *expect* students to learn something that doesn't make sense to them?

Where does all this essential prior knowledge come from? Not from systematic and specific instruction, which again depends on prior knowledge, but from general experience in the topic in which the learning is expected to take place. We learn by engaging in activities where we are helped to understand what is going on and helped to participate in the activities ourselves.

A classic experiment conducted by psychologist George Mandler in the early 1970s demonstrated how understanding takes care of learning and how the deliberate effort to memorize interferes. Three groups of college students were given the same amounts of time to study a pack of fifty-two cards, each card with a different word on it. One group was asked to sort the cards into separate piles that made some kind of sense according to the words printed on them. The members of the group could employ any system of categorization that occurred to them, such as putting all cards bearing names of animals into the same pile, and they could make as many piles as they liked. In other words, they were obliged to treat the task as meaningful. They were not warned that they would be given a memory test after the cards had been removed from their sight, to see how many of the words they had incidentally learned. The members of the second group were given the same task but also warned that they would later be tested to see how many of the words they could remember. The members of the third group were simply told that they would be given the memory test and not required to do the sorting into piles.

One might think that the experimental procedure was unfair to the members of the first group, who were required to do a lot of thinking and not warned that there would be a test, and that the procedure most favored the third group, who could concentrate on learning without having to do the sorting task. But in fact the unwarned first group did just as well on the memory test as the group given both the sorting task and the warning. Being told that there would be a test made no difference—the meaning-making activity of organizing the words into sets took care of the learning. The group that did worst was the one that received the warning but was not given the task. The members of that group devoted all their attention to trying to memorize the words on the cards, and as a consequence learned least. Nonsense activities—like rote memorization—result in less learning than the incidental learning that occurs when one is engaged in a meaningful task.

Memory, Motivation, and Effort

An excuse many people offer for failure to learn is that they have a poor memory. I don't want to argue about whether some people have memories that are less efficient in every respect than the memories of others, but rather want to point out that we can all remember some things better than others. And paradoxically, we tend to be much more aware of the things we can't remember than of the things we can. We may say we have a poor memory because of problems we have with names or dates, even though we have no problem remembering huge quantities of other things —like the details of the language we speak, the geographies of our homes and neighborhoods, and innumerable facts about the world in general. We may even overlook all the names and dates we do remember because of our concern with the few that give us trouble.

But even if individual memories may be weak in particular respects, what makes them function most efficiently is still not deliberate practice or determined effort, but meaningfulness. It is often argued that surely students who find learning difficult must be drilled in just one thing at a time and tested frequently. But if there are certain things that we have difficulty learning, it is all the more important that they make sense to us. We can only learn from drills or from rote memorization things we already understand.

Another frequent explanation for failure to learn is lack of motivation. It is true that we do not learn if we are not interested in something, if we just don't see ourselves as the kind of person who does whatever it is we are supposed to learn. But motivation, in the sense of deliberate and conscious effort, is a different matter. I think it is one of the biggest red herrings we hear from teachers. Most of the time we learn without motivation, without even knowing that we are learning. And motivation itself does not guarantee learning. Often we fail in the very things we are most motivated to learn.

We all learn things that we are not motivated to learn, like my friend who came back from Scotland with a Scottish accent. Children usually do not make a conscious effort to learn to talk, walk, and dress themselves like the people in the communities to which they belong. On the other hand, we can all fail to learn things we are highly motivated to learn, as I have failed with automobile engines. The most that can be said for motivation is that it puts us into situations where things are going on that we might be interested in learning. And motivation *not* to learn will almost certainly result in not learning. Motivation might raise the probability that learning will take place if the conditions are right, but it does not carry a guarantee of success.

The examples I have just given also demonstrate that effort will not take care of learning. We learn things without trying and fail to learn when we deliberately put our minds to it. All of this is contrary to another educational shibboleth, widely promoted by University of Chicago professor of education Benjamin S. Bloom (who will be met several times in the course of this book), that the amount of learning depends on the "time on task." The more time spent in studying something, Bloom believes, the more that will be learned. Bloom is right—but only for the kind of nonsense learning task that is involved in most psychological experiments. How much is learned by rote is a direct function of time and effort. But when the learning is meaningful we learn much faster and, without effort. Having to spend long periods of time in repetitive efforts to learn specific things is a sign that learning is not taking place, that we are not in a productive learning situation.

Why then, for all of us, should there be specific things we can't learn, even when our motivation and effort are high? The explanation is that we learn there are things that we can't learn. The brain functions too efficiently. Once we are persuaded, by ourselves or by someone else, that we can't learn something, no amount of dedicated effort will produce success. The hardest problem for the brain is not *learning,* but *forgetting.* No matter how hard we try, we can't deliberately forget something we have learned, and that is catastrophic if we learn that we can't learn.

Spelling offers a good example. Many people tell me they are poor spellers—and prove it by telling me the words they cannot spell. Their problem is not lack of effort to learn the words they can't spell. They are forever consulting dictionaries for the spelling of these words. The trouble invariably is that they have learned incorrect spellings as well. They have learned too much. Incorrect spellings as well as the correct ones come to mind whenever they want to write particular words. Writing out the correct spelling a dozen times to commit it to memory is a waste of time. The correct spelling has been learned, but it is just one of several alternatives. What these people are unable to do is forget the incorrect spellings they don't want to remember.

What I can't forget is that I can't learn about automobile engines. Other people tell me they know they can't learn algebra, music or bridge, recognize particular stars, or distinguish among different kinds of birds or flowers, even though they have learned far more complicated things in their lives. It is not a question of motivation or effort—the things that people say they cannot do are usually things they have tried very hard to do. And it would be absurd to suggest that they might lack unique parts of the brain that specialize in the understanding of algebra, music, bridge, stars, birds, or flowers. We have all excluded ourselves, or been excluded, from certain clubs, with the consequence that we approach learning differently. We have decided that we are not the kind of person who learns certain kinds of things, that we are not members of the club.

Exclusion From the Club

Why should deciding (or being taught) that we don't belong to a club have such a disastrous effect on learning? If we do not belong to a particular club, then we do not apprentice ourselves to people who are members of that club. Our minds fail to engage with the demonstrations that are provided for us—they do not become part of us. We cease seeing ourselves as "that kind of a person."

Our club memberships are our identity. The original basis for membership in any club, remember, is: "You're one of us." "I am [or can be] just like you." If we see ourselves as members of a club, then we can't help learning to be like members of the club. But if we regard ourselves as outside a club, then our brains will resist any learning that might falsely identify us as club members.

Teachers who try to get children to talk the way teachers do don't know this. Children know they don't belong to the clubs to which teachers belong. Many children know that they will never have the advantages of teachers, even if they talk the way teachers do. You don't talk like people in the clubs you don't belong to, even if you hear these people talking all day long. Teachers who try to talk like their pupils by deliberately learning a few bits of the slang of the school yard also don't know this. When teachers begin talking like children, children change the way they talk. The whole point of their slang is to show they belong to different clubs from their teachers. If teachers want to change the way children talk, teachers must show—if they can—that talking differently can make a difference to children, that a worthwhile club is open for the children to join. We all learn to talk like the kind of person we see ourselves as being. Teachers did not become what they are because they talk like teachers; they talk the way they do *because* they are teachers.

There is a suggestive phenomenon when English-speaking children learn French through "total immersion" in Canadian schools. After about three years of a totally French-speaking environment in their classrooms, these native English speakers speak a French that is indistinguishable from that of native French-speaking children. But then there is a marked regression. The children still speak French extremely well, but with an English accent, and perhaps with a few of the errors that "foreigners" typically make. The children would no longer be mistaken for members of the club of native French-speakers, but only as members of the English-speakers club who happen to speak very good French. The reverse occurs with French-speaking children who learn English under similar circumstances. All these children have made decisions about the clubs they belong to. When they decide they are not a particular kind of a person, they learn to not be like that kind of person.

There are occasional objections to the argument that children learn from what is demonstrated by the people around them. Parents in particular may be quick to point out that every day they demonstrate to their children how to clean their teeth, tidy their rooms, and close the door quietly as they leave, yet children rarely seem to learn these things themselves. In 1976, anthropologist Margaret Mead reported the explanation for this lack of learning, from her observations in New Guinea. When children see parents enjoying what they regularly do, children quickly learn to do the same things themselves, which is the reason they learn to do many things that parents would just as soon their children would not learn to do. But when children see grown-ups regularly doing something without pleasure, then children learn what is demonstrated—that the activity is not rewarding and that grown-ups can be very peculiar and even hypocritical people.

Children learn when they are told they do not belong to a club. They learn that they do not belong to the club and that there are things they should not expect to learn. When are people, especially children, ever told that they don't qualify as members of clubs, even as novices? These exclusions occur occasionally in the world in general, deliberately sometimes and by chance at, other times. But in school, people often go out of their way to tell children that they don't belong in certain clubs and that they are unlikely to qualify for them in the future. Tests are given to ascertain the clubs that children are unlikely to join. Programs are devised that convince children that they don't belong to the clubs of readers, writers, mathematicians, critical thinkers—all sorts of academic specialties.

And all of the tests have great predictive power—from a negative point of view. Our intellectual tests are abysmal at predicting success. Interests, preferences, and family background are much better predictors of professional achievement than the IQ.

But predictions of failure rarely fail. Tell children that they are likely to have a reading problem, and they will almost certainly turn out to have a reading problem. Tell teachers that particular children are likely to have reading problems, and those very same children are likely to have reading problems, because they will be given different kinds of things to do in the classroom, mainly nonsensical r-bbity exercises. They are denied access to the club of readers.

The Myth of Learning Disabilities

The brains of children are frequently blamed for the failure of programmatic instruction at school. It is taken for granted that something must be wrong with children who are confused or discouraged by school activities. Arguments like mine that the brains of children are superb learning instruments can even be taken as support for the proposition that a child who does not learn in school must be impaired in some way. Medical metaphors are frequently employed to support the fiction that school failure is a kind of sickness. Real or imaginary inadequacies are given clinical-sounding labels like "dyslexia," for difficulty with reading or "dysgraphia," for limited writing ability, and the shortcoming is attributed to hypothetical deficiencies in the brain. Medical terms like "diagnosis," "remediation," and "treatment" add to the impression that a physical abnormality must be involved. Often a physician or a clinical psychologist is recruited to give a stamp of authority to the dismal prognosis.

Everyone acknowledges that the key to learning is interest. Yet learning is made ritualistically dull. No wonder children become bored, apathetic, distractible, unsettled, and apprehensive. But instead of regarding such behavior as clear signs that something is wrong with our schools, it is decided that something is wrong with children's brains.

To ascribe difficulties with school subjects to "specific learning disabilities" is like saying that children cannot read because they cannot read. Solemn pronouncements about the kinds of brain disorder that result in reading or writing disabilities are made by medical practitioners who know nothing of language or learning and by educators who are similarly ignorant in matters of neurophysiology. In the absence of confirming evidence of a physical basis for the failure to learn, the "disability" is attributed to a "minimal brain dysfunction" too small and specific to manifest itself in any other way. This is like arguing that a child who cannot jump a certain height must have a special kind of defective leg, even though there is no direct evidence of fractured bones and the child is perfectly able to walk, run, and swim. The minimal brain dysfunction diagnosis says in effect: "We have decided that there must be something wrong with the child's brain even though we can't detect where or what the disorder is. We just assume that any child who fails to take advantage of the instruction provided at school must be short of something in the head."

It is, of course, indisputable that a few children seem unable to master reading, writing, or other school subjects, even though their general intelligence and learning seem adequate enough in other respects. But there is no reason for the automatic attribution of such failures to physical or mental defects. These children may not have experienced reading in an interesting or useful context, or they may have found the instruction confusing or punitive. They may have been intimidated by the pressure placed upon all children to succeed in school, or they may actively resent the pressure. Children may be antipathetic to the teacher or just downright cussed and resistent to learning anything adults try to teach them. All of these attitudes can cause enormous frustration to parents and teachers, but they are not indicative of anything fundamentally wrong with the children's brain.

Richard Wanderman, of Eugene, Oregon, was labeled as "learning disabled" at school. Now in his early thirties, he teaches computer-assisted design at the University of Oregon and writes a national newsletter for computer users. He thinks that he actually found the "learning disabled" label useful when he was at school, especially when he was depressed about his lack of success. The label gave him a reason for why he was finding it impossible to learn to read and to write. "I got some comfort in being able to identify what my problems with learning were," he wrote to me recently. "So the label worked, so to speak. But it doesn't quite fit in with my other ideas about learning and thinking in general. In particular, who decides who's learning disabled? Where's the line drawn? On which set of underlying assumptions about intelligence and learning are we basing the label and criteria?"

Richard Wanderman asks questions such as these because, like many other students identified as "learning disabled," he has discovered that he is not disabled at all. He began to read and to write when he was free of the cycle of test and failure at school—even though he still needed the reassurance of other people that he was in fact able to read and write and was not defective in some way. He credits the computer with making it easy for him to write fluently and extend his thinking about thinking and learning in general.

Here is "dyslexic" Richard Wanderman striving in remarkably articulate and competent writing to understand what went wrong in his own education. "Maybe what we call a learning disability is the reaction of a particular sort of learning style to the predominant one. Maybe learning would be easier if we weren't struggling to fit the ideal and allowed ourselves to learn more naturally. Maybe learning is a natural process, not one that has to be imposed on people. Maybe the reason we need to impose it in this culture is because the learning style we are teaching isn't natural. Maybe this is why I've learned more and functioned better since I've been out of school and its formalized, rigid, traditional learning situations. This is evidence for the idea that learning problems are the result of a reaction rather than simply a neurological difference. Maybe making mistakes, a part of learning that we are taught to avoid, is so central a part of the learning process that our culture in its avoidance of mistakes will perish for lack of new ideas, new adaptations. Maybe what we call a neurologically caused learning problem is evidence of a new evolutionary strain, a branch of the species that is breaking away from the mainstream to protect a part of human nature that's being slowly destroyed: the enjoyment of learning and creating."

Wastelands of School Instruction

None of us can learn something that we don't understand, that we are not interested in, or that we don't see as the kind of thing people like ourselves learn. Only membership in an appropriate club guarantees learning—not time, effort, or irrelevant incentives and rewards. Schools do not facilitate clubs. The drills and tests that pervade classrooms confront students of all ages with tedious, time-consuming and stressful nonsense, rewarding—or punishing—effort with pointless marks and grades.

Justin is a fourth-grade student in Sonoma County, California. He can read and write. Here is a story-poem that Justin wrote and illustrated:

> I am a ghost and that's no boast, as long as you don't look
> under me. I'm a host of another ghost that buys me candy free.
> He's a host of another ghost who pays him fruits and veges.
> I'm a host to all those ghosts and it gets kinda scary.

Justin's teacher made just one comment on the story—an unexplained circling of the word *He's*. In the same week Justin worked on sixteen duplicated worksheets from duplicated masters prepared by Prentice-Hall Learning Systems, Incentive Publications Inc., of Nashville, Tennessee, The Instructor Publications Inc., and his own teacher. For one exercise, Justin had to work through sixteen sentences like:

joseph cranston studied at harvard university

underlining the letters that should be capitals. Justin—whose story already showed that he could use capitals—got an A for this effort. He received only a B for a worksheet on a book he had read where he successfully located five action verbs and wrote a brief summary but failed to fill in blanks about whether the story was fact or fiction and the number of pages he had read. He had duplicated exercises in mathematics, spelling, handwriting, comprehension (more questions about stories), "brain stretchers" (more mathematics), and listening skills (more questions about stories). For all of his efforts Justin received letter grades and admonitions to be neater. What clubs was Justin introduced to? What was he *taught?*

Jonathan is a second grader in the same school district. In one week Jonathan averaged a dozen duplicated worksheets a day. On one sheet he had to copy twenty words ending with the letters *tch.* On another sheet his task was to color pictures for words that have the "long i sound," like "kite" and "bride." For coloring pictures whose words had a "long u sound," he was told (on a duplicated slip from "Rewards 'n' Stuff" produced by Enrich of Sunnyvale, California) that he had done a "bee-utiful job." What is Jonathan learning about reading and writing from the circus that is his reading instruction? What are the essential mysteries of long and short i's and u's that Jonathan, already a reader, must master?

Brook Higham, of Colorado Springs, could read when she began kindergarten. Her mother told me, "We never taught her, and we were surprised when she began reading to her three-year-old sister. At the age of three she would listen to a favorite book for as long as anyone would read it to her." Then Brook went to school. "Her first-grade teacher was determined to fill in the 'phonics gaps' she felt plagued children who had learned to read at home," said Jeanne Higham. In other words, her daughter had to concentrate on the meaningless drills that were supposed to make her a reader. Her teacher was frustrated because children like Brook spoiled the rationale for this type of instruction. Brook wrote a poem, and her parents bought her a blank book which she spent the year filling with poetry. She called her book "The Sky is Always Bluer on the Next Page," and she filled it with illustrations much like—naturally—those in her favorite book. She was adamant that she would not show the book to her teacher because the teacher would write comments on the pages and insist that the pictures be colored in.

University of Indiana education professor Carolyn Burke remembers her enthusiasm when she set off enthusiastically at the age of five for her first day in kindergarten—and her despair a few hours later when she learned that she would not receive her first reading book for a year. "Learning to read" would be a first-grade activity. Two professors at Teachers College, Columbia University, Denny Taylor and Dorothy S. Strickland, tell another kindergarten story. Shelly, who could read, write, and make books, was given the "C book," the "O book," the "G book," and the "L book" to work through and take home when she was done with all the exercises in each one. On the last page of each book Shelly's parents were told that she had now learned *one* sound for each letter and should not be confused by the introduction of other words. The "U book" taught the sound that came at the beginning of "up," "under," and "umbrella," for example; words like "use" and "urge" should be avoided. Shelly's parents were given exercises—hiding pieces of paper with words like *under* and *up* on them—to use in coaching her, to help her cope with her nonsensical work at school.

University of Michigan education professor Valerie Polakow has reported in the professional journal *Language Arts* that teachers told her that bright five-year-old Sharon "thinks the wrong way" because she does not follow the sequential logic of the prereading curriculum.

Children learn exactly what is demonstrated to them. Harvard Graduate School of Education researcher Barbara Eckhoff discovered in 1983 that second-grade children whose readers consisted of fragmentary sentences set out one on a line like:

> Ben said, "Stop, ducks!
> You can't eat this.
> No, you can't!
> No, ducks! No!
> You can't eat this."

wrote their own stories a similar way:

> A woman bought some tomatoes.
> She is happy.
> She is old.
> She is at the market.

Children whose readers contained more normal sentences, on the other hand, wrote stories like "The lady has just bought some tomatoes. She might make a salad or eat them raw. When she gets home she might give some of them to her friends."

Teacher-researchers Donald Graves and Virginia Stuart examined how children were taught to read and write all over the United States. In their book *Write From the Start,* they tell of a kindergarten child used to hearing real stories complaining that a first-grade reader had no story but a lot of words—words selected to correspond to what some distant expert assumed to be the child's reading skill. Such materials, in the researchers' opinion, provided no incentive for reading and poor models for writing—the opposite of what a child would be expected to achieve (though the blame for non-achievement would be laid on the child). Like many observers, Graves and Stuart conclude that kindergarten and first-grade children love to write, but "it doesn't take too many years of filling in blanks, copying words and diagramming sentences before children decide writing is no fun at all."

Graves and Stuart indict teachers and the publishing industry. They say that schools persist in the workbook approach to writing instruction because it is simpler and requires no writing ability on the part of the teacher. And educational publishers have a great investment in the materials. It might be argued that publishers produce only what educational systems will buy—but the publishers also persuade teachers that the programs they peddle are important. If it was decided tomorrow that children should read stories instead of doing exercises, then publishers would stop publishing workbooks and concentrate on stories. And teaching would change if school administrators expected teachers to be interested and competent in what they teach rather than dispensers of workbook materials.

Graves and Stuart also blame "the test-making business" for testing "component skills"—frequently at the rate of one a day. Because children are tested in this way, they are taught in this way. Instead of writing, children read a paragraph and then circle or underline "the correct answer" to questions, say Graves and Stuart.

When children do write, teachers concentrate on correcting errors, which is all they can do. All the red-inking makes the teachers feel better, but the child feels worse. Yet, Graves and Stuart decided, children who wrote instead of being primed for tests did better on them. And they are not talking about "privileged" children. They tell of elaborate and complex compositions on topics ranging from supersonic transport to the paintings of Van Gogh by children in some of New York City's poorest areas.

Susan Ohanian, a primary teacher in Troy, New York, for fourteen years, tells of asking a publisher's sales representative to show her the "readers" (educational jargon for stories) that children would read in the program she was selling. Ohanian describes the confused salesperson's response. "She kept showing me isolated paragraphs and the ubiquitous skill drills. 'No, no,' I insisted. 'Where's the reader? What do the kids read?' She replied, 'This program is skill based; it *prepares* the child to read.' I was looking for a sixth-grade program. Six years in school, and the child's day was still almost 100 percent skill filled. If one does not weep at that, what carnage does it take to fill one's eyes and heart with sorrow?"

Nobel prize-winning physicist Richard P. Feynman seethes rather than weeps at the math and science instruction imposed on teachers and children, especially since he uses math himself as a scientist. He describes his experiences as a member of the California State Curriculum Commission, which chooses the new textbooks for the state. "The books were so lousy. They were false. They were hurried. . . . The definitions weren't accurate. . . . They were faking it. They were teaching something they didn't understand and which was, in fact, *useless.*" Feynman describes pointless attempts to make mathematical exercises entertaining, even though what might be taught (like translating from one base to another) is "utterly useless." He talks about working through sentences full of minor errors (because "everything was written by somebody who didn't know what the hell he was talking about") to end with an absurd task, such as being given a "roughly correct" listing of the temperatures of stars and then being required to add the temperatures of stars together. "There's no purpose whatever in adding the temperature of two stars. . . . It was like reading sentences with a few typographical errors, and then suddenly the whole sentence is written backwards." Feynman resigned from the commission after failing to change its mind about science books permeated with nonsense.

Some Children's Opinions

The United States is not unique. Virginia Makins, a reporter with the *Times Educational Supplement* in London, invited British schoolchildren aged from five to eleven to tell her what they thought of the curriculum and teaching methods in their schools. Nearly 3,000 children from over 300 schools responded, and they were almost unanimous in their rejection of dull and ritualistic activities, even though the children acknowledged the importance of what they were supposed to learn. They just thought they could learn in more effective ways.

Tedium permeated the responses. One Manchester eight-year-old described a typical Monday morning: "After prayers we get out our spelling books and dictionaries. We look up the spellings and put the meanings in our spelling books. After that we get out our English books and put the sentences in it. After play we get out our math books. . . . After dinner [lunch] we come in and have reading laboratory." A West Glamorgan pupil reported: "A table test . . . then an English test which is wrote on the blackboard. The test is like name three kinds of meat and six things at a railway station. Then break, then number. Number is sums. Then handwriting, we are all on page six, book two in our class. Then we do five a day, five a day is five easy questions. Then we do spelling. Each week we have some spellings and the next week we have a test."

Hatred of English was almost universal in every junior-age school, said Makins. Instead of meaningful experience in the literacy club, the children reported: "Just the same boring thing over and over again." "My worst English is called *Basic Course in English,* it goes on and on." "The most boring and horrible subject is *Effective Composition.* " "I do not see what comprehension has to do with education, because all you have to do is answer questions." "We have to get the same answers, the whole class." Instead of "English" the children wanted poetry, drama, and more time for reading and writing "so we can really let our imagination roll and finish with a good long story." One child complained, "Our teacher makes me mad because she tells you to write a story and then after two pages she tells you to finish it even though you are in the middle."

The children liked mathematics and science, but only if they were taught by enthusiastic and interested teachers. Most children respected their teachers, especially the teachers who were concerned that the children understood and who could laugh with them. They liked clubs, experiments, practical activities, and would give up their lunch breaks to work in the school library or bookshop. The children made many sensible suggestions about how subjects might be better taught, continued Makins, and about what interfered with learning (like the growing shortage of books, rigid timetabling, crowded classrooms—twenty was the preferred number—copying from books, and extended mass practice on "basics").

Virginia Makins concluded: "The sad thing is that almost all the things children want to do could be geared to improving basic English and mathematics. The most extraordinary result . . . was the unanimity and conviction with which boys and girls aged eight to eleven called for a broader curriculum, with much more science, geography, history, art, craft, woodwork, electronics, cooking, and technology. . . . They wanted, above all, more work which allowed them to think for themselves. . . . They wanted to design and make things, to experiment, and to engage in first-hand observation."

But children were not getting very much of what they wanted. Makins summarized that "Most schools, on the children's evidence, have pretty rigid timetables which do not allow for sustained work on one enterprise. Basics, practised in isolation rather than in the course of other work, take up many hours—even for older children who know they are pretty competent. Work the children find interesting—humanities, science, craft—happens once or twice a week if they are lucky. Work . . . is not tailored to individual likes, talents, or aptitudes. In the few schools where children are trusted (or feel trusted) to plan their own work and choose, up to a point, what they do and how long they spend on it, they responded with enthusiasm." But such schools, Makins found, were "rare birds."

Of course, it might be argued that the children who responded to Virginia Makins's invitation were particularly bright and literate in any case, who would be bored by drills and needed the challenge of more complex activities. But is there any reason to think that less articulate children would find tedium more tolerable, or interesting and meaningful activities less stimulating?

Learning and Feelings

Learning is never divorced from feelings—and neither is failing to learn. We don't just learn about something, we simultaneously learn how we feel as we learn. Often the memory of the feeling lasts longer than the actual thing we learn. We learn about the ritual of going to the dentist on our first visit, and we remember forever after how we felt on that first visit, even though we may forget all other details of the event. We are unhappy on one occasion when we happen to hear a particular melody or smell a certain aroma, and every time we chance upon that melody or that aroma we feel unhappy, even though we cannot remember why. Even if we succeed in learning under conditions that are threatening, embarrassing, or punitive, then we will experience the same miserable feelings whenever we try to practice whatever we learned. Every advantage of learning can be destroyed by the circumstances in which the learning is expected to take place.

How can failure to learn be avoided, so that we and our children will not be taught *not* to learn? How can we ensure that schools are not places where worthwhile learning is doomed to fail? In the Learners' Manifesto that follows, I have summarized the essential conditions that must be respected if worthwhile learning is to be ensured.

The Learners' Manifesto

(1) The brain is always learning. We learn exactly what is demonstrated by people around us. Schools must stop trying to teach through pointless drills, activities, and tests.

(2) Learning does not require coercion or irrelevant reward. We fail to learn only if we are bored, or confused, or if we have been persuaded that learning will be difficult. Schools must be places where learning can take place naturally.

(3) Learning must be meaningful. If we understand, then we learn. Schools must change themselves, not try to change us, to ensure we understand what we are expected to learn.

(4) Learning is incidental. We learn while doing things that we find useful and interesting. Schools must stop creating environments where we cannot engage in sensible activities.

(5) Learning is collaborative. We learn by apprenticing ourselves to people who practice what they teach. Schools must stop trying to deliver instruction mechanically. If teachers cannot teach, there must be better teachers, not more tests and programmatic instruction.

(6) The consequences of worthwhile learning are obvious. We demonstrate the worthwhile things we learn by engaging in those activities. Schools, teachers, and parents should not have to rely on marks, scores, or tests to discover if we have learned.

(7) Learning always involves feelings. We remember how we feel when we learn and when we fail to learn. Schools must not treat learners like battery hens or like machines.

(8) Learning must be free of risk. If we are threatened by learning, then the learning will always threaten. Schools must recognize that continual testing is intellectual harassment.

CHAPTER 4

How Not to Create an Expert

R-bbits are prolific breeders. They have infested schools for so long that many people, including teachers, cannot imagine classrooms without them. The r-bbit philosophy of teaching and testing one predetermined thing at a time has made clubs all but impossible in schools. Children are too busy with the workbooks and activity sheets. A related philosophy plagues colleges and universities, where students may spend less time in critical thought and the collegial pursuit of worthwhile understanding than in assimilating and regurgitating required "information." R-bbits represent the rejection of every right in the Learners' Manifesto.

Where All the R-bbits Came From

R-bbits are not indigenous to education. They were not introduced into classrooms in any numbers until the 1960s, when they quickly proliferated to pestilential proportions. R-bbits were conceived in the laboratories of experimental psychologists and in the flow charts of systems analysts and project planners engaged in complex logistical enterprises like traveling to the moon. Research psychologists and systems engineers shared an obsession with the "programmatic" technology of breaking down complex activities into small parts, or "objectives," to be accomplished one at a time. The technology got man to the moon, but when extrapolated into education it failed, because it was tied to a fallacy about how people learn and how experts are created.

Learning has always been a difficult topic for research psychologists to study. How can experimenters compare how anyone learns French verbs, or mathematical formulas, or respect for their neighbors, when individuals approach learning situations with different backgrounds, interests, and prior knowledge? How can new learning be separated from what the learner might know already? Results obtained in one experiment elude replication in other experiments with different individuals or with different learning tasks.

Toward the end of the last century, experimental psychologists discovered that they could avoid all of the technical difficulties of learning studies provided they restricted their research to how individuals learned *nonsense*—meaningless shapes and symbols, or syllables like WUG, DEX, and TAV. Subjects in these experiments were given lists of nonsense syllables to memorize, and the rate at which they learned and subsequently forgot these syllables was compared with how much time they had been allowed for practice and rehearsal, their anxiety level, the consequent rewards or punishments, and any other factor the experimenter cared to investigate. No one could have prior knowledge of something that made no sense. With nonsense, everyone started learning from scratch. There were no uncontrolled variables or individual differences to "contaminate" the results and complicate the researcher's life. Every aspect of learning could be separated and individually monitored. Experiments could be replicated and empirical results verified. Indeed, it is often asserted that the invention of the nonsense syllable by Hermann Ebbinghaus in the 1870s made it possible for experimental psychology to become a science.

The nonsense syllable offered *control*. Experimental subjects could be given fixed amounts of time to undertake quantifiable amounts of learning and could be tested at regular and frequent intervals to see exactly what was learned and how long it was remembered. The results of such research studies made possible the formulation of *laws* of learning and forgetting, which could be represented by smooth curves on graphs and summarized by algebraic formulas. These laws could actually be used to predict how other learners would perform on similar tasks under similar conditions.

The fact that psychology's "laws of learning" are wholly based on nonsense is generally ignored. It is difficult to study meaningful learning under laboratory conditions, and precise predictions about experimental results with meaningful tasks are usually impossible. The most that can be said is that meaningful learning is always accomplished much quicker and persists much longer. But such learning produces no neat formulas, no satisfying graphs, that can be used to summarize and extrapolate the research findings. *Sense* makes havoc of carefully planned learning experiments. Experimental subjects seem to know that meaningful learning is more efficient than the rote memorization of rubbish. They are always trying to translate nonsense syllables into sense, no matter how bizarre. WUG, DEX, and TAV, for example, are much easier to remember if they are organized into an image of a drunken sailor trying to put a Wug (rug?) on the Decks of a Tavern. The history of the experimental study of learning has been a struggle between researchers trying to devise better nonsense and subjects trying to make sense of it.

The methodology of systems analysis similarly involves reducing large and complex activities to sequences of small tasks, or objectives, each of which has to be accomplished before there is progress to the next task. Individuals working on particular "en route" objectives need have no knowledge or understanding of the total plan, or even of the ultimate goal of the enterprise. Indeed, it is better that they concentrate completely on their own small set of prescribed objectives. When the Soviet Union first launched space satellite around the earth, systems analysis was the technology that was expected to ensure that Americans would be the first to walk on the moon—and it worked. The "giant step for mankind" of putting a man on the lunar surface was, in fact, a large number of small steps, each moving the astronauts and their life support systems one inexorable inch after the other to the moon and back.

The systems approach was successful in the space program because of the *control* that was imposed. Nothing was allowed to be overlooked or to get out of hand. To get to final goal Z, the spacecraft had to get to subgoal Y with enough equipment and fuel for the final step and for the return. To get to Y, it had to be sure of getting to X with everything required for the move to Y. And so on, all the way back to C, B, and the starting point of A. "Quality," in the sense of the successful attainment of limited but clearly specified objectives, could always be assured.

The same technology was also expected to eradicate illiteracy and other perceived defects of American education. Analyze what an educated person can do, break that expertise down into small parts, and deliver the parts to learners systematically. Psychology even had its laws to guarantee that learning would take place if instruction was systematically delivered one step at a time. Few politicians and administrators seemed to doubt that programmatic control, applied to education, could achieve major instructional objectives. If students were taught one thing at a time, and tested until they demonstrated that they had learned what they were taught, then students could be made experts.

Unfortunately, the philosophy of precisely controlled programmatic instruction ignores the fact that what is learned on any particular occasion depends on the prior knowledge, intentions, and state of comprehension of the learner, not on a system devised in advance by someone who is not on the scene. The journey to learning cannot be planned in advance and controlled like a journey to the moon. A teacher is not a redundant part of the system. There is no point in saying that disciplined study is good and even necessary for students. If they are required to learn something that does not make sense to them, then the learning will be much more difficult and pointless, in any case. This does not mean that teachers and other adults should do nothing, waiting around for students to make up their minds whether or not they want to learn to read, write, or anything else. The teacher's responsibility is to make learning a particular subject or skill both desirable and feasible; to depict the destination and to facilitate the route. Meaningful learning requires a club atmosphere, with the r-bbits, not the learning, strictly under control.

The Programmatic Control of Instruction

The preferred piece of instructional technology in the 1960s came straight out of the experimental psychologist's laboratory. It was the teaching machine, relics of which still gather dust in many school closets. B. F. Skinner devised his own teaching machine and wrote a book on the topic. The teaching machine was like a photographic slide projector with its own screen on which items of instruction could be presented one at a time to the learner, followed by an appropriate question. If the learner gave the correct answer, the machine moved to the next item. If the learner failed, there was a loop back to more instruction or to a repetition of the learning task. Exactly the same procedure could be followed on paper. In fact, there was a rash of books that were divided up into numbered sections rather than pages. For example, Section 18 of an introductory calculus text produced by Harvard physics professors Daniel Kleppner and Norman Ramsey presented in barely half a page an illustration of a graph of a particular function, a one-item test, and the instruction: "Check your answer. If correct, go on to 19. If incorrect, study frame 16 once again and then go to 19." On frame 19 the learner was told the correct answer, given a paragraph of instruction, and told to proceed to frame 20, and so forth, until sent into a backward loop by an incorrect answer. The test on frame 18 required circling the correct one of three given alternatives. Other tests involved filling in a blank.

Both the teaching machine and the programmed learning book have gone out of fashion, but not because the technique has been abandoned. Instead the techniques of programmed instruction—and many of its experts—were adopted and elaborated on by large publishing houses in the production of entire instructional programs which are frequently claimed to take care of all aspects of children's education in particular areas over a period of years. These programs were—and still are—elaborately packaged and expensively promoted, with glossy covers, high-quality illustrations, sophisticated graphics, and carefully prescribed learning sequences, together with workbooks, activity sheets, teacher manuals, and of course, tests. The *Lippincott Basic Reading Program* from Harper and Row, for example, claims to teach "all students *how* to read. . . . students master decoding skills early because every sound/ symbol is taught and reinforced before the next one is introduced. Each new skill is built on skills already learned." Ginn and Company tells teachers in its "totally new," 1985 program that "you'll find the actual instructions and directions you need to achieve the comprehensive goals you want. . . . Every skill is clearly defined for both you and your students. So there's never any guesswork about what you should do and why."

Everything is beautifully sequenced and systematic, and the programs are marketed at major conferences and in teachers' journals like automobiles. The current year's model is always the best, based on the latest research, with no explanation of why the product is better or even effective. The programs were primarily designed to appeal to teachers and administrators, although they were also made as attractive as possible for children. Everything is dressed up as "fun." Fill in the blanks, circle the correct answer, and go back if you don't get it right. Most of the larger instructional programs, produced by major educational publishing companies like Macmillan, Ginn, Scholastic, Prentice-Hall, Harper and Row, Houghton Mifflin, and Holt, Rinehart & Winston (CBS Publishing) aim at covering all bases, including books and stories for "meaningful reading" and an emphasis on "comprehension." But the reading materials are always supplementary to the repetitive skills instruction and accompanied by questions so that the students' "right" or "wrong" answers can be counted. And comprehension is reduced to a set of skills on which students can again be drilled and tested.

And now there is the computer, which can present programmatic instruction with sound, movement, and in living color, too. Computer manufacturers, computer software producers, traditional publishing companies, and a host of smaller enterprises propound the enticements of computer-based instruction. To select from scores of choices, American Educational Computer of Palo Alto, California, offers eight levels of "Micro-Read" for Apple computers, a "curriculum integrated reading program that talks!" The program is on seventy-three floppy disk sides, costs $1,795, and claims to cover all the skills that teachers want to teach. Bill Cosby has promoted Texas Instruments educational computer systems—which offer, among other things, an entire "basic skills and high school skills library"—as "the smart choice." IBM vigorously champions its own literacy program, which we will meet in the next chapter, designed by one man who claims he can take the place of all teachers. Rocky Mountain Educational Systems of Golden, Colorado, will for $485 provide a "manager disk and teacher's guide" for students with learning problems from preschool through junior high, with "1600 measurable objectives which cover 15 academic and social areas." Many companies claim that their regular programs can also be used with students requiring special attention, like the "gifted" and the "handicapped." In an unusual twist, Rocky Mountain claims that a "special use" of its materials, designed for students with difficulties, "will produce an instructional program plan, not only for handicapped students, but for all students from preschool through sixth grade."

The underlying theory is always the same. The instruction is fragmented into sequences of steps or "objectives" to be tackled one at a time, with tests all along the way to ensure that each thing is learned. Ironically, it is often claimed that this procedure facilitates "individualized instruction" where everyone can learn at his or her "own pace," although what is to be learned is rigorously predetermined.

Programmatic instruction—where someone outside the classroom who cannot see either learners or teacher decides what the teacher should do next—has never been successful beyond its own prescribed and limited objectives. The programs could never live up to their extravagant labels or advertising. No one would claim that students leave school today knowing more than students thirty years ago. The 1983 report of the ironically-named National Commission on Excellence in Education referred to a "rising tide of mediocrity" overtaking the nation's schools. The report, entitled *A Nation at Risk,* tells of about 23 million functionally illiterate adults, as judged by the simplest tests of everyday reading, writing, and comprehension, and falls in average scores on the College Board's Scholastic Aptitude tests of over 50 points on verbal items and nearly 40 points on mathematical items. All this was between 1963 and 1980, during the decade of the national "Right to Read" program, as programmatic drilling and testing became pervasive in American education.

In his book *Illiterate America,* teacher-reformer Jonathan Kozol puts the number of functionally illiterate adults at 60 million—nearly 40 percent of the adult population. The usual explanation for this colossal failure from the apologists for programs is that teachers still do not know how to use programs properly or that they circumvent them. In other words, the solution is to have more programs and tighter programmatic control (under the deceptive label of "teacher accountability"). But the real reason for the failure is that the technology that brought order to the research laboratory and put a man on the moon was not appropriate for education. It contains a critical fallacy about the nature of learning. The fallacy might be called "How Not to Create an Expert."

How Not to Create an Expert

The belief that supports all programmatic instruction is that the only sure way to transform a beginner into an expert in anything is to do a "task analysis" of what an expert can do and then to teach these things to the beginner one at a time (making sure always that they are learned). Step by step every American child would be made competent in reading, writing, arithmetic, science, and even in making ethical judgments.

And this was how the r-bbit was born. All literate people know how to fill in the blank in "r-bbit," therefore if children are drilled in doing this and similar things that the experts can do, then they will become literate themselves. Expert readers know the alphabet and the sounds of letters. Expert writers know spelling and punctuation. Mathematicians can add and subtract and perform all kinds of more complex operations on numbers. Therefore to construct a literate person make sure beginners learn the alphabet and the sounds of letters, and the rules of spelling and punctuation. To construct a mathematical expert, drill children in addition and subtraction. It is all sheer superstition. Understanding is expected to be a consequence of all this learning, not a prerequisite. And the r-bbit has proliferated despite a chorus of informed opposition from experienced educators.

Roger W. Shuy, a professor in the Center for Applied Linguistics at Georgetown University, examined research studies into how children learn about language, both spoken and written, and reported in 1981: "This research shows that good language learners begin with a function, a need to get something done with language, and move gradually toward acquiring the forms which reveal that function. They learn holistically, not by isolated skills. Such learners worry more about getting things done with language. . . . they experiment freely and try things unashamedly." He goes on: "For reasons unclear and almost incomprehensible, we have developed a tradition of teaching reading, writing and foreign language which goes in just the opposite direction . . . from part to whole."

In 1972 mathematics teacher Richard Skemp suggested an explanation why teachers might prefer programmatic instruction. He distinguished two forms or purposes of mathematics understanding: *instrumental* and *relational.* Instrumental understanding, he said, is knowing how to do something, like the cross-multiplication of numerators and denominators in the division of fractions, without necessarily knowing why it is done. Relational understanding means comprehending the reasoning behind mathematical operations, for example why cross-multiplication results in division. Instrumental learning has limited applicability, results in monumental errors of misunderstanding, and rarely leads to useful insights. Relational understanding, by definition, produces learners who know what they are doing, who can evaluate results, extrapolate from them, and even work out likely new strategies independently. So why is so much school instruction instrumental? Skemp argues that instrumental operations are much easier to teach and to drill, especially for teachers who lack any mathematical understanding themselves. Instrumental instruction lends itself perfectly to the mindless repetition found in workbook and computer exercises.

In a keynote address to the Annual Symposium for Science and Mathematics teachers held by the Illinois Science Lecture Association in May 1984, Victor F. Weisskopf, emeritus professor of physics at M.I.T., pointed out that science is not an accumulation of facts, of correct answers to definite questions about formulas and names. "Science is curiosity, discovering things, and asking why, why is it so? . . . We must always begin by asking questions and not by giving answers. . . . Youngsters and adults cannot learn if information is pressed into their brains. You can only teach by creating interest, by creating an urge to know. The knowledge has to be sucked into the brain, not pushed into the brain. First you have to create a state of mind which craves knowledge. . . . Avoid, as much as possible, frontal learning: teacher talking, students listening."

Many teachers will immediately object: But what about the students who aren't interested? Surely those students have to be drilled. Many program developers have told me that it is the student in difficulty who most needs the "frontal learning." The truth is that these students can tolerate it least. As Weisskopf asserts, it is the teacher's prime responsibility to make the subject interesting.

Weisskopf says, "When I start a course, I always say at the beginning, 'I will not cover the subject. I will uncover part of it.' " He tells classroom teachers, "I know that you have to face principals, tests, SATs, Achievement Tests, etc. But we must work together to reevaluate the whole problem of necessary knowledge. Students don't need to *know* so much. . . . You don't need to know the details if you know where to find them. . . . Interest students, and then they will become eager to know more, not to know less, as they are most eager today."

There are two essential flaws in the notion that the way to construct an expert is to catalog everything that an expert can do, and then to teach the learner to do these things one by one. The first mistake is that the approach overlooks *why* the expert learned to do such things in the first place, and the second is that it ignores *when* the expert learned them. Programmatic instruction (sometimes misnamed "programmed learning") ignores why and how people actually learn.

Competent readers did not learn the alphabet and the sounds of letters so that they would be able to read; they acquired the "basic skills" as a consequence of reading (and of being helped to read). No child ever learned to put together the "sounds" of the word "McDonald's" in order to be able to recognize it. But recognizing the word enables children to make sense of instruction concerning the sounds of those letters. Arithmetic drills do not help anyone to understand addition and subtraction, but understanding transactions involving numbers results in learning to add and to subtract.

Experienced people do not learn useful skills when they are engaged in activities that they do not understand. People become expert when they are doing something that makes sense to them. Making sense of situations takes care of the learning. And in any case, sense is always easier to learn than nonsense.

Turning Sense and Nonsense Upside Down

A myth that supports all of the effort to drill into children things they do not understand is that learning has to precede understanding. To understand something you first must learn it, or learn to understand it. And there is no point in studying something you already understand. These are common assumptions, and totally wrong; the reverse of how things actually are. To learn you have to understand. There is no point in trying to learn something you do not already understand. The myth confuses understanding something with knowing it already. We are capable of understanding many things we do not already know; we probably do so every moment that we are awake and not bored or bewildered.

We do not usually persevere in reading an article in a magazine or newspaper if we do not understand it—that would just be confusing. But we also do not read an article if we already know what it has to tell us—that would be boring. What we do is read something that we understand, that we can make sense of, but that we do not know already. And as a consequence, we learn. The only thing we are likely to learn if we are confused or bored is that the article is confusing or boring. And if we continue to read material that is confusing or boring, we shall quickly learn that reading itself is confusing and boring. To understand something does not mean that we know it already, but that we can relate it to what we know already, that we can make sense of it.

I understand when my morning newspaper tells me that my local team lost another game last night. Every word in the report makes sense to me, but not because I already know the result of the game. I also learn as a consequence of my understanding of the report—I learn the result of last night's game. I do not have to memorize the result, to deliberately put it into memory, because my understanding takes care of that. I would only have to memorize deliberately if I were dealing with something I did not understand —but if that were so I probably wouldn't be reading the report in the first place. I do not have to learn anything in order to understand, but my prior understanding results in my learning.

All of this is totally contrary to a monument of theorizing that has influenced and justified educational psychology and instructional development for the past thirty years, formally known as Bloom's Taxonomy of Educational Objectives. Benjamin Bloom and his academic associates at the University of Chicago developed their taxonomy, or classificatory scheme, of levels of learning complexity in the 1950s, when the systematic analysis of learning and instruction was beginning to gain momentum. Bloom's proposal was that complex types of behavior (like the kinds of things humans generally do) are based on more simple kinds of behavior (like the kinds of things generally done only in experimental studies), and that instruction should similarly proceed in the same direction. Bloom's six categories begin with simple "knowledge," with relating one thing to another, like getting a fact out of a file. Learning and remembering that Lima is the capital of Peru, or that seven squared is forty-nine, are examples of the "knowledge" at the bottom level of Bloom's hierarchy, scarcely different from the rote memorization of nonsense syllables. This type of learning is also called "stimulus-response" learning, reflecting the origins of this kind of theory in the animal-conditioning experiments of the Russian physiologist Pavlov and in B. F. Skinner's behaviorism.

Next up the scale from such "basic" learning in Bloom's hierarchy is "comprehension" of the very simplest kind, like being able to use a fact in some way without necessarily understanding its implications or relating it to any other knowledge. The ascent of the scale continues through *application, analysis,* and *synthesis* until the pinnacle is reached at *evaluation,* where the learner is able to make judgments about the value or utility of what is learned. For instructional and testing purposes, the six steps on Bloom's ladder are commonly reduced to three or four, starting with fact learning and rising through inference to application and then to evaluation. Each successive step is supposed to be harder than the earlier one. Midwest Publications Company's "Basic Thinking Skills" series, which has been adopted for both English and math instruction in California and other states, claims to be "related to Bloom's Taxonomy" because the programs lead children from following directions and recognizing patterns to thinking about problems and making judgments.

Bloom's is not the only hierarchical learning scheme in educational psychology, but it is the most influential. Unfortunately, all hierarchical schemes represent the world turned upside down. They are based on learning that is essentially nonsensical, determined by the experimenter rather than by the learner, and rely on data collected in controlled experimental conditions. In the real world, "fact learning" is the most difficult kind of learning, unless it is embedded in something that is understood. The recall of nonsense is much less efficient than the recollection of situations that were comprehensible. Children learn through what they do rather than doing things as a result of what they know. They do not learn from the club members they apprentice themselves to unless they can infer why club members behave in the ways they do and unless they evaluate the behavior as worth emulating. They learn when they decide they would like to do something themselves—a judgment that is at the peak of the hierarchy.

In language learning, in mathematics and in science generally, teaching the "skills" or the "basics" first and hoping that understanding will come later may be the easiest kind of instruction for teachers who do not really comprehend what they are doing in any case. But children learn to read and to write when they are engaged in activities that naturally involve reading and writing, as a whole, not in bits. Children learn math and science when engaged in enterprises that involve math and science—when they are shopping, building, creating, and exploring, and they can see a purpose and a value in what they do. For learning that occurs spontaneously and continually, the hierarchy and the taxonomy should be upended.

The Rise and Decline of Mastery Learning

Bloom's theories have also been directly translated into a program called "Mastery Learning" that has been adopted by over 1,500 school districts across the United States, one of them being its home territory of Chicago where it has recently been withdrawn as a failure. While his hierarchy is widely taken in support of the absurd position that something children can make sense of and use is more difficult to learn than something they cannot, Bloom has an underlying view that is insightful and indisputable. For thirty years he has argued against the widespread belief that there are good learners and poor learners, and in favor of the notion that there are faster learners and slower learners. Bloom has also pointed out that individual differences are not so much between *learners,* as people, as between *what is learned,* and that in fact the same individual might be a fast learner for some things and a slower learner for others. The realization that everyone could learn anything if given enough time led Bloom to the notion of mastery learning, which is one of the most influential ideas behind programmatic instruction today.

The way Bloom proposed that mastery learning could be translated into practice in schools was the familiar one that subjects in the curriculum should be broken down into parts, which he called units, and students should not be permitted or expected to proceed to the next unit until they had mastered the one they were working on. The idea sounds reasonable enough, but at this point a number of things go wrong. The first snag is that subjects are typically broken down into units, or objectives, without any regard for sense or for how children actually learn. Subjects are broken down on the principle of "what makes an expert," so that instead of having an opportunity to master one thing at a time—if indeed that is what children normally do—in a meaningful context, children are expected to progress from one meaningless chunk of learning to another. And in practice there is usually no more sense in the sequencing of units than there is in their content. Children "do" addition before subtraction, fractions before decimals (or vice versa), without understanding how the different parts of what they are doing relate to each other or to anything else.

The second difficulty is that while schools have avidly introduced the "mastery" part of mastery learning, they have not adopted the "different speeds for different learners" philosophy, which of course does not fit with the notion that children should achieve particular objectives by the time particular tests are administered or be labeled "failures." So while children are forced to struggle to master "units" that make little sense to them, standardized tests that they are not ready for come along at regular intervals to confirm that they are in fact poor learners.

In a comprehensive volume on the research and practice of mastery learning—and of how it can be administered to children disguised as play—Daniel Levine, professor of education at the University of Missouri in Kansas City, credits Bloom with being "the major theoretician and promulgator" of the system. Levine goes on to indicate clearly how students who fail to cope with such concentrated instruction are regarded as inadequate: "Mastery learning can be generally defined as instruction organized to emphasize student mastery of specific learning objectives and to deliver corrective instruction as necessary to achieve that goal. Mastery learning that involves formative testing of initial skill acquisition followed by corrective instruction for nonmasters has become increasingly popular during the past ten years. Thousands of school systems are now utilizing mastery learning as defined here to define student achievement."

One of Levine's associates, Herbert J. Wahlberg, describes the methodology of mastery learning: "Students, alone or in groups, work through units in an organized fashion at their own pace and must *master* a given amount of one unit, typically eighty percent on end-of-unit or formative tests, before moving on to the next unit." There is little logic involved in deciding what constitutes a unit (which might be the name of a letter of the alphabet or the recognition of a number) or in deciding how units should be sequenced.

There is certainly no concern with how much sense or purpose any particular child might be able to detect in the unit to be learned, only with ensuring that there is sufficient time for the child who is a "nonmaster" to persevere with efforts to learn. The notion that children work at their own pace, which superficially sounds as though the program is responsive to the rate at which individual children learn, instead means that there is no escape for the child who is having difficulty; who must just keep trying until reaching "eighty percent" mastery. It is not surprising that mastery learning enthusiasts are anxious to get as much time for their drills as possible, by lengthening and increasing the number of school days.

Other Levine associates—Beau Fly Jones, Lawrence B. Triedman, Margaret Tinzmann, and Beverly E. Cox—provide "Guidelines for Instruction-Enriched Mastery Learning to Improve Comprehension." They offer four principles which could be taken as the essence of all programmatic instruction: (1) Organize the overall curriculum in terms of stated objectives. (2) Deliver day-to-day instruction in units with a four-phase cycle of teach, test, reteach, retest [teaching meaning primarily the specification of what the student is supposed to recapitulate on the test]. (3) Align testing and curriculum. (4) Keep records unit by unit. The curriculum has to be "aligned" with four kinds of tests that are at the heart of the mastery learning philosophy: (1) Pretests, which have the effect of priming the student for the regime of tests that will follow. (2) Formative tests, to "diagnose" learning errors. (3) Retests, at the end of every unit "to document mastery." (4) Summative tests, to assess how much learning has been done after a series of units. It is the results of all these tests that have to be scrupulously recorded.

Phyllis R. Pringle, in "Establishing a Management Plan for Implementing Mastery Learning," outlines how management plans should be written at the district level—as far away as one can get from the actual classroom. She says that the plans, usually written by a management team centered on the superintendent's office, should set student learning goals for all staff. Teachers have to design their teaching to match the district objectives. Mastery learning can be an administrator's delight—until it, too, obviously goes wrong.

Mastery learning instructional materials were first developed by Chicago school personnel in 1975 and are now sold by Mastery Education Corporation of Watertown, Massachusetts, under the name Chicago Mastery Learning program. They were mandated for use in Chicago schools in 1981. Student workbooks emphasized specific skills, such as "learning to follow directions" and under-standing consonants and plurals. Mastery of the materials was the basis for promoting students to the next grade and for evaluations of teachers. Charles Munoz, president of the Chicago School Board, eventually acknowledged that a basic problem was that children were not allowed to read books. Even parents complained that children were bored by the exercises, and a study of the 1984 graduating class reported that only 6,000 of the 18,500 who gradu-ated had reached the national twelfth grade level of reading ability; 5,000 were reading at or below the national junior high school level. These figures took no account of the fifty percent of the children who entered high school but dropped out before gradua-tion.

Dr. Manford Byrd, Jr., Superintendent of Schools in Chicago, decreed in July 1985 that in the future teachers should employ Mastery Learning materials only on an optional supplementary basis, for both reading and mathematics. Students would primarily learn to read by reading from books. But another commercial program—the one published by Lippincott—was adopted to fill the programmatic gap, and it remains to be seen how much teachers will be able to break free from years of programmatic instruction —and where they will turn to cope with the continuing emphasis on demonstrating progress. Meanwhile, Mastery Learning materi-als are still extensively mandated for use elsewhere, including all New York City schools.

Confusing Teaching and Learning

A lot of subtle brainwashing is going on. Almost all of the educational programs, activities, and materials that I have been talking about, especially the computerized ones, are accompanied by the word "learning" rather than the word "instruction" or "teaching." "Learning systems" are produced and advertised, not "teaching systems." The program is called "Mastery Learning," not "Mastery Teaching" or "Mastery Instruction." According to an advertisement by the biggest producer of educational software, "Spinnaker games aren't just computer games. They're learning games." Edu-Ware Services of Agoura, California, advertises that "The microcomputer is the ideal learning companion." American Education Computer has "Easyreader" programs, including "Learn about sounds in reading" and "Learn about words in reading." Computerland pictures a child at a computer saying, "Don't bother me, I'm learning," and McGraw-Hill employs the same slogan. Milliken Publishing Company claims to be the leader at "Turning computer systems into learning systems." Reader's Digest Educational Software, we are told, "is enhancing and improving learning on many levels." Mattel, the toy company, promotes "teach and learn computer systems." At least the old teaching machines never claimed to be learning devices, but such scruple (or lack of marketing sophistication) is rare today. Like health foods and diet drinks, educational products take for granted the condition they are supposed to bring about. Why bother to look for evidence that an educational program will produce learning when the word "learning" is in the title of the product? There is no sense even in asking whether learning materials will produce learning; what else would they do?

The situation is not clarified by the fact that in school, teaching and learning are generally regarded as the same thing, or at least complementary. Although teachers may be heard complaining that they have taught something four times but some students still have not learned it, there is a general assumption that teaching should result in learning and that learning is the consequence of teaching. The problem with this assumption is that the student tends to be blamed for failure to learn. The thought is rarely entertained that teachers might not be teaching what they think they are teaching, or that programs might teach something other than what their labels claim. A teacher or program may be teaching "reading skills," but the student might be learning "reading is boring" or "I am a dummy."

The truth is that a good deal of teaching goes on without

children learning anything that they are intended or supposed to learn, and enormous amounts of learning occur without conscious teaching or formal instruction. Most learning takes place without anyone even suspecting that it is occurring. That does not mean that the learner alone should take credit for the learning. Teachers and parents should be given the credit when children learn, just as they must be open to blame when children fail. Their responsibility may not be to provide direct instruction, but to arrange the situations in which learning will take place. The adults who help children learn are those who ensure that the appropriate clubs are available for children to join. Paradoxically, the adults who worry most about providing instruction for the children in their charge may be the ones who most deprive the children of the opportunity for learning.

The distinction between teaching and learning must be clearly drawn because r-bbit educational systems and programs are misleadingly named. They are not learning programs, but teaching programs. They are not learning systems, but systems of instruction. And teaching no more guarantees learning than preaching guarantees conversion. Instruction that is misconceived, irrelevant, or inappropriate will have the contrary effect to what is expected, no matter how imaginatively it is labeled.

Confusing Education and Entertainment

The trend toward labeling every instructional activity "fun" is a related piece of artful marketing. The computer manufacturing company Atari makes the point—and puts teachers in their place—by advertising that through its programs "students will learn more because they have more fun learning . . . without constant teacher supervision and involvement." The advertisements for Sprout educational software (by Mindscape of Northbrook, Illinois) claim that "while kids are having fun at home, they're reinforcing what they've learned at school." The creatures in their computer games "represent one of the most serious approaches to home education you've ever heard of." The headline bluntly introduces these computer creatures: "Meet your kid's new teachers." And the text explains: "These amazing teachers are called Tink and Tonk. They come from Sprout. Software for kids 4 to 8. The beauty of Sprout is how we balance entertainment with a healthy dose of education." Eric Software Publishing "makes it fun to learn" in software called "The learning line." In IBM's "Writing to Read" program, "students have fun with pictures and games while they learn letters and sounds with a computer that talks." Scott Foresman has a software program called "Reading Fun." Milliken Publishing Company has an entire division called "Edu-fun" producing such programs as "Mathfun" and "Wordfun." Barnell Loft of Baldwin, New York, has a series of vocabulary exercises called "Fun with New Words" ("Rosa and Don can jump. They can run too. Rosa and Don can run and jump"), and "Reading for Fun." Fearon Teacher Aids, a division of Pitman Learning of Belmont, California, announces that in its "Birdseye Writing Skills: Sentences" (Grades 4–6), "40 fun-filled, reproducible lessons help students master good sentence structure, including subjects, predicates, simple and compound sentences, punctuation, and more." A different component of the same series offers "a super-nova collection of 40 reproducible lessons . . . reinforcing correct punctuation," and a third promises "a fantastically fun assortment of 40 reproducible lessons to involve students in the building blocks of writing" (presumably including the use of the word "fun" as an adjective). Fearon's mathematics materials are "a math-a-thon of fun!" Nothing escapes the frenzy. In Fearon's "Logic, Anyone" (Grades 5–8), "165 logic problems mean fun and challenge! Exercise thinking, analytical, and reasoning skills. Includes reproducible worksheets and answer key."

What is wrong with all this concern with fun? Does learning have to be miserable? Of course not. But the underlying implication of "learning should be fun" is that learning *will be* a painful and tedious activity unless it is primped up as entertainment. Learning is never aversive—usually we are not aware of it at all. It is failure to learn that is frustrating and boring, and so is having to attend to nonsensical activities. Children do not learn things because they are fun, but because they enable them to accomplish ends, and they learn in the process of accomplishing those ends.

It is another libel to suggest that children need rewards for attending to tasks, apart from intrinsic interest and satisfaction.

Children work very hard in their purposeful endeavors in the world, when they have ends they want to accomplish themselves. It is meaningless teaching, not learning, that demands irrelevant incentives. Children who do not attend to instruction are not necessarily obstructing their own learning, nor need they lack the essential "listening skills" that are such a concern today. They are not out of touch—the teacher is.

Many teachers still do not perceive a student's boredom or confusion as a danger signal that no worthwhile learning can possibly take place. All of us have enormous difficulty learning when we do not understand what we are expected to assimilate, and our recollection of what we learn in such circumstances will be fragile indeed. Rote memorization is the worst strategy for trying to learn anything we do not understand, including poetry, multiplication tables, and historical dates. Yet so many well-meaning teachers seem to regard confusion and boredom as challenges or as flaws in students: Whatever a student finds confusing or boring has to be taught, and the student should just buckle down and learn it.

The danger in making instruction indistinguishable from the Saturday morning cartoons or the Sunday comic supplements is that nonsense is dressed up as something worthwhile. It becomes easy enough to get students to spend more time on task, to apply themselves more to learning, but what they learn is that education has to be entertaining rather than useful or thought-provoking and that teachers have a very cynical view of what is required to bribe students to learn.

If children cannot become expert readers, writers, and mathematicians by being instructed programmatically, how can they become competent at the things we want them to do? I outlined the solution in my discussion of "clubs" in the previous chapter. Children must be permitted to learn naturally—by apprenticing themselves to people who do better those things that children are inspired to want and to expect to be able to do themselves. It is through apprenticeships with people they want to emulate that children become literate, learn to talk and ornament themselves like their friends, and occasionally try to hold up gas stations. Children, like adults, become interested in a way of life when they see someone else engaging in it, and they learn when someone else involves them in that way of life. The programmatic approach to education ignores the relationship that learners must have with more experienced people. How can anyone have a personal relationship with a computer or with a teacher who delivers systematic instruction no differently from a computer? The power of complex and delicate brains withers from undernourishment.

Children can't learn anything worthwhile one fragmented, trivialized, and decontextualized bit at a time. But an industry has developed that is dedicated to confining children in precisely that way, supported by administrators and professors of education who do not trust teachers to teach. The myth of how to create an expert has became validated by government and academia, and implemented by a vast and influential industry.

CHAPTER 5

The Nonsense Industry

The curious belief that experts can be constructed from instructional blueprints might have remained a minor educational oddity, had it not been piggybacked onto two other myths. The first, which might be called the myth of quality-controlled education, holds that instruction in all subjects will succeed if it is delivered to students of all ages in the same systematic way that the parts of industrial products like bicycles and aircraft are brought together and assembled, with constant monitoring all along the production line. The second fantasy, the myth of the omniscient outsider, is that people outside the classroom can make better instructional decisions than teachers who actually know and see the students involved.

The combined myths have constituted an ideal philosophical basis for the growing political illusion that standardization will improve education. The consequences of the myths and their implementation are rapidly becoming more acute with the arrival of computers on the educational scene.

The Myth of Quality-Controlled Education

The systematic transfer of classroom control from teachers to external authorities began in the United States in the panic of threatened national esteem that followed the launch of Sputnik, the first Soviet space satellite, in 1957. (The Russians are responsible!) During the fiscal years 1958 and 1959, appropriations to the U.S. Office of Education nearly tripled and the National Science Foundation allocations to "course content improvement activities" increased nearly tenfold, according to a history of federal intervention in education published by the National Center for Educational Research and Development in 1969. The anonymous author confirms that the spur was "the educational concern which accompanied the shock of the Soviet space success in October 1957." There is no further detail about who precisely in education was concerned or shocked by the fact that the Russians threw a dog into orbit, although I doubt whether many students or classroom teachers were included.

Title IV of the Elementary and Secondary Education Act of 1965 authorized the Commissioner of Education to support educational research and the "dissemination of information derived from educational research." Among a plethora of agencies, institutions, offices, centers, and bureaus that sprang up to implement this mandate—or to take advantage of the enormous funds that became available from government and private sources—were seven university-based national research and development centers and twenty off-campus regional development laboratories intended to bring commercial, community, and school people together with the academics. The largest regional lab, in New York, started with an annual budget approximating $2 million, and so did the second largest, the Southwest Regional Laboratory (SWRL) near Los Angeles. SWRL (pronounced "Swirl") was the birthplace of early computer-based classroom management systems, instructional programs for teaching reading, English, and critical thinking to young children, and also of a creature named Sam the Fat Cat, which I came to know well.

The success and survival of these regional laboratories depended upon their writing research and development proposals that would attract federal funds, according to the author of the National Center for Educational Research history I have just quoted. In a recent book on ideology in educational research, Thomas S. Popkewitz relates how ad hoc decisions were made to get the university centers operating and to acquire and maintain the grants that became available from the Office of Education. Although the centers were expected to coordinate theory and practice to achieve educational goals through the science of management, says Popkewitz, there was little research underlying the basic assumptions. The "concepts" that were to be taught were taken for granted, the method of instruction was to be behaviorism, and the science of organization was "systems," based on the identification and achievement of specific goals.

Popkewitz speaks from personal knowledge about the center at the University of Wisconsin at Madison, set up to "improve the efficiency of cognitive learning and to translate that knowledge into instructional material and procedures." A research procedure that involved dividing students into groups of from 100 to 150, in order that small differences would become statistically significant, became an assumption about how schools should be organized. The title of the program, "Individually Guided Instruction," was selected to provide nominal differentiation from the competing "Individually Prescribed Instruction" program of the Research and Development Center at the University of Pittsburg. Reading was selected as the core of the curriculum project because teachers wanted a management scheme so that they could cope in the classroom with all the objectives they had been told were important.

There are now ten university-based research and development centers and seven remaining regional laboratories, all actively engaged in producing educational programs. The 1980s have seen the establishment of a Center for the Study of Reading at the University of Illinois and a brand new Center for Educational Technology at Harvard, both plums that have been keenly competed for. In fact, the Harvard one became the subject of a lawsuit.

Education's Moon

The national "Right to Read" program was launched in 1970 by James E. Allen, Jr., Assistant Secretary for Education and U.S. Commissioner of Education, who referred to national literacy as education's "target for the seventies" and "education's moon." He was confident. "With the same zeal, dedication, perseverance, and concentration that made possible man's giant step of last July 20 [when a human foot first disturbed the dust of the moon] this moon too can be reached," he said. The commissioner's peroration was significant. "Necessary will be committed participation and support of the Congress; state and local political leaders and legislative bodies; business, industry, and labor; civic and community groups; publishers; advertising organizations; television, radio, and the press; research and scientific organizations; foundations; the entertainment industry; the sports world; and perhaps most essential of all, the understanding and support of an enlightened and enthusiastic public." Everyone was invited to the literacy education party, except schoolteachers and children.

Sending man on a return trip to the moon was accurately seen as a complex logistical problem that could be solved one painstaking step at a time. The relatively new techniques of systems analysis and linear programming would be employed to reduce the complex task into sequences of manageable components. Similarly, new program planning procedures, involving constant monitoring and quality control, would ensure that every objective was achieved and thus would eliminate all possibility of a failing link. Identical procedures would deliver literacy and other academic skills to all American children. The theory seemed beautifully foolproof: Teach one small thing at a time and test constantly to ensure that each objective is achieved before the learner moves onto the next. The regional labs were confidently expected to put together the programs to propel every American child inexorably toward the outer space of literacy. The appropriate instructional modules would be constructed by university specialists, together with a new breed of experts in "instructional planning and development" and, low on the totem pole, school practitioners. Teams of test constructors were simultaneously employed producing instruments of quality control to ensure that no child proceeded to a new objective without first demonstrating mastery of the preceeding one. Instruction and tests became inexorably linked, with a program component for every test item and a test for every program.

To prepare the groundwork, massive research programs were launched in the mid-1960s, such as Cornell University's Project Literacy, modeled in concept as well as in name on Project Mercury and other space ventures. The intention was to coordinate experts from a variety of disciplines, such as psychology, linguistics, sociology, and education, in compiling "task specifications" of the skills and knowledge of experienced readers and writers, and in flow-charting sequences in which such skills and knowledge might be taught to beginners in the programs of the regional laboratories.

The aspirations were laudable, financial support seemed limitless, and hopes soared in a blissful union of patriotic enthusiasm and unsullied faith in technology. Many of the most experienced and best-intentioned educators and academics in the United States joined the enterprise, no matter how tangential their expertise. They were joined by "consultants" from other countries, who quickly exported the philosophy, jargon, and techniques of programmatic instruction to the rest of the English-speaking world and, in time, to just about everywhere else. Small entrepreneurs began producing their own educational programs. "DISTAR," a mastery learning program which in its teacher manuals tells teachers the exact words they should address to children, and even when they should smile, rapidly gained enormous influence. Soon, the largest educational publishers introduced their own programs, all promoted as the latest and best despite the fundamental similarity of their colorful graphics (to appeal to teachers), carefully sequenced instructional and test procedures, and extravagant claims to provide everything that any child might need in years of literacy education.

Harper and Row, for example, one of the world's biggest educational publishers, began inviting teachers to inquire about their English program, which claims to provide everything students and teachers need to build "communication skills" and "SUCCESS!" from kindergarten through eighth grade. Their advertisements proclaim that "the program introduces, develops, and refines language arts skills through every lesson." The Teacher's Editions "make teaching easy." They "offer clear teaching plans with simply stated objectives, step-by-step lesson development, learning activities for different abilities, and suggestions for class discussions." One wonders why there should be any problems left in education at all. Of course, all of Harper and Row's competitors make similar claims. "Meeting each student's needs," declares a Ginn and Company advertisement for their English program (also for grades kindergarten to 8). "That's every teacher's goal. It's our goal too. The new *Ginn English Program* is designed to make meeting the challenge of whole-class instruction easier and more successful. . . . Consistent organization, well-designed lesson plans, and abundant practice add up to effective teaching."

The "abundant practice" is always the same: Present some item of knowledge to be learned (the name of a letter of the alphabet, one of the "sounds" of a letter, the spelling of a word); test whether the item has in fact been learned (by requiring the student to fill in a blank or to select among multiple-choice alternatives); and move on or do it again, depending on whether or not the response was "correct." As long as the student's performance achieved the prescribed level of the specified objective every step along the way, the student would finish up an expert. This was the system that was guaranteed to put a man on the moon.

By the end of the 1960s, the International Reading Association could confidently announce that the end of illiteracy was near because the National Aeronautics and Space Agency had agreed to lend its expertise to the construction of programs for reading instruction. In effect, systems analysts would make all the important decisions about what and how children should be taught in classrooms. Technology would take the place of teachers, who would now assume the classroom role of "instructional managers."

Politicians and school administrators were universally enraptured by the idea and its promises. Programmatic instruction seemed to guarantee results that would be both demonstrable and measurable. Even if children did not learn to read they could be shown to have made some progress. The language and concepts of programmatic instruction were insinuated into every corner of education, even when the words "program" or "systems" were not used. Everyone was supposed to specify and achieve *objectives*—not vague generalities like "helping a child to love literature," but hard-nosed, rigorous, en route objectives, the mastery of specific skills like learning that *b* is pronounced "buh," and that *c* is pronounced "kuh" or "suh" or is silent, and so forth, in endless pointless tedium.

Theories were developed to support and justify the new fragmented approach to education. "Subskills" theories were proposed that argued that anyone who wanted to read and write should master a lot of subskills, which in themselves might be meaningless but which when put together would somehow result in proficiency. This was the myth of how to create an expert. The usual explanation given for why no competent reader or writer was ever aware of these subskills (like identifying and putting together the sounds of all the individual letters in words) was that they were eventually done so fast and so automatically that they required no attention. In time, these subskills became raised to even greater heights as "the basics" of literacy, with emotional assertions that education ought to get back to them. And the underlying argument was always the same—that the pathway to learning was a terrazzo trail of meaningless fragments.

Some Personal Confessions

I worked on Project Literacy at Cornell University for a year and spent another year at the Southwest Regional Laboratory, both in the late 1960s, while I was still a graduate student. At that time, my ignorance and incompetence in education could scarcely be exaggerated. I was a writer and former newspaper reporter who had developed a practical language-user's interest in cognitive psychology and linguistics. My dissertation at Harvard had been on a narrow area of visual perception, selected as a specialized and abstract topic that could be disposed of expeditiously. I knew nothing of teaching at any level.

But familiarity with children has never been a requirement for planning instructional objectives in major educational research and development projects. Anyone who could combine a theoretical knowledge of language with research on the way the eyes worked had to be an expert in reading and therefore in specifying educational objectives for learning to read and for telling teachers how to teach reading. That was the thinking in the days when there were many more vacant positions in research laboratories than there were qualified people to fill them. People who actually worked with real children were considered amateurs and given routine tasks. The "experts" were the Ph.D.s, especially those who could speak the arcane languages of systems analysis and of program planning and budgeting. My subsequent career—working with children and with the actual teachers of children—has been one of constant disagreement with everything I observed during those first two years.

The regional educational laboratories were set up to provide bridges between theory and instructional practice. The expectation was that experimental psychologists and other theorists would make discoveries about learning and about particular subject matters that could be exploited to improve educational practice. Not much thought was given to the possibility that new ideas could be given directly to teachers for them to implement (or ignore) as they saw fit in their classrooms. There was a widespread conviction, which is still current, that teachers do not know how to handle theory, that they do not have time for it, and that what they must be given is "practical suggestions." Instead, the plan was that the theory should be translated into "curricula," or programs of materials and activities, which all teachers could apply, whether or not they understood the theory behind the programs. The teacher would be an "instructional manager." Instruction would be delivered to children in the way that the astronauts were delivered to the moon, through task analysis, the specification of objectives, program planning and quality control. Everything would be achieved by programmers, planners, accountants, and designers, all properly coordinated to work single-mindedly according to quality-controlled flowcharts and schedules, just like the materials they were expected to produce.

All this sounds bleak—and indeed much of the initial work

was. SWRL's beginning reading materials were based on vacuous "stories" like, "Sam the fat cat sat on a flat mat," constructed with the sole purpose of validating a drill designed to teach children the sound of the first letter of the alphabet. The fact that such a rule was completely useless for a sentence like "What did Mary say when she saw Charles fall?"—where none of the a's has a "fat cat" sound—were left aside as too complicated (for the program developers, not for learners). Also ignored were the facts that children did not need to be instructed on the sounds of letters in order to learn to read words like McDonalds, and that it was learning to recognize significant words that made learning the sounds of letters easy and meaningful, rather than the other way around. But instruction in the alleged sounds of letters could be delivered in the form of drill and test exercises—known as *phonics*—while knowledge of the words that individual children knew or were interested in was of course unattainable by the programmers. Right from the beginning, the programmers' concern was with the constraints and possibilities of the instructional technology rather than with the immediate needs and abilities of learners.

Sam the fat cat—like his littermate the r-bbit—is representative of all kinds of nonsensical materials, largely based on fallacies about how children learn language, and claiming justification from the upside down hierarchical schemes of theorists like Benjamin Bloom. There were, for example, the beliefs that short words are easier than long words for children to learn, that short sentences are easier to understand than long sentences, and that brief stories hold children's attention better than longer ones. In reality, long words are much easier for children than short words—the long words offer many more clues. It is much easier to tell the difference between "banana" and "cucumber" than between "cat" and "dog," and children generally know more three syllable words than monosyllabic ones. Long but meaningful sentences are much easier to understand and remember than elliptical telegraphic sequences. When language is normally used the richness of detail in longer sentences helps the reader to understand the gist; short sentences are a strain on both memory and patience. Real stories written by experienced authors, rich with plot, narrative interest, and character development, are easier to comprehend than a few truncated sentences put together by instructional technicians. Artificial language is required only to make nonsensical instruction look good.

It might be objected that children love nonsense and can be enchanted by "Hickory dickory dock" and the dish running away with the spoon. But poems, stories, and games with exotic or fantastic words and sounds are not nonsense, in the sense that children might not be able to relate them to anything they already know. The nursery rhyme kind of "nonsense" is replete with rhyme and rhythm, with action and with imagery, the opposite of tedium. The fabulous cat in the hat about which Dr. Seuss wrote is a totally different animal from Sam the fat cat. Dr. Seuss's cat is part of a real story told in real language, a fantasy rather than a travesty. The cat in the hat is a poetic image, not an exercise in sound-spelling relationships. Dr. Seuss's aim was to help children to enjoy reading, not to engage them in a learning exercise. Children will sit and read or listen to the tale of Dr. Seuss's cat time and time again. But jazzy graphics, extrinsic incentives, and more direct forms of coercion are required before teachers or children attend to r-bbity fat Sam.

The Entry of the Publishers

Producing educational programs that schools would actually adopt was demanding and expensive, the regional educational laboratories discovered. It was not enough to have personnel with the expertise and dedication to spin seemingly endless skeins of programmatic material. Schools would not buy instructional products unless they were properly packaged and marketed, a demand that involved different sources of funds and talent than those available to the regional laboratories. Some programs were put into the public domain, and some of the program specialists established their own publishing companies or moved into partnership with commercial concerns. "DISTAR," for example, which was developed by a group of academics led by Professor Siegfried Engelmann at the University of Oregon, became a commercial program marketed by Science Research Associates of Chicago, now a subsidiary of IBM. Several of the largest educational publishing houses had already been producing their own reading programs, some with historic antecedents, but these were usually little more than sets of readers and an occasional alphabet book. Now a whole new technology was available, and it came with a U.S. government seal of approval. It was almost a patriotic duty to purchase the new instructional programs. Didn't everyone want to eradicate illiteracy from the Western world?

Commercial publishers took over the technology of the r-bbit and many r-bbit experts as well. Actual teachers continued to be employed at the low end of the scale—composing "stories," activities, and test items in accordance with the specifications of the instructional designers and layout specialists. Educational programs began to be packaged and marketed like patent medicines. Some of the publishers continued to publish children's stories and poems of literary merit and artistic quality, just as some continued to publish textbooks for teachers, including some of my own, that argued for a different point of view. But this was less schizophrenia or accident than the hedging of bets and picking up of any slack that might remain in the market. There was no doubt where the major rewards lay and the major efforts were to be made.

And the rewards continue to be huge, especially for companies large enough to invest in the production of integrated multigrade programs and willing to mount major marketing campaigns based on hyperbolic and untestable claims. Programs are produced that cover up to ten continuous years of schoolwork, with teachers' manuals, lesson plans and record sheets, student readers, exercise books, activity kits, and tests—everything that is required, according to the promotion, to make a child a reader (or writer, or mathematician, or social scientist, . . .). Most school jurisdictions prefer "comprehensive" programs; they want everything taken care of. With 40 million students in 85,000 public schools in the United States, textbook "adoptions" offer goldmines to successful bidders. A single adoption by a state or provincial education authority can mean an order for hundreds of thousands of copies of textbooks, and even of programs worth hundreds of dollars for each child. Total textbook sales, from kindergarten to college levels, totaled $1.5 *billion* in 1980, an average of about $40 for each student. Adoption of a program in California or Texas can mean up to half a million guaranteed sales in every subject at each grade level. There is intense competition among publishers to discover and conform to the latest requirements and "objectives" of the largest state education authorities. The rest of the nation—together with many other parts of the world—finds itself having to choose among programs designed to meet the specific requirements and idiosyncracies of the bigger states.

The job security of entire divisions of major educational publishing houses depends on such large-scale adoptions. Their companies have been absorbed into multinational communications conglomerates whose accountant managers are guided only by the balance sheets. Publishers must strive desperately to discover what the potential consumers want, what the "guidelines" are. The concern is not with what research demonstrates but with what sells. Most educational publishers of my acquaintance are idealistic, if not romantic, people who would prefer to be dealing with storybooks that schoolchildren would like to read. But a book that is not part of a complex program, that does not contain questions that can be scored, and that is not fitted into a lock-step instructional sequence has very little chance of getting into many classrooms—from kindergarten to graduate school.

While even small companies can turn a profit getting some of their specialized materials into one or two classrooms, a few major programs have been enormously successful, especially as they have to be updated and replaced every few years (so as not to be left behind by the "latest research"). The 1985 Holt, Rinehart and Winston catalog announced a number of "new and updated texts and programs" because "in our fast-changing technological society, nothing seems to change faster than the way our children learn." Just as automobile manufacturers bring out the coming year's models months in advance, so the Holt catalog announced that "new and revised" 1986 editions of their reading, algebra, science, social studies, Spanish, and French texts would be available in the spring of 1985.

The companies that produce these programs have not achieved their success by being different and innovative, but by being the same. Often they employ the same designers and editors, whom they hire from other companies to produce an almost identical product. As soon as the new Macmillan Series-R reading program began achieving dramatic sales in the early 1970s, Holt, Rinehart and Winston hired many of the Macmillan editorial staff to produce its own kindergarten-to-eighth-grade "Basic Reading" program. A relatively small core group of consultants from the educational and academic world advises the creative staff of publishers on instructional aspects of the multimillion dollar enterprise of devising or updating a major educational program. Some "consultants" simply lend their name to a venture. The main thing is to have visible credentials—a name that is known, a Ph.D., or an elevated position in the educational hierarchy, preferably as a superintendent, but in a pinch a principal will do. Consulting editors need never have taught a child, provided they know how to design instructional programs. People who have never written a real story write "stories" for children—if they can put together sentences of standard length and minimal grammatical complexity from limited vocabularies. People who know nothing about history or geography construct tests on history and geography—they know how to construct tests. R-bbits are generally bred by educational amateurs or by professional entrepreneurs.

After I had published my first books for teachers about reading and writing, I began to be invited to be a consulting editor on the development of literacy programs. When I pointed out that I had a totally opposite point of view and could only condemn programs, I was told that my "input" would be welcomed. Once I tried to decline gracefully by saying I had no free time to participate. That would be fine. I would still receive my fee, even though I contributed nothing, provided my name was listed as a consultant in the promotional material. I was even credited as a consultant on a brochure for the Children's Television Workshop when the only question asked of me was whether I would like to be involved in the project and my only response was, "No."

Whether penny plain or tuppence colored, whether massively produced and marketed or modestly duplicated and insinuated, the printed materials of programmatic instruction have flooded education. Many teachers could not teach without these materials. They would not know what to do with all the free time that became available and with all the student energy that was released.

Recognizing the R-bbit

It is easy to recognize programmatic instruction. There is always something for every child to do—to memorize or practice and learn. There is always a response that is required so that the child can be adjudged right or wrong, some question to be answered, some blank to be filled in. There are always scores, which will be counted, compared, and contrasted. There are always some children who are "behind." There is always a next step to move on to. The activities are always decontextualized, fragmented, and trivial, engaged in only for the sake of the mark and for getting through the day. The activities have no immediate utility, relevance, or sense, and they do not create the kind of situation in which children normally and sensibly learn. Programmatic activities are instruction for the sake of instruction.

Curriculum Associates, Inc., of North Billerica, Massachusetts, has a reading program extending from kindergarten to tenth grade. For Grades 1 to 3 the materials include a "short book" and a "long book." The "short book" is full of "short-vowel" r-bbits: "Dr__p the d__st cl__th, dr__p the m__p! It's time for f__n, so work m__st st__p." The long book comprises "long-vowel" r-bbits: "k__y, s__a, thr__e, p__anuts, b__an." Not untypically, the last five examples all happen to be technically incorrect; the missing "e" is not a vowel that can be considered separately from the letter that follows it.

No potential consumer is overlooked. Scott Foresman has a nine-year reading program, called "Focus," for students who don't succeed with the regular "basal" program. These, presumably, are the children who cannot make sense of the standard instruction. The aim of "Focus" is "the gift of reading independence" and transition into the regular program. To those ends, it provides "motivating reading materials of a lower readability" (which means shorter words, shorter sentences, and shorter sense) plus work on "language and/or English" skills, background knowledge and concept development, vocabulary growth, better word study skills, better comprehension skills, more "time on task" (meaning drills) to learn new skills, and "clear organized instruction" (meaning directions for the teacher) that leads to "reading independence."

There is nothing shoddy about any of these materials. Like all the basals and other instructional programs of the major educational publishers, the booklets of the "Focus" series are well printed, with bold text, contemporary graphics, and lavish illustrations. It might be thought that the product is a little too sophisticated, patronizing, and even distracting for children, but the aim is to make an immediate appeal to adults. Activities are provided for every minute of every lesson. Children start on page one of every workbook and work through to the end—breaking words into syllables, underlining letters, and circling pictures—and then move on to practice pads and duplicated exercise sheets if they get through the workbook. When students do get to read a short passage, "Immediately following the selection, students answer comprehension questions that develop thinking skills on the literal, interpretative, evaluative, and creative levels. And another set of comprehension questions about the selection is provided in the workbook." There is no escape. There is not even the possibility that a serendipitous teacher might stumble on something interesting—or decide that an activity is boring—because the answer to every question is provided in the teacher's manual. And also for the teacher there is the inevitable provision for recording the "score" on all of this question answering, to ensure that the child's achievement for the day can be compared with that of other days, other children, other teachers, other skills, and discriminatory "norms."

As for "clear organized instruction," teachers are told "None of your precious time is wasted finding appropriate materials or planning alternative instruction." Leave everything to the program. One wonders how the teacher's "precious time" ought to be spent, if not in finding appropriate materials or planning alternative instruction. The programmatic answer is, of course, in ensuring that the children work their way through the program every day. To that end "Every lesson step begins with an easy-to-spot Overview in a pink box that summarizes the objectives, goals, and materials for the day. Teachers . . . will appreciate this handy time-saver." A card from the pink box for a Grade 5 teacher specifies as the day's teaching goals: "Have pupils read pages about the Great Pueblo Period. Teach time sequence; use Sharpen Your Skills. Have pupils practice skill in reading. Introduce Unit vocabulary: *canyon.*"

To argue that teachers need not follow every step of programs like this is beside the point. Many teachers have no choice; the program is imposed upon them. Even if teachers can choose, they must have *some* program. They are expected to be able to say what they are working on today, what they have "covered" in the past, what they will be doing next week. They are expected to make "objective" reports to administrators and "progress" reports to parents. Teachers in the next grade up will expect them to have brought students to a certain point (but not to have taken them so far that they have already done some of the following year's work). Most teachers have been *taught* to teach in this way; they would be lost without a program.

Other publishers claim to meet every contingency in one program. The "philosophy" of one version of the Holt, Rinehart and Winston *Language Patterns* series says that "to meet the needs of today's children [that is, to satisfy teachers and administrators] it must meet the needs of the gifted pupil with his high conceptual resources; it must offer the creative child the opportunity to satisfy his restless need for innovation. At the same time, it must not ignore the needs of the child who does not learn by traditional or conventional methods." Then, modestly, "The needs of the gifted, the average and the perceptually handicapped child are all met through the psycholinguistic approach of *Language Patterns.*"

The word "psycholinguistic" is jargon, which in the context means nothing. (Some of the originators of psycholinguistic analyses of reading would argue that the phrase 'psycholinguistic program' is a contradiction in terms.) There is no shortage of jargon as the Holt promotional materials continue. "Pupils are introduced to reading through the multi-sensori-motor method. This method is combined with intensive audio-visual activity to sensitize children to the sound-symbol relationships of our language." There is no need to worry if such language seems incomprehensible; it is basically meaningless.

Promotional writers are not above borrowing reflected glory from distinguished individuals who have had nothing to do with the program, especially if even a tenuous local connection can be claimed. The advertising for the Canadian version of the Holt, Rinehart and Winston program from which I am quoting avers that its authors were indebted to a number of writers "whose works in neurology have illuminated the field of learning. Among these are two world-famous Canadians, Wilder Penfield and D.O. Hebb. The former has emphasized the central role played by the integrative areas of the brain and the latter has emphasized the functional grouping of neural units in learning." It would have been just as meaningful to say that the program reflected the latest advances in heart transplant surgery, since there is no way that anything brain researchers have discovered about the organization of nerve cells in the cerebral cortex can influence the manner in which exercises or reading passages are set out in the worksheets. It is difficult to see how neurological research led to a first-year skills sequence that begins with tracing letters, learning their sounds, and exercises on such "structural parts" as "the plural s and verb inflect s, possessive 's and 's as a contraction for is."

Staggered Sentences

One of the favorite devices of English teachers hoping to give older students systematic instruction in writing is the sentence-combining exercise, in which fragments of short sentences must be combined into longer ones. Publishers like the exercise because it is easy to produce by the bookfull, and such books have to be bought for every student in the class. Teachers like the exercise because it keeps students quiet, and the work is neatly organized into chunks suitable for one class period or a homework assignment. Administrators like it because records can be kept of student "progress," and the aim sounds important. Researchers are not sure about the exercise. Some research claims to have demonstrated that some students who work on this type of exercise end up writing longer and more complex sentences but not, of course, that they become more competent and more interested writers. (The exercise claims only to teach how sentences can be combined, not when they should be). Other research has been unable to find a difference. In any case, students are likely to think that the entire procedure is unnatural and boring nonsense.

Schools in the Montebello Unified School District near Los Angeles use the second edition of a popular sentence-combining book written by William Strong, of Utah State University, published by Random House. For exercise after exercise, students are required to work on clusters of phrases like:

> 1.1 Hills surround the lake. 1.2. They are flat-topped. 1.3. They are rugged. 1.4. The lake is clear. 1.5. The lake is turquoise.
> 2.1. Many hues are reflected in the water. 2.2. The hues are reddish-brown.
> 3.1. The sky is hot. 3.2. The sky is mottled. 3.3. The weather is hot.

First the students must read the sentences and try to understand them; then they work out how the sentences might be combined into one or more "complex" sentences like, "Rugged flat-topped hills surround the clear turquoise lake," which they write in their workbooks. This kind of activity is so common that most teachers do not see how artificial it is. Experienced writers never begin by writing a series of short sentences that they then combine into more complex forms. Many of the phrases the students are given are not even sentences, since by themselves they are meaningless. At best, sentence combining is part of the revision and editing authors engage in *after* they have written something; it is a consequence of being a writer, not a part of learning to be one. Students learn nothing if they can already do the exercises. And if the students have difficulty with the exercises, they are required to spend more time on them, so that they learn that writing is a boring and point-less activity which can never be of interest.

Here is a cluster from another set of exercises:

> 1.1. Young children are remarkable. 1.2. They have an ability. 1.3. The ability is natural. 1.4. The ability is to remain "in touch." 1.5. They are in touch with their feelings.

Reading these sentences is like reading a deliberate puzzle. The intent does not become clear until the final sentence is read—that young children are in touch with their feelings (whatever that means). Everything that comes between sentences 1.1. and 1.5 is a distraction, an imposition on memory, especially for anyone who has difficulty reading or focusing attention on obscure texts (yet this is supposed to be a writing exercise). The student is hardly helped by an "invitation" at the end of the five exercises in this group to try splitting the first cluster (the one I have quoted) into two sentences connected by a semicolon. Now students have to carry a semicolon in their minds as they try to make sense of the fragments.

A later set of exercises, ironically entitled "Thinking About Writing," could represent a coup de grace for confused students:

> 1.1. Think of writing as a conversation. 1.2. The conversa-tion is "one-way." 1.3. The conversation is with an audience. 1.4. The audience is invisible. . . . 3.1. Your links must be clear. 3.2. The links are among words. 3.3. The links are among sentences. . . . 7.1. Communication is the goal. 7.2. The goal is primary. 7.3. Writing must make sense to readers [an assertion that is difficult to relate to the exercise as a whole].

The language of these drills is that of the basal reader of reading instruction—it is not really "language" at all. The vocabulary is jargon, with its references to "links" and "one-way conversations." The meaning is muddled and the intent obscure. How can the activity help a student with any residual desire to learn to write?

And the drills take up days and months of valuable teacher and student time that could otherwise be spent in actual reading and writing.

The Duck That Became an R-bbit

Research that is perfectly respectable (but educationally irrelevant) can be translated into instructional practice in totally inappropriate ways and made the subject of programs and tests. Take as an example the case of The Duck That Faces the Wrong Way.

I must begin by admitting that I was part of the start of this travesty. My graduate studies into visual perception (and my desire to dispose of a dissertation quickly) had led me to the rather esoteric question of how the brain decides what the eyes are looking at when we see a letter of the alphabet. At the research project at Cornell University I used to give seminars for instructional developers on how the visual system operated during reading.

Put very simply, the specific question concerned what the brain has to do to recognize that the shape *A* is the letter called "a." The answer, according to my studies and those of many other researchers in a variety of fields, is that eye and brain make a detailed analysis of the shape of every letter, looking for particular patterns of straight lines, curves, corners, intersections, and a dozen other "distinctive features" that distinguish letters from each other. It is the presence or absence of particular patterns of features that enable eye and brain jointly to decide which letter of the alphabet we might be looking at. Another term for distinctive features is "significant differences," since a feature is, in fact, a difference that enables a distinction to be drawn, a difference that makes a difference.

Enough of the technicalities. We have all learned to see without this kind of intimate knowledge of what goes on behind the eyeballs. The analysis of significant differences is totally unconscious and not amenable to any kind of observation or control. And the distinctive feature theory could be wrong in any case. So how did a Duck That Faces the Wrong Way become involved?

It was a classic case of trying to transform children into experts by teaching them, one thing at a time, some of the knowledge that experts possess. One thing that expert readers can do is recognize letters of the alphabet, so the plan of some Project Literacy researchers was to start systematic reading instruction by drilling kindergarten and first-grade children in recognizing the letters of the alphabet. This was to be done regardless of whether the children had any idea of the relationship of letters to words, or even of any meaningful use of words in written language. Indeed, the work on the alphabet was seen as a *preliminary* to reading. Children were not even expected to get to stories until they completed the obstacle course of learning to recognize unrelated letters. The letters, in other words, were to be taught as nonsense shapes—this squiggle is called "a," this one is called "b," and so forth. Not surprisingly, many of the children became totally confused. They could not distinguish one squiggle from another, let alone remember their names.

At that point, most intelligent teachers would have called time out. What is the point of driving bewildered children further into the ground? Intelligent reading teachers would probably provide a solid dose of listening to interesting stories just to restore a child's faith in the meaningfulness of written language. But not the researchers who wanted to ensure that children learned the letters of the alphabet systematically. If some children were unable to benefit from the instruction, perhaps they were not aware of the distinctive features that constitute significant differences among letters. The remedy was to design a program to teach distinctive features. Instead of being drilled to distinguish A, B, and C, the children who failed were now confronted by exercises in telling the difference between straight lines, curves, corners, and intersections.

Once again some children failed, and the researchers now diagnosed a serious problem indeed. If children could not tell the difference between distinctive features, they were obviously deficient in the basic skill of telling the difference. They needed remedial exercises in difference-telling. And so a set of en route objectives was devised that required the children to look at sets of different shapes and objects, one of which was always different from the others. One of the sets consisted of three ducks, two facing one way and one the other, and the children's task was to put a ring around The Duck That Faces the Wrong Way.

The researchers recognized that their aim of systematically teaching all the letters of the alphabet as a prerequisite for reading might involve many children in lengthy frustration and disappointment. Was it necessary that all children should be obliged to try to learn the difference between letters, if some would fail because they could not distinguish distinctive features, or even ducks that were facing in different directions? Wouldn't it be more efficient to construct a test to identify in advance children who were lacking in telling-the-difference skills and therefore unlikely ever to profit from reading instruction?

A "reading readiness" test was therefore devised that teachers could administer to identify any children who might not be intellectually prepared for the experience of reading (or rather, for programmatic reading instruction). Any child who had difficulty on the test of distinguishing the Duck That Faces the Wrong Way could be immediately identified as having a telling-the-difference disability and singled out for special instruction in distinctive features skills.

Any parent who thinks that the account I have just related is too ridiculous to be true need only go to the nearest school reading center or educational psychologist's office where tests of "reading readiness" are administered. Curriculum Associates begin their kindergarten-through-eighth-grade reading program with a "Sound Start" segment in which children are shown sets of four jumbled up drawings—three boats and one dog; two noses, a cat and a house; two toes, a coat and a pot of paint—and instructed to "circle the pictures that are alike." (Has anyone ever met a child who could not tell the difference between a boat and a dog?) "DISTAR" has an entire segment teaching children to discriminate between boxes that are full and boxes that are empty. The duck and its descendents are still hard at work identifying children who may be disqualified from joining the literacy club before their foot is in the door.

Bringing the Nonsense Home

Many children can never escape the r-bbit. They can bring additional drills home from school, or their parents go out and buy them at the supermarket or local bookstore.

Golden Books have long been favorites of many parents and children, with interesting stories, fact or fiction, and attractive illustrations. Now produced by Western Publishing Co. of Racine, Wisconsin, Golden Books has introduced a "Step Ahead" series with over fifty titles, from beginning reading to computer literacy, from kindergarten to Grade 6. For less than two dollars, parents can buy a handful of r-bbits, together with push-out colored stickers like "Smart kid" or "Super star" to reward a child for completing a page of drills. In "Word Building, Level 1," children must underline the letter that represents the beginning sound of a pictured object, or fill in the missing letters of dr__m, t__b, c__p, and s__n, assisted by a picture clue. Advice to parents at the beginning of the booklet is "Working with your child at home helps him or her to develop skills and build confidence." A similar series of twenty-four workbooks that were produced by Grossett and Dunlap Inc. asserted that "Modern parents understand that education does not end when a child returns from school in the afternoon. . . . One or more pages may be assigned every day. Each page represents a complete lesson. Regular use of the lessons will provide a systematic diagnosis of individual weaknesses and insure mastery of important facts for systematic skill training [or] a strong remediation program."

The same promises are extended to adults—even teachers. An advertisement in the magazine *Learning*—headed, with typical abandon, "Anyone can learn to read!"—promises "A new self-help reading program . . . for illiterate adults, teenagers and foreign-born who can't read English. They can learn in private." In contrast to the complex and costly instructional systems of larger corporations, this unnamed $39.95 program by an anonymous entrepreneur working out of "Department 3" at an address in Modesto, California, is contained in eight one-hour cassette tapes and a phonetic workbook. "The teacher on the tapes teaches the workbook lessons. Teachers who are not sure of their phonics are buying it for themselves. It teaches them everything they need to know."

Television evangelists are entering the scene. In February 1986, the "700 Club" was promoting on its morning television news a "Sing and Spell Heads-Up Program" which was being placed in churches and schools to eradicate not only illiteracy, but crime as well, among disadvantaged populations. Phonics—teaching children the sounds of letters—has long been a popular resort for people who want to get reading instruction properly organized. It looks so simple—once children know the sounds of letters they will be able to "decode" from the letters of written language to speech. Unfortunately reality is far less simple. The spelling to sound correspondences of English are inordinately complex—there isn't one letter that represents just one sound or one sound represented by just one letter—and cannot be relied on. Furthermore, until a child can read, talking about letters and about the sounds of letters is sheer jabberwocky. Thorough knowledge of letters and their sounds is not required in order to read words; phonic skills come with reading.

Prophets and Messiahs

The self-appointed leader of the phonics movement is Rudolph Flesch, who thirty years ago published a popular book entitled *Why Johnny Can't Read.* His patent-medicine prescription was that every child could be taught to read provided that all parents and teachers employed scrupulously the method outlined in his book, which was drilling children in the sounds of letters. Twenty-five years later he concluded that since many children were still not learning to read, it must be because his good advice and generous offer had been ignored. In fact, in recent years more parents and teachers have been trying to teach children the Flesch way than in any other period of history, urged and supported by the federal government, abetted by the regional research and development laboratories, encouraged by the publishers of elaborate commercial tests and programs, and browbeaten by politicians and administrators. What has failed is phonics.

Loathe to blame himself and his method, Flesch instead constructed a false enemy, the "look-and-say" method of teaching reading, which in its most extreme form proposes that children should learn words "as wholes," on sight, preferably from flashcards or else in "stories" like the notorious "Look Dick Look. See Spot run." that have as little resemblance to how anyone actually uses or learns language as Flesch's drills. The teachers who oppose the meaninglessness of phonics oppose the meaninglessness of flashcards, too, and the pointless exercises and "stories" that accompany them. Nevertheless, Flesch achieves frequent quotation in popular magazines, including a flatteringly uncritical article in *Reader's Digest* (November 1985) with reprints distributed free, full-page advertisements in the *New York Times* (October 24, 1985), and dissemination through a "Reading Reform Foundation" in Scottsdale, Arizona.

Flesch is not alone in thinking that he has the complete answer to educational problems, provided teachers allow him to make their decisions for them. A former math teacher, Dr. Caleb Gattegno, has a company called Schools for the Future Foundation, Inc. In one of its programs, called "Words in Color," he claims to make children into readers by teaching them a color code for a small number of distinct sounds and an algebraic procedure for combining the sounds. In a short article published in *Harvard Educational Review* in 1970 entitled "The Problem of Reading Is Solved," Gattegno offered, "Illiteracy can be wiped out at a far smaller cost than any wild dreamer has ever dreamed. I am prepared to do the computation if asked."

Gattegno has attracted a following in education—including, evidently, the editors of the 1970 *Harvard Educational Review*—as a consequence of his enthusiastic and confident manner, expansive claims, and esoteric way of discussing education. For example, he says the problem in reading instruction is "to provide awareness that a system of signs isomorphic to the system of sounds of one's language exists and can play a certain number of the roles of the system already owned." He also has a math program based on similar principles, which he explained in an interview in *Computer Classroom News* in 1982. "We have a program which will take a child—four- or five-years-old—from scratch to a level of competence in mathematics that is rarely achieved today," he said. "The program consists of 122 modules on ten disks. It will take a child about two years to complete the program. It is totally automated for the child. The teacher simply makes the proper selections."

Gattegno described the program: "It is truly a lovely program, and this is a beautiful way to learn." The first disk on the program teaches the digits "one to none." Commands are flashed on the screen to which the child responds with a light pen. If the child doesn't respond, the computer waits, then reminds the child to do something. The computer tells the child immediately if there is a mistake. Next the child learns the tens, then the hundreds, then intermediate combinations of digits, then operations with numbers. The child is not pressured, but the child's attention is not permitted to wander, and results are demonstrated.

The interviewer asked about the role of the teacher. Gattegno replied "The teacher? The teacher is the computer. All that is needed is some adult to read the menu and make a selection." The interviewer asked if he was planning to take the classroom teacher out of the picture for mathematics education for young children. His reply was, "I am the teacher, and the computer is me at the disposal of everybody. I've made myself available to everyone. The child doesn't have to interact with any other teacher."

John Henry Martin also has an offer that he thinks no teacher should refuse, and in addition, he has excellent connections. His computer-based "Writing to Read" program is being promoted by IBM and has been adopted—or accepted—in many school systems. When Martin was interviewed in *Educational Leadership* magazine in 1981, its readership of educational administrators was blandly told, "With a simplified alphabet and interactive computer programming, John Henry Martin has developed a system by which children learn to read and write far better than usual. In this interview with Executive Editor Ron Brandt he explains his approach, which could revolutionize the teaching of English language arts."

Martin's revolutionary notion is to teach children to read by teaching them to spell, or more precisely to write letters that represent the sounds of words. And since he acknowledges that the forty or forty-two sounds of English "are represented 500 different ways in print," his approach is in fact to get them, first of all, to spell them wrong. He first teaches them to write words the way they sound, like writing *boi* for "boy," and later "suggests" they spell words the way they are in books.

My intention at this point is not to argue with Martin's theories of reading and writing, which are about as sophisticated as those of most instructional program developers. Instead I want to focus on how Martin proposes to teach. The interviewer asked why Martin wanted his program to be delivered by computer. Martin explained, "Classroom teaching is mass education. We know the importance of the tutorial relationship between teacher and learner, but we can't have 50 million teachers for 50 million children. With the computer as tutor—as interacting agent with the learning person—we come closer to the ideal teacher than ever before." Like Gattegno, Martin thinks he can replace teachers entirely—and IBM agrees with him. In place of his "50 million teachers," Martin would have none. Or rather, just one—himself, controlling every child through the computerized extension of his ideas in the classroom.

Martin is just as optimistic about teaching subjects other than reading and writing, which he regards as "the most complex curriculum problem we have." (He likens teaching reading and writing to the "problems" of curing cancer and the common cold.) "Now I have developed a pedagogical design using high technology for treating both these problems with a higher degree of effectiveness than we've previously been able to accomplish," he says modestly. "If we can do that, then composing computer curriculums for biology, history, and science should follow without major difficulty. It's complex, but in terms of what has already been accomplished, it's simply the next step."

Martin is evidently serious in believing that electronic technology can take the place of teachers, in fact he told the interviewer he thought curriculum people should begin working with social scientists to address the question of what will constitute schooling when much of the drudgery of teaching can be taken over by an efficient piece of technology. His presupposition all the time is that teaching is drudgery and that learning must be boring, which is only the case when it is believed, as Martin believes, that becoming a reader and writer involves learning fragmented rules and procedures rather than making sense of print. Martin clearly indicates the direction in which computers are taking the r-bbit. In the spring of 1986, Warner Books announced that Martin's program, "presently used by 200,000 children in over 4,000 classrooms nationwide, is now available for home use."

The Entry of the Software Producers

Far more forests have been sacrificed to provide the paper for the fat cats, perverse ducks, and ubiquitous r-bbits of workbooks and activity kits than have ever gone into stories for children to read. And now all the junk learning can be delivered by computers. The technique remains the same—present a "fact" to be studied (except that the fact is now likely be called "information" or "data"), ask a question, move the learner on if the response is appropriate or back to try again if not, with further "instruction" if a sufficient number of responses is wrong. But the new r-bbit is animated and in color, there may be sound of one kind or another, the responses are made on a keyboard or with some other electronic device rather than with pen or pencil and paper, the exercises are addressed to the student "personally," and there are many more tests, scores, and comparisons.

Each of the lessons in Milliken's "Spelling System"—this is the one where an egg hatches for every word the student gets right—is composed of three separate exercises. To quote the brochure, "First, the student receives a brief introduction to the 'fact' being presented. Then, he works through three practice activities aimed at consolidating his understanding of the pattern demonstrated. Finally, the student tests his mastery of the lesson words. . . . The management program will maintain records of all test scores, and print-outs may be generated, if desired." An example of the kind of "fact" children must learn before they are allowed to become readers is that "some short vowels are spelled with two vowel letters." Computer programs have to resort to devious tricks with spelling because they need learners to write words without first having seen them. The Milliken program employs three typical strategies to test the short-vowel "fact"—presenting words that are mixed up, such as "LTAHEH" when they want the learner to write "HEALTH," or words that are a code, like "BNTMSQX" for "COUNTRY," or words that are misspelled, like "BIRD BATHE" for "BIRD BATH."

The Milliken "Comprehension Power" program previews a reading selection for the student—*Moby Dick* is an example given in the software catalog—followed by the reading selection "presented either one line at a time at a preassigned rate, or page by page with the student advancing the pages on the computer screen manually. The timed rate may be set from 50 to 650 words per minute." After reading the selection at the assigned rate, the student then tries to answer "comprehension" questions in multiple-choice format, such as "AHAB is to PEQUOD as a Captain is to his (a) crew, (b) ship, (c) sails, (d) uniform." Immediate feedback tells the student "Your reading rate was 300 wpm. Your comprehension rate was 75%. Your reading index is 225. You reread 1 time. Four questions—five tries. . . . three out of four questions correct." The teacher is assured that "the management program will total performance data for an entire diskette. Student difficulties in one or more of the 25 skill areas can be readily identified and corrective activities can then be assigned."

Each unit of Milton Bradley's instructional software for language and math instruction has a built-in "management system" that holds up to 125 student records on the same diskette as the actual skill programs. "All skills . . . can be managed by this system. The Mastery Quiz and Instruction Mode update the student's record for each skill. Once mastery is achieved, the computer automatically moves the student up to the next skill level." When Mike types in the correct answer the computer says, "Right on, Mike." If the response is incorrect the computer says, "Bad news, Mike." Milton Bradley, of Springfield, Massachusetts, claims that its software meets "every student need."

Many of the same large companies that publish instructional programs in print are involved, and so are the surviving regional laboratories and federally-funded educational research centers. Major educational publishing houses, sensitive to every shift in the direction of educational winds and often steered by holding companies with a primary interest in "communications" technology, have rapidly diversified into software development. Houghton Mifflin, for example, launched its "Dolphin" computer software series in 1981, with reading, language arts, and math programs across eight grade levels "based largely on proven Houghton Mifflin paper-and-pencil materials." Once adapted for the computer, they have been proven "to significantly increase skills performance—in some cases by three times!" Dolphin computer-based instruction, according to the promotional material I have been quoting, "joins a century of Houghton Mifflin curriculum expertise with breakthrough, state-of-the-art technology to create one of the strongest skills mastery packages ever offered to the serious educator." All of the teacher's traditional chores are provided for. In addition to a comprehensive management system for keeping all the scores, "the Dolphin even offers the *Guidance Information System*, the world's favorite computerized guidance resource!"

New companies, large and small, have also come into the educational market from the computer technology side—and made fortunes in a few years. Spinnaker Software Corporation, one of the most successful new educational software companies, advertises directly to parents: "Finally, computer games you *want* your kids to play." Spinnaker has "Early Learning Games" (for ages three to eight) and "Learning Discovery Games" (for ages six to twelve), sold through local retailers, "written by top educators who know how to make learning fun. And by expert game programmers, who use colorful graphics, animation and sound to make our games so exciting, your kids may not even realize they're learning. They're having too good a time."

Here is how Spinnaker's president Bill Bowman described their corporate strategy: "We developed a business plan aimed at the home educational segment, because the companies in that market were basically technology- or educator-led companies and not market driven companies. We felt that by really changing the product, making it with good color graphics and sound combined with terrific packaging, heavy advertising, and professional promotion and selling, we could become a major supplier of home educational software." The absence of any particular educational aim or philosophy extending beyond the appearance of the product was clearly no handicap. Spinnaker now has annual sales of about $30 million, half of the home educational software market.

The most that might be claimed of educational merit in such programs is that they give teachers and parents what they have been persuaded they want. The programs themselves are trivially easy to produce. Even amateurs can join in. IBM advertises in computer journals, inviting backroom programmers to write educational software. IBM will reprogram professionally anything it considers marketable, copyright it in the author's name, promote and market the new package, and pay the author a royalty. John Henry Martin's "Writing to Read" program is an example. For a while, programmers who bought a particular brand of floppy disk in England were offered another package free if they returned a single disk with an educational program on it.

How to Write Instructional Software

Whether the procedure is called "programmed learning," "drill and practice," or "electronic page turning," instructional software programs are constructed in essentially the following manner: An item of "information" is displayed on the screen, such as:

Lima is the capital of Peru.

Some time later the computer asks,

What is the capital of Peru? *or*
What country is Lima the capital of?

and depending upon whether the answer is right or wrong, the computer says:

Well done *or*
Bad luck [and the student's name].

The computer then moves on to the next item or repeats the previous one, totals the score, reports the score back to the learner and the teacher, keeps the score for the next day, the next week, or the end of term, and makes all kinds of comparisons—whatever the teacher or an administrator wants. Just to make sure the student keeps on task, commercial television techniques of animation and sound are employed. R-bbits abound. Everyone is entranced.

I am not saying that students need not learn that Lima is the capital of Peru, but that computerized drill is a perverse way of trying to cram into their minds the wrong thing at the wrong time in the wrong way. And this is exactly the kind of instructional programming that is done by educational outsiders adept in the simple techniques of presenting "learning materials" systematically.

First, the "databank" of facts to be learned is loaded into the computer—not even in complete sentences, but in appropriate pairs:

A.	B.
Peru	Lima
Argentina	Buenos Aires
Chile	Santiago
Brazil	Brasilia

[and so forth . . .]

followed by the instructional framework—"B is the capital of A"— and the testing frames—"What city is the capital of A?" or "What country is B the capital of?" The particular items taught and tested can be selected randomly by the computer or determined in advance by the teacher or (more often) the programmer. Additional material can always be included, and the technique can be employed to generate items for any subject matter. First the "information":

4 is the square root of 16
la chaise is the French word for "chair"
barium is the 14th chemical element

Beethoven composed the *Moonlight* Sonata
1821 was the year of Napoleon's death.

Then the test:

What is the square root of 16?
What is the French word for "chair?"
What is the 14th chemical element?
Who composed the *Moonlight* Sonata?
When was the year of Napoleon's death?

or

————is the square root of 16.
————is the French word for chair.
The 14th chemical element is————.
The *Moonlight* Sonata was composed by ————.

There is no end.

This programming technique can be employed by anyone with the slightest acquaintance with computers, and it is. There is no need to know anything about the subject matter being covered—an encyclopedia will give you everything you want to know (or it can be "adapted," with minor modification, from something someone else has done in printed materials or in other computer software). There is no need to know anything about education, and it is impossible to know anything about the individual students who will be confronted by this instruction. The cottage industry of instructional program development works behind the scenes and blindfolded.

Few of the people who should be the most involved in education—administrators, teachers, and parents themselves—look beyond the packaging of these programs, which now exist in tens of thousands. It is ironic that there are even instructional software programs for schools on "consumerism" when so little consumer intelligence is exercised in the selection of the software for schools. The programs look good, they look professional, they look interesting and manageable. They make students more tractable. Why look at the content of the programs, at what they actually do, when the goals they supposedly accomplish are so glittering and desirable? The r-bbit bounds along the road to El Dorado.

When Experts Become Naive

So many extravagant claims are made in the advertising and promotional material for instructional software that it is hardly necessary to find professional educators to give them authority, but it is also not difficult to acquire such testimonials. The programs can be made to look particularly authoritative by employing teachers or (more often) professors to say what the content should be. This is a trap. "Vague" responses are not accepted; statements like "I would like students to learn to love reading" are rejected as too subjective, unscientific, and wishy washy ("hand-waving" is the pejorative jargon). Precise behavioral objectives are demanded, like "knowledge of the letters of the alphabet." In other words, the teacher must supply something to suit the program, not the student. The programmer still manages to finish up with:

> A is the first letter of the alphabet. . . .
> The first letter of the alphabet is . . . ?
> What is the missing letter in r-bbit?

Knowing something about what they are supposed to be teaching doesn't always protect people within the educational profession from foolishness. The experts themselves can forget everything they are supposed to know about their subject matter and about learning when they are in the grip of enthusiasm to apply computer technology to instruction. At two conferences recently, one in Toronto concerned with second language teaching and one in San Francisco concerned with special education, I watched special committees of linguists and experienced teachers discussing the development of computer "learning modules." All the time they talked of right and wrong answers, of immediate feedback, multiple choices, random presentations, continual testing, and mountains of scores. These experts did not realize that they were talking all the time of obstacles that would be put in the way of learners, many of whom would be having trouble making sense of school in any case. The experts were thinking of record keeping, administration, and of how they could best use the computer. They overlooked what they were trying to achieve: the development of language fluency.

Although many of the experts were linguists, they even ignored what they knew about language. If a student had asserted in an assignment that a predominant characteristic of language was that it did not make sense, the student would have been given a low mark and told that the statement was ridiculous. Yet the experts wallowed in the ways in which the computer could produce language that was nonsense.

Blanks abounded. These committees of experts were carried away by the fact that the computer could produce endless sequences of sentences with bites taken out of them. Give the computer a passage of text or a list of sentences, and it could leave out every second noun, every third adjective, every fifth or seventh or ninth word, anything they wanted. In fact, the computer could itself generate endless lists of sentences for fragmentation.

This device of leaving out words for the learner to replace is a well-known research technique called the "cloze." The technique enables statements to be made about how easily a piece of text is understood or how well a particular reader understands the piece of text. (The higher the replacement rate, the greater the comprehension). But this is nothing like the way language really works. Real language doesn't have holes in it.

But with the help of the r-bbit the computer could have students filling in the missing words every day of the week. Or more likely, it would have them not filling in the missing words, because many students would not do very well at such a strange activity in the first place, and in any case these programs are designed to "challenge" students, which means always to move them onto a level of confusion where they are bound to make mistakes. And the students who have the most difficulty are labeled as having learning problems and are put on an even more concentrated diet of absurd experience.

The committees of experts at the conferences I am discussing did not stop with the blanks; they reveled in other ridiculous things that computers can do with blinding ease. For example, not only can computers take words out of sentences, they can also put words in. It is no trouble for a computer to put randomly into sentences words that do not belong in them. The learner's task, of course, is to detect the intruding word, so that the computer can evaluate the answer as right or wrong, report the score, move to the next item, and so forth. Once more, the computer will be able to compare all the scores, decide which students are learning and which have learning problems, compare current rates of progress with last week's and last year's, and set targets for the future. And it is all done with nonsense. Computers can even be programmed to generate infinite numbers of totally jumbled sentences for learners to reorganize into grammatical form. There is no end to the meaningless tasks that computers can orchestrate, and since there will always be some students who cannot do these tasks as well as others, there will always be a need for more programs claiming to train "disabled" learners to perform marginally better on what, in any case, are pointless activities.

Teaching Students to "Think"

It is not difficult to find examples. (It's only difficult to stop quoting them.) The companies and materials I have so far cited as illustrations, both in printware and computer programs, were picked almost at random from a pile of alternatives that was growing out of control on my study floor. I did not select them as being particularly good or bad, only typical. Any current parent, teacher, professional, or computer magazine could provide scores of alternative possibilities. None of the materials or advertisements I have quoted from is shoddy. All represent enormous investments in time, expertise, capital, and expectation—full-page full-color magazine advertisements, multiple-page full-color brochures on heavy stock, more substantial and impressive than the promotional kits for cars, computers, or television sets. And the scale is enormous. Let me describe the material from one more company, which I have selected because it is involved in an area that is becoming a particular concern in education (although I do not think that this or any other company has the answer)—namely, thinking.

Midwest Publications of Pacific Grove, California, specializes in producing "critical thinking supplies" for schools. Its 1984 catalog introduced a "new comprehensive thinking skills series" for second to seventh grades that would make it easy for teachers to introduce the skills into the classroom. Many of the exercises are on computer disks, and more are being produced. The rationale for the manner in which pages and pages of exercises are supposed to "build thinking skills" is that "before an individual can develop the more sophisticated concepts of order, class, or analogy, the learner must be able to distinguish similarities and differences in shapes or words." In other words, children who since birth have been effortlessly distinguishing and classifying cats and dogs, tables and chairs, knives and forks, an average of twenty new words a day and countless faces and places, are assumed not to be able to distinguish shapes and words. This is the Duck That Faces the Wrong Way again. The children are therefore given exercises on nonsense shapes, meaningless lists of words, and complex verbal puzzles, all selected to ensure that some students will fail, otherwise there would be no point in the exercises.

Nothing is actually *taught,* except that nonsensical activities are important. For example, under Midwest Publications' impressive heading of "Sorting into Classes," students have to work their way through an unbroken paragraph of thirty-two words and phrases beginning "all, always, anybody, downstairs, downtown, early, everybody, everyone, far away . . . ," writing them in one of three columns according to whether the words refer to who, when, or where. It is easy to be critical of detail in activities like this—to point out how much reading ability and test sophistication is required even to find out what is supposed to be done (common sense provides no clue), and that the instructions themselves are misleading (some of the "words" to be sorted are in fact phrases, and a student taking the instructions literally could regard "far away" as two entries). But the essential fact is that the exercise is totally meaningless. In real-world language, words are never "sorted" into categories the way sports teams and socks might be. It is absurd to

suggest that children cannot "sort"—they demonstrate this innate
mental capacity the first time they distinguish friends from strangers
or say something is their own and not anyone else's. All that children can learn from such an exercise is that "learning" is boring
nonsense and quite possibly that they have a mysterious and probably incurable learning defect.

In new Midwest Publications computer software called
"Mind Benders," designed to "sharpen deductive thinking
skills," one of the first of the "easiest" items is, "A cat, a small
dog, a goat and a horse are named Angel, Beauty, King and
Rover." Learners must read a set of clues to find each animal's
name. In real-world language no one would deliberately produce
such a complicated sentence; language is not supposed to confuse.
If such a sentence were produced, it would be assumed that the
order in which the animals are named is the order in which they
are listed, so that Angel is the cat's name and so on. Thus anyone
who does this test has to forget the way language is normally used
and develop a new assumption (quickly learned by all schoolchildren) that educational language is intentionally meaningless and
confusing. Instead, students are supposed to work out each animal's name from the following three "clues": "King is smaller
than either the dog or Rover. The horse is younger than Angel.
Beauty is the oldest and a good friend of the dog." To help the
learners, a chart is provided with four columns headed A, B, K, R
(you have to work out that the letters represent the initial letter of
the animal's name) and four rows labeled C, D, G, H. It is more
of a problem to deduce what has to be done with the chart than
to "solve" the puzzle itself.

But once again, what is the point of this exercise, and page
after page of similar exercises? Students will either be able to do
the task or they will not. The fact that they can do the task proves
nothing, except that they may be good at the kind of puzzles adults
engage in only occasionally, as a pastime, if they do so at all. If
students can't do the exercises, they will have to spend more time
on them (and less on more meaningful activities), and teachers and
students will become convinced that they have an intellectual problem. Word puzzles of this kind, incidentally, are a staple of the
hundreds of different kinds of books and sets of materials on the

educational market claiming to teach "thinking skills" of various kinds.

It has never been demonstrated that people who cannot do these puzzles are unable to think as they go about their daily business, or that being able to do the puzzles indicates some special kind of intellect that makes one a more efficient physician, truck driver, schoolteacher, or even just a better or happier person. The underlying rationale is about as sensible as suggesting that ability to do crossword puzzles or to solve chess problems indicates a valuable and generalizable intellectual talent, and that drills in crossword puzzle solving will increase anyone's mental capacity and work efficiency. But when I come to mention crossword puzzles, I realize that they also are a part of many instructional programs. It is just about impossible to imagine a nonsensical activity to serve as an analogy for what goes on in schools. Instructional programmers have preempted every pointless activity one can think of and included it in an educational ritual.

The problem is not primarily with the students who can do these puzzles—although for them the constantly repeated activity will be a crushing waste of time. The problem is with the students who are bored or confused. They will not learn anything except that school and learning are boring and confusing, and they and their teachers will quickly come to believe that they have a particular kind of learning problem. Getting the student to complete the nonsensical task becomes a challenge to the *teacher;* in fact, the teacher will usually be held "accountable" for keeping the student on task and evaluated on how well the student eventually does.

In another Midwest "Basic Thinking Skills" series there is a set of worksheet drills labeled "Patterns." This type of exercise is very popular and is often employed under the heading of "concept formation," which is supposed to be a useful and difficult thing for students to do. Midwest claims that these exercises "sharpen analytical thinking for better reading comprehension, math, writing, science, test-taking, etc." (The "etc." is thrown in to cover any form of instruction the programmer and copywriter might have overlooked.) It is suggested that teachers read the problems aloud to the entire class, which should work through them together, to enable the teacher to help develop listening skills and permit weak readers to participate in the thinking process. A typical problem requires students to "figure out what a *gurnet* is" from diagrams indicating whether various geometrical shapes are or are not gurnets. All of this is once again supposed to teach something to children who have had no problem figuring out whether far more complex real-word objects are or are not shoes, hamburgers, bicycles, or telephones.

The r-bbit is never far behind of course. Midwest has a program called KLOOZ (the "cloze" technique mentioned before), available in either software or book and ditto form, "designed to improve your students' reading, writing and mathematics skills. . . . Players are presented with a paragraph from which most of the words have been deleted. The goal in KLOOZ is to deduce the meaning of the paragraph, using the fewest number of word and letter clues."

For mathematics there is a collection of "math amusements" providing "an ideal combination of extensive practice exercises embedded in cross-number puzzles, line designs, decodes, graphs, optical illusions and others." Under the heading of "equivalent fractions," a book entitled *Mathamerica* contains fractions in which letters replace numbers. Students must solve the fractions in order to find out a coded word. If this sounds complicated, it is; it is a devious device for getting students to engage in drills on fractions. Once again one has to ask what it will achieve if it is successful— students who can do fractions will spend more time drilling on fractions—and what the consequences will be for students who cannot do them—what will they have learned? The code is the r-bbit in disguise.

It is a little invidious to pick on Midwest when there are scores of publishers promoting identical materials and making identical claims. But that is the point. Midwest is representative, and Midwest is doing well. According to the *U.S. News and World Report* of January 14, 1985, the business of Midwest has increased tenfold over the past ten years. The materials it produces are popular, and they are being used more and more, especially with computers. "Teaching thinking" is in—more work and more profit for the program developers and promoters, more work for the r-bbit, and more pointless and discouraging busywork for the teacher and student.

The Myth of the Omniscient Outsider

The unspoken assumption behind the production and promotion of all programmatic instruction is that someone outside the classroom can make better decisions than the teacher in the classroom. Johnny has just completed one task; now the program dictates what he moves to next. Jane is having difficulty at the moment, and the program or test determines what she needs by way of "remediation." It is taken for granted that such choices can better be made by someone who will never know Johnny and Jane than by the teacher on the spot.

The assumption is that what matters is "the acquisition of information"—the communication and learning metaphor of the electronic age—regardless of the order or relevance of the information that is presented. It is not surprising that programmatic instruction is so congenial to computer software designers, whose professional speciality is the construction of information control systems. Every piece of software controls the behavior of the computer on which it is run, precisely and unambiguously, with no room left for unplanned variation. And every piece of educational software also controls the behavior of the teachers and students with whom it is employed, with no allowance for ambiguity or unplanned variation. There is no opportunity to seize a magical moment of enlightenment or to assuage an anxiety, to write a poem or to discuss a concern.

Few experienced teachers would claim to have such special skills that they could do a better teaching job from a distance—say over the telephone—than a competent teacher actually in the classroom. How can anyone who cannot see a child know why the child learns or fails to learn? Children who know things learn them for different reasons, in different circumstances. They will be able to demonstrate what they know in different ways. For a variety of reasons, children are sometimes unable to demonstrate knowledge or ability that they possess, for instance because they are confused, apprehensive, bored, suspicious, tired, hungry, out of sorts, or out of sympathy with school or the teacher. Students can perform equally well (or equally poorly) on tests for different reasons. And students who do not know something may have failed to learn for a variety of reasons. They also may be apprehensive or rebellious, timid or assertive, overconfident or overcautious. How can anyone who does not know a student *teach* that student, especially in highly structured, controlled, and monitored ways with penalties attached for "failure"? There are no omniscient outsiders in education. There never could be.

A Question of Trust

Why then should a few people set themselves up as experts or be regarded by others as qualified to make critical pedagogical decisions, sight unseen? And why are they so often supported by administrators, politicians, and the authors of editorials, sydicated articles, and letters in newspapers? The answer is very simple: *None of these people trusts teachers to teach.* This is again a matter of control. The very notion that programmatic instruction can ensure excellence in education is an indictment of teachers. This lack of confidence is frequently explicit, as it is in programs where teachers are admonished not to vary the procedures that have been laid down. Some instructional systems have actually been advertised as "teacher-proof." I have been told that my expectations for teachers are too high, that most teachers do not have the experience or skill (or even desire) to make decisions in their own classrooms.

All this may indeed be true. There are doubtless many teachers in schools today who could not manage their classrooms without programs to guide them. (Teachers who depend upon programs are teachers who do not trust students to learn.) Teachers have asked me what they would do with their time if programs were taken away. They have been trained for the past thirty years to be dependent upon programs. They have not been trusted or taught to be able to make their own decisions. Professors in faculties of education have told me that student teachers are not "ready" for theory—and that most practicing teachers are not either. These professors argue that student teachers must be given "survival skills" to get through the day and that they must be prepared for the way schools are, not for the way schools ought to be. Teachers, like students, behave in ways that reflect how they have been taught.

But even if it is true that many teachers today cannot be trusted to teach, programs cannot be the solution. Programs are not an alternative, they will not do the job that good teachers are supposed to do, namely help students to learn in a worthwhile manner. If teachers are inadequate, then the solution must be better teachers, not more programs. Computers cannot take over from teachers. Print programs and software programs will only make the situation worse—and continue to undermine the confidence and ability of the teachers that we have.

Arguments for programs tend to be emotional rather than rational. The proponents of programmatic instruction claim to be objective and scientific, but they play upon ignorance and guilt. Parents are asked, "Can you afford to let your child fall behind?" or even "Does your child deserve less than the best?" Some of the most coercive programs are categorized benignly as "direct instruction" or "precision teaching," which simply means *ensuring* that the student learns at every step. Who would not be in favor of such a thing? Programmatic instruction claims to be "research based." But there is no conclusive research evidence that children ever learned anything worthwhile as a consequence of programmatic instruction, certainly not what the labeling claims.

There never *could* be proof that programs were responsible for making children literate, for example, unless children were denied every opportunity of experiencing print in meaningful situations (a situation unlikely to arise unless computers take over instruction completely). So the possibility can never be excluded that children have learned in some other way and are making programmatic instruction look good. Instructional programs are not compared experimentally with real-life experiences—with meaningful learning. The experimental controls would be inadequate. Instead programs are compared against each other for how well they teach specific things, such as "subskills" and isolated fragments of "information." Not surprisingly, when children are tested under such conditions, those who have been drilled on specific skills and facts tend to demonstrate better knowledge than children who were not drilled on those particular items.

On the other hand, there is a wealth of evidence that children succeed in learning without the benefit of programmatic instruction. All children learn to talk and to understand spoken language without prepackaged direction. There is no omniscient outsider deciding the order in which they should learn about their culture or the particular world in which they live. Most children have learned a good deal about reading and writing before they come to school, as a consequence of being inducted into the literacy club, not because of exercises and drills and tests. Not all children are apprentice members of the literacy club before they come to school, of course, and those children who are not are even more in need of literacy clubs when they get to school than those who are. There is no evidence that programs will take the place of clubs in assisting these children toward literacy. Another common assertion that "some children"—usually "slow learners" or members of minority groups—need highly structured teaching defies logic as well as research evidence; programs simply add to any relative deprivation these children might already suffer.

The idea that any outsider is required to ensure that students learn is a myth and an insult, to students and to teachers. The quality control of education has become the enforced administration of an unbroken diet of nonsense. The people who try to assert every detail of what teachers should teach are not really in the business of helping students to learn at all. Their business is the control of education, and their method is the topic to which I must now turn, the mania for testing.

CHAPTER 6

The Tyranny of Testing

Programmatic instruction and testing are inseparable. Every item in an instructional program is followed by a test. Almost everything that students produce—poems, essays, projects—is given a mark, a grade, or a "score," so that everything students do becomes a test. Little escapes numerical "evaluation." Two assumptions underlie the "quality control" of continual testing: (1) that children will learn more and (2) that teachers will teach better. Both assumptions are flawed. Children do not learn better as a consequence of incessant testing; they learn not to learn. And teachers do not teach better as a consequence of the testing; they learn not to teach. Yet the tyranny of testing increases, because testing is the means by which education is controlled.

Tests are built into every program as part of the drill and test ritual, and teachers give other tests weekly and even daily to check on student progress. Schools usually require tests annually or more frequently, sometimes for explicit purposes of "monitoring progress" and sometimes simply from force of habit. It is widely believed that examinations and tests are good things; that they encourage students to learn. Every two or three years most children are confronted by state-imposed standardized achievement tests or competency tests that occupy much of their attention, and their teachers', for months in advance. It is through testing that politicians, administrators, and supposedly omniscient outsiders exert the control that they expect will achieve excellence in education. As Professor W. James Popham, an expert on educational testing at the University of California, Los Angeles, has written "In an evidence-oriented enterprise, those who control the evidence-gathering mechanisms control the entire enterprise."

Teaching to the Test

The control is achieved because teachers have little choice but to teach to the tests. When master-teacher Donald Graves and co-author Virginia Stuart complained that children quickly decide that reading and writing are no fun at all, they accused teachers and publishers of employing a workbook approach to instruction. But primarily they blamed "the test-making business" for testing "component skills—frequently one a day" so that teachers teach in this way. Instead of writing, according to Graves and Stuart, children read a paragraph and then circle or underline "the correct answer" to questions. When children do write, teachers concentrate on correcting errors, which is all they can do. All the red-inking makes the teachers feel better but the children feel worse. Yet, Graves and Stuart decided, children who wrote instead of being primed for tests did better on the tests. And they are not talking about "privileged" children. They tell of elaborate and complex compositions on topics ranging from supersonic transport to the paintings of Van Gogh by children in some of New York City's poorest areas.

Many teachers believe that children cannot write unless they learn "basic skills"—which means they expect children to be secretaries before they can become authors. Programs assist such teachers. Milton Bradley Software has one program to teach commas and another to teach the period, question mark, exclamation point, semicolon (taught as two separate skills), and colon. Two other software programs are devoted to sentences, including the recognition of sentence parts, predicates, complements, and clauses. Other subjects receive similar treatment. The same company's "Division Skills" program begins with "90 basic facts." There are math programs "especially suited for remedial practice" where "speed drills let students master basic concepts before starting the regular program" and there is "only one try per problem, computer corrects mistakes immediately." A built-in "application mode" with every program includes pretests to "diagnose" student ability and posttests to measure student progress. The computer automatically identifies students as, M, P, or I on every skill, to indicate whether mastery has been achieved, or practice or instruction is required.

Similar help is available for courseware based on textbooks, workbooks, and paper-and-pencil exercises. Holt, Rinehart and Winston's "Math 1000" program—"A high octane program to tune up your general math students"—includes "diagnostic and prescriptive tests [that] identify and eliminate skill deficiencies with whole numbers, fractions and decimals." And now the company offers "CLASS"—an acronym for Computerized Learning and Scoring System—which "allows one computer to manage the testing and scoring of all grade levels for all Holt's basal programs . . . increased flexibility in reporting, increased automation in record keeping, and increased customization of student tests and reports." The latter include a "class status report, class activity report, student report card, grade status report, school status report, district status report, student diagnostic test results and student history report." A test bank that accompanies the "CLASS" program for math "provides a set of tests for all key objectives of major basal mathematics programs, automatically generates an individual second test or homework assignment for each student based on objectives not mastered in the chapter test, automatically scores each test and updates the student's files, provides a complete, up-to-date record of each student's progress and achievements [and] automatically generates new sets of questions customized to the individual needs of each student in the class." Who will be in charge of the classroom?

Ginn and Co. makes a similar offer for teachers overwhelmed by record-keeping. "If too much paperwork is complicating your teaching of reading, here's a simple solution. It's the Ginn Computer Management System, the software package that helps you organize, store, evaluate and report all that vital information on your students' achievements. . . . No more adding up correct answers on tests and figuring out percentage scores. No more writing class or individual student progress reports or reports for unit, level or mid-level tests. And no more long hours spent writing parent reports. The [system] takes care of all this paperwork, more quickly, efficiently and effectively." The "vital information" is of course scores and test results. Even reports to parents are written more effectively by the computer, not simply as a record of scores, but as a "personal" letter chatting about where Johnny has strengths and Jane should demonstrate more effort. The risk of bias in a teacher's report will be replaced by the risk of bias built into a machine.

Programs like these from major publishers are not driving education where it does not want to go, they are not radical. These publishers are producing what they know state and local education authorities will buy.

The Roots of Testing

It was through the testing movement that psychology gained its initial hold over education. At first, experimental psychologists needed educational data for their own research, and then test results were used to make instructional decisions concerning the placement of children and type of instruction they should receive. Educational research was almost entirely a matter of testing children, until a decade ago when a few radical researchers began looking at the ecology of classrooms and the behavior of teachers.

The systematic testing of school children that began in Britain in the early years of the present century was closely linked with an influential eugenics movement, primarily motivated by a fear of uncontrolled fertility and inherited intellectual inadequacy among the poorer classes. The preferred solutions to what in those days was seen as a potential threat to the race were usually birth control and sterilization. Some of the most historic names in statistics and educational psychology were involved in both the eugenics movement and the mass assessment of schoolchildren's abilities. Germaine Greer recently documented the association in her book *Sex and Destiny* in which she asserts that "modern society is unique in that it is profoundly hostile to children." She points out that the geneticist Francis Galton, who proposed that the state should deliberately breed its most gifted men and women to increase the genius of the race, was the first person ever to carry out a systematic examination of a school population. Galton developed methods of mathematical analysis that are the basis of contemporary testing statistics. His work was continued by Cyril Burt and Karl Pearson at University College, London. Pearson, another mathematician and biologist, devised many early tests and gave his name to a correlational statistic on which many comparisons of test results are still made. Pearson announced in 1903: "The mentally better stock of the nation is not reproducing itself at the same rate as it did of old; the less able and the less energetic are more fertile than the better stocks. No scheme of wider or more thorough education will bring up in the scale of intelligence hereditary weakness to the level of hereditary strength. The only remedy, if one be possible at all, is to alter the relative fertility of the good and the bad stocks in the country."

Raymond B. Cattell, director of the Schools Psychological Clinic in Leicester, author of *The Fight for Our National Intelligence,* and—according to Greer—"a fervent supporter of the sterilisation campaign," was offered an award by the Eugenics Society in 1935 "for the investigation by tests of the intelligence of a typical urban and a typical rural population of school children with a view to determining the average size of the family at each level of intelligence." Cattell's teacher at University College, London, was psychology professor Cyril Burt, who was knighted for his nineteen-year service as a designer of mental and scholastic tests for the London County Council schools (and subsequently discredited for faking his data). Burt was convinced that the intelligence that his tests measured was inherited, and was lowest and declining in the "general population" which also tended to have more children, a fact that he was concerned "might produce serious cumulative effects if at all sustained."

It is the descendants of these tests, predominantly produced and promoted in the United States since the time of Sputnik, which underlie the efforts to evaluate constantly the learning of children today, no matter how trivial and disruptive that learning might have to be to facilitate the testing.

The Short Right Answer

The basis of all tests and of programmatic instruction is what critic Walter Karp has called "the tyranny of the short right answer." In a review of eight recent books and official reports on the current state of American education, including research by John A. Goodlad, former dean of education at the University of California, Los Angeles, which involved observation in over a thousand classrooms, Karp summarizes: "From the first grade to the twelfth, from one coast to the other, instruction in America's classrooms is almost entirely dogmatic. Answers are 'right' and answers are 'wrong' but mostly answers are short." He cites Linda Darling-Hammond's Rand Corporation study that when "important decisions are based on test scores . . . teachers are more likely to teach to the tests and less likely to bother with nontested activities, such as writing, speaking, problem-solving or real reading of real books." The most influential promoter of standardized tests, according to Karp, is the "excellence brigade" in the Department of Education. "Consider the current cry for greater use of standardized student tests to judge the 'merit' of teachers and raise 'academic standards.' If this fake reform is foisted on the schools, dogma and docility will become even more prevalent."

The short right answer has come to dominate education, but only because of the mania for teaching and testing by the most mechanical means possible—"objectively." The theory is that to teach and evaluate learning in any way except by numbers would be unscientific and unreliable, and to allow scores or grades to be allocated on the basis of personal judgment would be "subjective" (a pejorative term) and biased. Ironically, the endeavor to remove the personal and possibly prejudicial from educational evaluation has resulted in the totally arbitrary and distorted procedure of teaching and testing only those things that can be cleanly scored right or wrong, and counted. The cost of removing human error has been the removal of all humanity and the reduction of education to trivia.

Chester Carlow, a professor of curriculum at the Ontario Institute for Studies in Education in Toronto, describes what happens when math teachers become more concerned with right and wrong answers than with how students get those answers. He says that thirty years ago, one student went to the front of the class and worked out a problem on the chalkboard, while the teacher critiqued the process and helped the student where necessary. Today eight students go to the chalkboard, all work simultaneously on their problems, and the teacher critiques the results. Students don't even try to understand why they are doing what their teacher tries to get them to do, says Carlow. They try to copy what the teacher does and hope they get the right answer.

At a school in New Hampshire where Donald Graves and his associates were trying to teach teachers and children what it was to be a writer, I noticed that while third-grade children were indeed writing fluently and competently, their writing was all factual; there was no fiction, no fantasy. Two teachers explained why: One said that surely fantasy was harder than fact—you couldn't look it up but had to make it up. (What sort of a brain did she think children have?) The other teacher was more frank. Children could write fantasy at home if they liked, but in school she wanted facts. How could fantasy be marked right or wrong?

Even the deepest emotions of students are subordinated to the obsession to find something to mark. A teacher told me about a poem and a short story, both on the subject of death, in a statewide English examination. The teacher had thought such a topic might be upsetting to students taking the examination, especially any who had recently been bereaved, and had raised the matter with the committee who selected the examination items. One committee member agreed that the poem had reduced her to tears—but she would not take it out of the examination. Another member of the committee said that poetry was *supposed* to affect the emotions. So the teacher asked why the committee couldn't select poems that were cheerful and optimistic? The answer was that happy poetry frequently dwelt upon taboo subjects and that, in any case, it was difficult to find poems that contained figures of speech, factual information, and other characteristics which could be the basis of multiple-choice questions. Upsetting students in the middle of an examination was of minor consequence compared with being able to construct test items with quantifiable short right answers.

I talked with a professor at the University of California, Santa Barbara, who taught "freshman composition." He was a member of a group of professors and teachers participating in the Bay Area Writing Project, a scheme in which teachers of writing examine and discuss what takes place when they themselves write, and who try to bring these insights to bear in helping students to write. These teachers are more aware than most that writing is learned from engaging in reading and writing, not from drills, tests, and other activities that exclude students from the meaningful use of written language. So when I asked the instructor what he had been doing with his class that morning I expected to be told how they had all been using written language like members of the reading and writing club. But I was wrong. "We've been preparing for the midterm exam," he said. He had been engaged in what he thought was most relevant for the college's purposes, and what was most on the students' minds, even though he knew this was a waste of yet another day as far as helping his students to become writers was concerned. What exactly had he been doing? "Two things," he said. "Going through how the items in the tests are scored, and trying to reduce student anxiety." He did not disagree when I suggested that the two aims might be in conflict. But he saw no alternative. If he ignored the examinations, he would be accused by most of his students and colleagues of ignoring the most significant event on the student horizon.

The Universal Currency of the Grade

The problem goes right through education. When I was a professor of education I used to tell my graduate students—all far more experienced teachers than I was—that I expected to learn from them and that they would learn from each other in the course of our studies. Many students didn't like the notion of learning from each other. Wasn't the instructor supposed to be the expert? Administrators among my students especially wanted to get down to business. I should tell them what they were expected to learn, they would then learn it, and no one's time would be wasted, they told me.

Everyone at the university, instructors and students alike, seemed to me to be so busy coping with course content and program requirements that no one had any time to read or to write in any productive way in pursuit of personal interests, let along to talk or think. So I used to give my students time to do all these things. I would tell them that their next assignment was to read a book. Which book, they would ask. I replied: any book that interested them, that they thought worthwhile. Most of the students would look puzzled, even anxious. How would I test them if they all read different books? I told them there would be no test; I would ask no questions. They responded: *If there will be no questions, why should we read the book?* I asked them to write a paper. What about? They could choose. How long should it be? As long as they thought appropriate. I knew that if I said seventeen and a half doubled-spaced pages I would get seventeen and a half double-spaced pages, whatever the topic. And then the key question: How would I grade them? I said there would be no grades. And the response was: *If you aren't going to grade us, why should we write anything?*

These were not "disadvantaged" or learning-disabled students —not in any formal sense at least. These were teachers, the cream of the crop, experienced, dedicated, and working for their masters or doctoral degrees. Where could they have learned that there is no point in reading a book unless someone is going to ask them questions; no point in writing something unless someone is going to give them a grade for it? The answer, of course, is in school. It is only in school that people read in order to answer questions or write to get a grade. These teachers were demonstrating what they had learned and what they were teaching their own students.

My students were disturbed to think that they might indeed be teaching children not to read and to write, so they went back to their own classrooms to find out. They gave children as young as second graders the same invitation—read a book, write something. And second graders produced the same objections as graduate students: If there will be no questions and no tests, why should we do it? It is obviously not just failing students who are damaged; the attitudes of the "successes" are just as warped. Everyone learns. The lack of interest is so compelling that some teachers have told me that children are born this way—as if babies will not learn unless they are given a grade for doing so. But children learn all the time, and what they learn in school is exactly what they are taught.

Bryant Fillion, a professor in the faculty of education at Fordham University in New York, calls it "information dumping." Teachers dump facts on students which they expect students to dump back on them. Fillion, a teacher who has worked with hundreds of other teachers, even has a theory of how information dumping is perpetuated. He tells of Johnny, who is told to write a project on Japan. The child goes to the library and looks up "Japan" in an encyclopedia. He reads that Japan is comprised of four main islands and writes that down. He reads that the population of the country is about 100 million and writes that down. He reads that fish forms a large part of the Japanese diet and writes that down. And depending on whether he comes from a four- or five-fact classroom, he writes down one or two more facts, carefully avoiding any words he does not know how to spell, and dumps it all on the desk of his teacher, who gives him an A, commending him for his neatness and the absence of factual errors. If Johnny continues to be tidy and factually correct he will continue to receive As throughout his grade-school years. If he is very good at doing the same thing in college he may become a teacher himself. And if he can maintain his success when he goes to graduate school he will in turn become a professor and teach teachers himself.

Susan Ohanian, an outspoken teacher who taught grade school for fourteen years in Troy, New York, says that children will not learn if they are not willing to take risks—like giving a wrong answer occasionally. "Do we want to be too quick to label such risks as error?" she asks. "I am not grateful to the guys who bring me the nasty combination of silly questions and speedy corrections. I find no charm in immediate numerical gratification."

Learning and Thinking

In an article entitled "Are Your Kids Learning to Think?" in the educational magazine *Changing Times* in December 1983, Don Carriker, assistant superintendent for instruction in Marion, Ohio, was reported as complaining of students: "By third or fourth grade they're convinced that the teacher will feed them the answers and they'll have to memorize them." However, the superintendent clearly thought this was the students' fault. To remedy the situation, fifteen "thinking programs" had been introduced into Marion schools from kindergarten to third grade, where Dr. Carriker hoped to form students "who would not wait to be spoon-fed but would frame their own questions and know how to find their own answers"—to do, in other words, what all children have done out of school since infancy if they have learned to talk like their friends and to find their way around their own community.

Richard Paul, director of the Center for Critical Thinking and Moral Critique at Sonoma State University, was quoted in January 1985 as saying "We need to shift the focus of learning from simply teaching students to have the right answer to teaching them the process by which educated people pursue right answers," which means presumably that children have not been taught to be educated people. But the problem with much of the critical thinking movement, of which Dr. Paul is a leader, is that it believes critical thinking is a special set of skills that must be taught, rather than a way of thinking that has been suppressed. The result has been more tests and more skills programs.

The report of the National Assessment of Educational Progress in 1980 blamed schools for teaching students "an emphasis on shallow and superficial opinions at the expense of reasoned and disciplined thought." Once again one might wonder where students are expected to see "reasoned and disciplined thought" demonstrated in schools. Predictably, states have begun to pass laws mandating instruction in critical thinking (six by the end of 1984, according to a survey by the American Federation of Teachers). California has included "thinking skills" items in its reading, writing, and math tests for sixth and eighth graders and is adding an eighth-grade examination on history and social science with forty percent of the questions devoted to critical thinking. It is predictable that many students will do poorly on these items and will be diagnosed as having thinking problems, which teachers will then be expected to solve by adding thinking skills to the curriculum. Peter Kneedley, a consultant with the California Assessment Program, explained the rationale: "Assessment is a very powerful tool to encourage schools to teach critical thinking."

The mania to test, compare, and classify has spread from the United States back to Britain, and to other parts of the world as well. In the schools of British Columbia, the "Canadian Tests of Basic Skills" are widely used—in the words of University of British Columbia educator Sydney Butler—to "camouflage the familiar monster of standardized testing to separate the sheep from the goats." The tests are not Canadian by origin, however; they are American. And Butler's observations have a general application.

"It would be extremely naive to think that these tests measure the student's mastery of language skills," Butler remarks. "At no point does the student generate language. Simply, the tests face the student with examples of the examiners' language and their contrived errors. . . . The reading comprehension test measures a very narrow sector of the student's ability in reading . . . the student scans or plods through a reading passage to find answers to trivial and meaningless questions. There is no attempt to make the student aware of any real purpose for reading other than answering questions about matters of less than passing interest. The effect of the test is to help students become non-readers in the true sense. . . . The reading comprehension test provides the usual, dull, disjointed paragraphs typical of these tests. Under pressure of time the most successful test-taker does not, of course, attempt to read the passages, but merely takes each question in turn and scans the passage for a clue to a right answer."

The spelling test requires students to guess what incorrectly spelled "words" are supposed to be, just as they have to make sense of "non-language as produced by the craziest of compositors" to correct punctuation errors, and—in a "usage" test—make sense of sentences full of "supposed errors that do not occur normally in the language of children or any native speaker of English." Instead of evaluating the student's mastery of language, concludes Butler, such tests "deal only with the student's ability to recognize the test-makers' misuse of the English language."

Butler says the tests put teachers in double jeopardy. On the one hand, the test results "can be misused to label individual students according to their supposed deficiencies. On the other hand, even conscientious teachers will feel that they have to give their students a fighting chance to defeat the tests. With such coaching and cramming for commercialized tests we will have given up control of our school curriculum, and decisions about what our children are learning will have been made in the publishers' offices in Toronto and New York, whose main interest is to sell their test booklets and answer sheets."

The Consequences of Tests

Of course, no one escapes judgment. Our behavior and ability are almost always subject to evaluation in our daily lives, especially when our relationships to other people and our work are involved. But in these contexts the evaluation is always with respect to fitness for purpose. We are judged on how appropriately we behave and on whether what we do is appropriate for what we intend to do or are expected to do. But our competence in social and occupational matters is never assessed with a number or a grade. The test of what we do is always relative to the circumstances in which we do it— and so is the reward. Making mistakes is not generally equated with failure, unless the result is catastrophic. Normally when someone can't do something as well as circumstances require, someone else assists. Most of the testing that takes place in our lives outside school occurs in clubs. When evaluation that seems inappropriate or arbitrary occurs, then we are properly outraged.

Educational testing is the opposite of the way people behave, learn, and are evaluated in clubs. This testing prevents the formation of clubs. It precludes apprenticeships by destroying the role of the person who would normally be the guide and mentor to apprentices. Teachers behave differently when they are expected to teach to test and through tests. Teachers become obsessed with errors, which have to be eradicated, while at the same time forcing children more and more into situations where mistakes are bound to be made. One of the prime purposes of tests is to move children away from what they can do into areas where they will find difficulty and confusion. Tests probe for difficulties the way a dentist probes for cavities. In educational jargon, finding something that a child cannot do is called "challenging the learner" (just as "meeting the child's needs" is an educational euphemism for fulfilling the requirements of a program).

Discrimination Against the Confused

Purdue University researcher Patrick Shannon has collated evidence that teachers rely heavily on test results when putting children into reading groups, often overlooking other relevant information and making the grouping decisions on test scores alone. Children allocated to "low-ability" groups are placed at different tables and receive different instruction, involving more drills and less meaningful reading. Not surprisingly, children placed in low-ability groups rarely get out of them. Unless teachers get to know students before they receive their test results, the teachers trust the tests even more than their own knowledge of the children, which is why it can be disastrous when students' test results precede them up the grades. Teachers are ready to discriminate against students with poor test results before they even meet.

Expectations become translated into practice and self-fulfilling prophecies. Teachers expect different behavior and achievement from particular students; the teachers therefore behave differently toward those students; thus the students receive different messages which affect their achievement, motivation, and self-concept; so that in time teachers succeed in shaping student behavior to meet the teachers' initial expectations.

What are teacher expectations? According to research summarized by Shannon, students in low-ability groups are more likely to have their attention directed to the sounds of isolated words, letters, and other meaningless fragments, while comments to high-ability students deal more with the context surrounding the troublesome word—they deal with sense, in other words. Fourth-grade students in low groups (after three years of drilling) were still found to be spending twice as much time on phonics drills in isolation compared with students in high groups (who can in any case read for themselves out of school), half as much time on reading in context, and more time in nonreading activities. Furthermore, children in groups labeled "high-ability" are often asked to read texts that are easy for them, while those in low groups are more generally given materials that are difficult for them. They often misread one word in ten when reading aloud, forcing them to pay attention to individual words rather than context and triggering more interruptions from other students and the teacher.

Exactly the same conditions and consequences can be found in math, science, or any other subject area. Teachers allow students in low-ability groups less time to correct themselves, rushing in with the right word or right answer to keep instruction moving, with the result that the students become even more hesitant, appeal for help if it doesn't come, and are reluctant or unable to monitor their own reading. The process is completely circular and self-fulfilling. It can begin with a completely false diagnosis—a student's bad day or a clerical mistake—but the test result can color the remainder of the student's academic career.

Often the results of tests can move students out of the "mainstream"—the term is educational jargon again—into side channels from which they can rarely escape. The moment children, or populations of children, are termed "special," they are in effect segregated from the very clubs they are supposed to be learning to join. This discrimination was forcefully demonstrated to me at two particularly emotional conferences I participated in within two weeks in February 1985, one in a warm climate and the other in a cold one.

At a convention of bilingual educators at the Sheraton Universal hotel in Universal City, Los Angeles, 3,000 bilingual educators heard distressed retiring president Lorenza Calvillo-Craig declare that she and their organization had failed: Another generation of Mexican-American children had been lost. She was referring to a series of political decisions cutting funds for bilingual education, which enabled children to receive some of their education in their own language, and reaffirming that English was the only language that could be spoken officially in California. From Los Angeles I went to Grande Prairie in the north of the Canadian province of Alberta, to a conference of teachers of handicapped students and of some of the students themselves. I was taken to see beautiful facilities with specially designed swimming pools, libraries, and classrooms where handicapped youngsters could get a special—but segregated—education. One bitter teacher told me, "All this is conscience money. It's a way of hiding the students away. When they leave here at eighteen, it's the end of their lives for many of them. There's nowhere in society for them to go." But there was nowhere in schools for them to go either.

I heard exactly the same arguments at both conferences. The terms "handicapped" and "Mexican-American" could have been interchanged. The dilemma was the same in both situations, since there was really nowhere for either group of students to go where they would have a chance. If they joined the regular classes—if they were mainstreamed—they would inevitably finish up at the bottom of the class. Their language or physical differences were too great for most of them to be able to "compete" at the tests they must all take. They were labeled as educationally and even intellectually deprived. But if they were separated into groups of their own, then not only did they continue to suffer from being classified as educationally different, but in fact they were excluded from the wider society that education was supposed to bring them into.

The cause of the dilemma is popularly supposed to be the

"difference" of these students, but it is not. The problem is testing, which systematically sorts out students and puts the ones who are "different" or "special" at the bottom of the heap. They are automatically classified as failures. The solution is not to treat some students as "special," which is no solution because it immediately makes them outcasts from the group as a whole. The solution is to treat everyone as "special," as unique, and not to expect anyone to fit into an arbitrarily designed mold. If there were no tests in the classroom and no comparisons made in order to segregate students, then everyone could find a place and have an opportunity to learn without having to learn that they did not belong.

It is a fallacy to believe that students have to be separated on the basis of age and ability into groups as alike as possible in order to learn. It is not true that children learn best when they are segregated with others of equal ability (or equal inability). Children learn best when they can help each other, when they do not always have to look to a teacher—or to an answer sheet—for help. The sorting of children, like commodities, into similar groups is done for the benefit of programs, not of children. Programs and tests cannot function when learners of varying degrees of experience and ability are intermixed—when there is a club situation in other words. But in the club situation, programs and tests are not required.

The Involvement of Parents

Teachers sometimes tell me that parents object if the teachers do not grade every piece of children's work or send home their test results. This may be true, but it cannot be used as justification of teachers' behavior. The parents are responding to teachers' behavior, to what they know to be the currency of school. They know the importance of test results and of progress through programs. The test results and programs are brought home to parents directly.

When teachers who follow programs report to parents, they tend to emphasize negatives, asserting that a child has "weaknesses" in certain skill areas simply because the child is not up with the rest of the group. Positive comments tend to be bland, related to "satisfactory progress" on program components that a parent does not understand. The negative comments are meaningless, too, but parents do not know this, and the mystery only makes the comments sound more impressive, especially when there are pathological overtones to the jargon employed—"Johnny has difficulties with auditory discrimination" (which probably means that he does not understand teacher talk about the sounds of letters), or "Jane's visual acuity requires special attention," or even comments about the child's ability to concentrate or comprehend.

Ann Adams, of the reading center at Duke University, has observed parents to "fly into a panic" when told their children know this skill but not that one.

Concern in the Colleges

The journal of the American Association for the Advancement of Science, *Science,* responded to the dismal findings of the National Commission on Excellence in Education with an editorial written by David Pierpont Gardner, president of the University of California, on June 29, 1984, proclaiming that "the good news is that this country is ready for educational reform. Many encouraging developments have occurred, at least partly in response to various reports issued last year." Among these encouraging developments are more and tougher tests: "(i) 47 states have proposals to increase high school graduation requirements, and 34 states have enacted them; (ii) 34 states are in the process of raising college admission requirements, and 22 have done so . . . (v) 273 state-level task forces have been established in 50 states, including among their members professional educators, parents, legislators, employers, and other concerned citizens. A gratifying number of local school districts have begun comprehensive planning efforts, reviewing the curriculum, studying the status of teaching, and improving school leadership."

The implication seems to be that educational standards have declined because students have been trying to sneak into college without being qualified, and because teachers have not had enough comprehensive planning and review of their curriculums.

The blind drive to control and monitor student learning has infected colleges and universities as much as grade schools. Professors are expected to set out in advance the "content" of what will be covered, for approval by committees and coordinators. Frequently such detailed specifications lead to restrictions. Professors are expected not to poach on each other's preserves, so that, for example, a professor giving a course on "reading" in a teacher training institution will be expected not to discuss "writing," which is the subject of another professor's course. This happened to me. This constraint is as absurd—and as commonplace—as one elementary school teacher objecting to a teacher one grade lower "covering" material that should be withheld until the higher grade (otherwise the higher grade teacher will be left with nothing to teach). Professors are regarded as interchangeable and are expected to "teach" a variety of courses (from the appropriate textbooks), instead of demonstrating interest and expertise of their own. But above all, the emphasis on properly spelled out course content leads to the usual plethora of examinations, assignments, and tests in which students are required to regurgitate what they are supposed to have learned.

I have already discussed some of the consequences, and others are well-known: students unwilling to read or write anything that is not directly related to the content of the course, who are reluctant to collaborate with each other, who do not think it is their responsibility to bring any ideas or experience to the course, and who have a total and competitive preoccupation with grades, leading occasionally to plagiarism and the deliberate hiding of books in libraries to handicap the opposition. "Content" can be delivered by a single professor, and now by computers, to large groups of students. Many "introductory" college courses have classes of 200 or more. And grading of specific content can be done mechanically with little or no opportunity for student contact with the professor.

Such consequences have been acknowledged many times, recently by the Association of American Colleges—who, from some points of view, might consider themselves to be the culprits. Early in 1985 the association published a report of a three-year-study by representatives of eighteen colleges and universities. The report, summarized by Colin Norman in the March 1, 1985 issue of *Science,* is entitled "Integrity in the College Curriculum." The committee declared that "The curriculum has given way to a market place philosophy where students are shoppers and professors are merchants of learning. Fads and fashions, the demands of popularity and success, enter where wisdom and experience should prevail. Evidence of decline and devaluation is everywhere." The committee, not surprisingly, tended to fault professors for preferring research to teaching (knowing where the career rewards and personal satisfactions lie), but acknowledges that not all is well with what is taught. Remarkably, after criticizing faculty curriculum committees who make centralized decisions about course content because they frequently "suffer from chronic paralysis," the committee suggested that they be given more power. The committee was on target with what is usually wrong with the curriculum—courses that offer "too much knowledge with too little attention to how that knowledge has been created and what methods and styles of inquiry have led to its creation."

The committee lists nine elements that should be embedded in all aspects of undergraduate education—and fails to note that the gaps the new elements are supposed to fill are the direct results of the movement away from courses requiring the personal involvement of professors. The nine essential elements are listed almost as additional content to be added to the curriculum, whereas, in fact, each requires personal demonstration and example, which is necessarily absent in large classes focused on the presentation and examination of "facts."

The nine elements are: (1) Inquiry, abstract thinking and logical analysis (which the committee correctly notes "grow out of wise instruction, experience, encouragement, correction and constant use"); (2) Literacy (the committee unfortunately believes that students can be "taught how to read actively, arguing along the way with every word and assertion" without pointing out that *people* are required to demonstrate the purpose and practice of reading in such a way); (3) Understanding numerical data (including such concepts as degree of risk, uncertainty, confidence levels, and interpretation, which are sterile if presented as abstract procedures and definitions, without demonstration of their *use*); (4) Historical consciousness; (5) An understanding of the way scientific concepts are developed, the limitations of science, and the "human, social and political implications of scientific research"; (6) Values; (7) Art; (8) International and multicultural experiences; and (9) Study in depth. ("Today's majors are not so much experiences in depth as they are bureaucratic conveniences. . . . they allow deans to control the flow of student traffic.") Half at least of these elements make little sense as part of the content of the curriculum, but rather refer to the way the courses should be taught. This is evident from the ninth element, which actually isolates the cause of the problem.

What the committee is discussing, although it does not appear to recognize the fact, is the dehumanization of the university and the total distortion of learning into the acquisition of information, of short right answers. Professors and students alike become demoralized and cynical when higher education is regarded as nothing more than the trafficking in miniature packages of information that can be allocated and evaluated numerically. The committee says, in essence, that students have no way of discovering what it is like to be a learner at a university. But how could they gain any inkling of this, when their professors themselves do not demonstrate learning activities in their courses, where there is no room for apprentices (except for a favored few students in menial roles on research projects), and where all the rituals are bureaucratic?

Controlling the Classroom

There is one reason only for the insistent control of programmatic instruction and tests in classrooms. That reason is *lack of trust.* Teachers impose programs and tests when they do not trust children to learn, and politicians and administrators impose programs and tests when they do not trust teachers to teach.

The dependence of many teachers on programmatic instruction is perhaps understandable. Teachers frequently have large classes, reluctant students, constant pressures from outside the classroom (and sometimes from other teachers in the same school), and a fragile sense of their own authority and ability. The public image of teachers is not high, and they often see themselves as underpaid, undervalued, and beleaguered. Teachers uncertain of how to do their job adequately tend to prefer pathways that are clearly defined, especially teachers who have been trained to rely on programs and tests. They fear that classrooms without programs would quickly degenerate into chaos, and have little idea of how to assure themselves that children are learning without the tests. It matters little to such teachers that none of their anxieties is well-founded, that teaching is easier in active learning environments, when interested children help each other and collaborate with the teacher, continually demonstrating their learning in meaningful enterprises. But this is something many teachers have not learned. Most teachers do not have a good theory of learning and teaching. What they know is what they have been taught about the mechanics of teaching. And when they are in doubt, when they are under pressure or losing commitment, they stay with what they know best.

But programs and tests are also demanded when outside authorities do not trust teachers to teach. "Accountability" is the standard term for the belief that teachers will teach better if they are constantly and publicly confronted with the consequences of their teaching, in the form of numerical test results. I am not against accountability. I think society has a right to expect teachers to promote student learning to the utmost, just as society demands that physicians do everything possible to advance and maintain the health of patients. But society does not tell physicians how to practice medicine. Teachers are given responsibility without autonomy; they are expected to teach according to schedules of tests and examinations. The tests control teachers far more effectively than occasional visits from inspectors and other supervisors. Through tests, teachers can be controlled without anyone ever entering their classrooms. And ironically, the procedures that are supposed to ensure that teachers teach effectively prevent them from doing so.

Control through tests is lowering standards and reducing expectations. The deterioration is clouded by an educational jargon that is literally doublespeak, saying one thing while meaning another. I have already referred to the use of the word "learning" when instruction is the topic, and discussed how the term "mastery" is employed for the acquisition of fragments of knowledge rather than broad ranges of ability. Making teachers accountable means taking responsibility away from them. "Growth" is a favorite word we are about to meet; it is used to describe the development of children but really relates to keeping up with programs. There is a cluster of expressions, such as "basic skills," "the basics," and "minimum competencies," that are frequently attached to the concept *learning* when what is actually being referred to is *deprivation of experience.* And "excellence"—a vogue word in business and industry at present— has long been used in education when the primary aim is to optimize returns on the least expenditure through maximum regulation. Doublespeak itself is accompanied by doublethink when politicians and administrators persuade themselves —as I shall show—that despite falling standards, talk of "excellence" can actually take the place of money.

Control Through Evaluation

The development of federal control of education through testing has been traced by Thomas S. Popkewitz, whose description of how one university-based research center scrambled to get a share of federal funds I have already cited. Popkewitz points out that the research centers—and the associated regional development laboratories—marked a substantial increase in the federal government's role in educational policy. Management techniques in education were expected to bring about changes in society. School intervention was expected to redress social inequalities. Title 1 of the Elementary and Secondary Education Act, passed in 1965, for example, was specifically designed to "break the cycle of poverty and equalize lifetime opportunities." Popkewitz says that "Faith in the expert guided the social amelioration efforts. . . . Legislation included evaluation as an essential part of the effort to improve the conditions of the poor and to produce curriculum that responded to changing economic conditions."

Thus a major tool of this educational intervention was to be evaluation—the constant monitoring of student progress as a measure of the success of teachers and of schools. Evaluation, according to Popkewitz, became a science and an ideology, not something that can be done by everyone, but only by "experts." Evaluation was taken out of the hands of classroom teachers and established among the educational managers.

Referring to the "inevitable accountability" aspect of evaluation, Popkewitz notes that schools became regarded as "production-oriented institutions to be managed by precise standards and techniques that direct, predict and control all the activities of the organization. . . . The view leads to behavioral or performance-based objectives setting out what a student will be able to do after a prescribed unit of instruction. . . . By focusing only upon what is observable and quantifiable, accountability obscures and trivializes our view of life by creating a one-dimensional lens. To consider history as 'a list of three major factors causing a war' is to mystify the process of *doing* history."

Teachers Versus Technocrats

An insider's description of another university research and development center's endeavors to drag out increased efficiency from teachers through the imposition of planning and testing techniques has been provided by Harry F. Walcott in a book entitled *Teachers vs. Technocrats.* Walcott was "project ethnographer" on a program run by the Center for the Advanced Study of Educational Administration located at the University of Oregon. The program had the support of the Office of Education and, later, of the National Institute of Education. Guinea pigs for the field test of SPECS (a typically cute acronym that stood for School Planning, Evaluation and Communication System) were teachers and children of the nearby South Lane School District. The project, says Walcott, was not instigated because the teachers or children at South Lane were regarded as inadequate, but because the center itself was being criticized by the funding agency for failing to engage in "development," which meant tangible products and observable results. The center decided to concentrate on management, and the SPECS project eventually became the largest part of its program. The proposal was specifically written to employ center staff, according to Walcott, who was told by one student at the party held to celebrate the funding of the proposal that he was "in it for the bread."

The project, Walcott continues, was "an outgrowth of the trend towards accountability." Its aim was "to help schools to budget, operate and evaluate their total educational system." To get the project under way, teachers had to specify general objectives that would be translated into "performance objectives" so that "actual student performance data could be collected." Everything had to be "coded." There was a mass of materials, procedures, and worksheets, so verbose, according to one teacher, that "even an elephant could understand it—but it doesn't say anything." Teachers were required to distinguish not only objectives, but five levels of mastery and three levels of effort.

Walcott says he was distressed by the heavy-handed manner in which the project was imposed on teachers and dismayed by the way in which the resources of his institution were poured in to *make* the project succeed. He was also impressed by the courage of a group of teachers who "regarded the project as an inadequately designed and oppressively imposed system that greatly infringed on their professional autonomy." But stubborn opposition by teachers was confronted with stubborn determination to make the project work. Superintendents insisted that they could see progress being made. Few teachers gave the project credit for anything, however, and even then they complained about the effort, says Walcott.

Among comments made to him by the teachers were: "The developers [worked hard but] are so far removed from those of us at the 'peon' level." "If we did all the pretesting we're supposed to do [when the children arrived at school in September], we wouldn't finish until Christmas." "It's the Mickey Mouse in triplicate that gets me." "This business of testing . . . junk, junk, junk. I just throw lots of it into the wastebasket." "The whole program looks marvelous on paper, but things just don't work out according to the plan."

Walcott documents the long miserable process of teachers becoming exhausted, suspicious, and disenchanted. The teachers objected that administrators were the primary beneficiaries of the

program, not the students. The teachers objected to threats requiring conformity with the program, which adversely affected the
morale of seventy-five percent of the teaching staff. They also objected to evaluation of the project by the people who had designed
it. They tried to take their problems to the Board of Education and
then complained that they were ignored, sidetracked, and delayed.
They were not successful in getting the matter considered to their
satisfaction until they took it to the press (to the consternation of
the project officials). When eventually there was an Oregon State
Department of Education investigation, says Walcott, it came down
firmly on both sides of the fence. The program had good and bad
aspects, the department of education decided, but there was no
challenge to the basic assumption that program planning was a good
thing. The project persisted for six years and cost almost a million
dollars. At the end it withered away, concludes Walcott, although
it was officially declared a success by its organizers at a closing
conference in 1975 because "every project has to be a success."

In a foreword to Walcott's book, the center's director, Max G.
Abbott, acknowledges that some teachers felt they had been victi-
mized and that their appeals for relief from interminable objective
writing were ignored. "Unplanned consequences" caused the project to take on a life of its own: increased federal support brought
increased federal control, with demands for detailed planning and
anticipation of results. Abbott sums up: "Accountability stifled
spontaneity and creativity."

The Downhill Pursuit of Minimum Competencies

The days when outside intervention was expected to produce
significant improvements in learning have gone. The pressure of
programmatic control has not been relaxed, but the aim now is
more of a holding action, a desperate hope to demonstrate at least
some success. In place of major objectives, many state and local
school administrations now look for the achievement of "minimum

competencies." These are also known as "the basics" and, occasionally, "survival skills." Minimum competencies refer to such attainments as sufficient reading and writing ability to study the "Situations Vacant" column and to compose a job application; sufficient math to total a fast-food order and complete a tax return.

The triple thrust of minimum competencies is that by reducing what children have to learn to as little as possible, by specifying exactly how this pittance is to be taught, and by holding teachers accountable for teaching in this way, success will be universally demonstrated. Kenneth Goodman of the University of Arizona at Tucson, a leader of literacy teachers in the drive for humanity and intelligence in education, has provided a caustic analysis of the rationale.

Goodman begins with a parable. A student complains that he has a problem. He is not too good at reading, writing, or arithmetic, and will graduate from high school soon. He'd like help. His teachers are sympathetic, but they also have a problem. The teachers have done their best, but their students haven't achieved very much. The teachers would also like help. The school district administrators are sympathetic, but the low achievement is reflecting badly on them, too. They want help as well. The state legislature steps in to solve everyone's problem. No student will ever graduate from high school without minimum competencies in the basics. How will that goal be achieved? Administrators will be held accountable for testing all graduating seniors and for withholding diplomas from any who can't pass the basics at the tenth grade level. The administrator will hold the teacher accountable for getting students ready for the test. How will that be done? By eliminating frills. What are frills? Anything that is not on the test. "Now then," the teacher says to the student, "we can look at your problem. Put your book away, we've got exercises to do." The student says, "I think I've got two problems now."

Goodman concludes that minimum competency testing would be effective only if some or all of the following propositions are true. *However, all these propositions are false:* (1) Failure to achieve is due to a lack of school standards. (2) Student failure is largely the result of lack of teacher concern for student success. (3) Solutions for teaching/learning problems are built into current materials and methods. (4) Test performance is the same as competence. (5) Students required to succeed will succeed.

Goodman's analysis appears in a pamphlet published in 1978 by the International Reading Association, of which he was once president. The board of directors of the association, which represents scores of thousands of reading teachers throughout North America, typically does not take a position on the issue. Instead it presents three points of view. The way in which these three points of view are presented is itself instructive. Goodman gets a subtly dismissive introduction: "Because Dr. Goodman is not a stranger to many thousands of IRA members, it should not surprise them that he supports a humanitarian, idealistic view of minimum competency standards." There is no reference to Goodman's arguments. To be humanitarian is to be idealistic. Roger Farr, a test expert from the University of Indiana, is by no means against the tests, but is worried that they might be misused. He is introduced in a more neutral, respectful manner: "Writing from a well-recognized background in evaluation and measurement, Dr. Farr expresses concern over the limitations of testing procedures prescribed to determine whether the competency levels have been attained." Jack Cassidy is an administrator. He simply offers ten guidelines on how teachers should develop minimum competency programs. His introduction is: "Dr. Cassidy, perhaps because he is currently most closely tied with a public school system, accepts minimum competency programs as a fact of life and then proceeds to consider how professional educators can live with them." In other words, there is little point in expecting administrators or the executives of teachers' associations to take a stand against the encroachment of centralized control on teachers. Even the most vacuous of schemes must be accepted as "a fact of life."

A typical minimum competency approach is that of Leo D. Leonard and Robert T. Utz, two University of Toledo professors who wrote a popular handbook for teachers on competency-based teaching. They acknowledge as the basis of their philosophy the educational objectives of Benjamin Bloom's taxonomy, which they say has had the greatest impact of any single model of education in the last decade. Leonard and Utz want to employ this model for "developing a competency-based curriculum . . . structured to allow maximum growth for *each individual* student." The italics are theirs. The way they propose that such "maximum growth" will be achieved is through "behavioral objectives, pretests, individualized learning activities, and posttest problems." Behavior modification techniques are suggested because "they provide a systematic means of modifying behavior in the classroom. The competency-based model is based on the philosophy that curriculum can be written in discreet [*sic*] units of instruction (behavioral objectives) so that the student's performance can be easily measured during the course of instruction."

Leonard and Utz present a flowchart to demonstrate exactly how teacher and student should interact. By following the arrows, as if in a board game, the teacher selects objectives, pretests, instructs, evaluates, and then either "synthesizes" and moves to the next objective or "remediates" and retests. Every object has to be expressed in terms of behavior. As an example of a good terminal objective, Leonard and Utz recommend, "The student will be able to complete a 100-item multiple choice examination on the topic of 19th century American literature. The lower limit of acceptable performance will be 70 correct answers within an examination period of 90 minutes."

The language should be noted. The cages of systematic instruction are decorated with sentimental and even noble verbal embellishments. Who would not be in favor of individual instruction, growth, and development (although the notion of "growth" always bears watching, with its implication that any student who does not progress through the instructional sequences is stunted in some way)? The words "diagnosis," "intervention," "remediation," and "treatment" are particularly common in competency programming and testing, reflecting the belief that anything on a program or test that a student is unable to do indicates a defect of a medical nature. Leonard and Utz actually talk about "recycling" students who do not get something correct the first time.

Like most proponents of competency-based instruction and testing, Leonard and Utz are aware of the objections. They note the fears that the instruction is mechanical, the tests arbitrary, and the procedures inhumane, that teachers will teach to the tests, and that whatever is taught will be devalued. But all of these apprehensions, they respond, relate to *improper* or inefficient procedures; they are not really relevant when the instructional development is done correctly. How the ideal competency-based instruction and testing will actually overcome all the handicaps and adverse consequences is left as a matter of faith.

From Mastery to Minimums

Purdue University's Patrick Shannon has examined the way in which dependency on "mastery learning" leads to the setting of goals at a minimal level. He looks particularly at the claim that universal literacy can be reached if "(1) reading instruction is segmented into separate skills which are arranged hierarchically according to difficulty, (2) teachers engage in a teach/test/reteach/retest instructional cycle, and (3) students are given unlimited time to learn one skill before progressing to the next skill in the hierarchy," as outlined by Benjamin Bloom. "With the recent popularity of 'direct instruction' and the 'back to basics' movement," says Shannon, "many school districts are foregoing the debate of basic assumptions and are attempting to translate mastery theory into current school practices."

Shannon cites research showing that because even the slowest students in the program must become "masters" of reading within established time limits, reading goals are set at a minimal level and are restricted to easily definable and testable skills. He quotes the experience of a middle school teacher: "The Tests of Basic Skills [in the mastery program] are designed to enable a teacher to know whether each one of his or her pupils has learned what it is that has been taught at each level of instruction through the use of the materials which compose the reading program. We are required to record the skills test scores and the dates that the tests were taken on student file cards. These cards are reviewed every other week by our reading teacher. Sometimes the principal looks at them and announces whose class is doing well over the loud speaker. Every eight weeks or so we fill out report cards by checking off the objectives that have been passed and send them home to the parents. Of course, there is pressure to hurry students through the materials.''

All students are expected to learn the same skills throughout their districts, Shannon continues. Schools create or more often purchase a packaged set of objective tests, books, and instructional manuals and seek to standardize teachers' use of these materials. Administrators can monitor teachers' application of materials and student progress through the materials with periodic reviews of the test results. Thus, the application of packaged materials becomes the only acceptable instructional practice, the materials transcend teacher judgment, and teachers have control of their reading instruction taken away from them.

Administrators explained to Shannon why a single set of materials was needed in their district—to accommodate students who move from one school to another and to ensure that teachers all teach the same thing. Over ninety percent of 445 classroom teachers questioned, and eighteen principals, agreed strongly that the administrators would not tolerate reading instruction without commercial materials.

Shannon reports that when the Chicago superintendent of schools was confronted by evidence that reading test scores were low and declining rapidly, he appointed a task force of administrators to make recommendations to improve high school performance. ''After several weeks, rather than repudiate the mastery learning reading program which produced these [low-scoring] readers, the committee recommended an extension of the mastery learning reading program into the high schools. These administrators were unable to look beyond their refined reading program to find a solution to this formidable problem.''

Shannon's conclusion was harsh and unequivocal: ''Students are rendered almost powerless, either they learn to read critically outside of the classroom or they accept the teachers as a model and follow explicitly the direction in the packaged mastery learning materials. To correct these injustices, teachers must accept responsibility to become their own experts concerning literacy and learning, they must engage in discussions of first principles, they must act collectively to regain control of their instruction, and they must find ways to help students become self-reliant readers and learners.''

Unlearned Lessons From History

Most administrators who promote minimal competency testing believe the idea is novel and are not aware of previous experiences —and inevitable failures. George F. Madeus, a professor at Boston College in Massachusetts, and Vincent Greaney, of St. Patrick's College in Dublin, recently pointed out that Iceland, Belgium, Denmark, Italy, France, Switzerland and Ireland have all tried without success to improve education by requiring children to sit for achievement tests at the end of Grade 6 or 7, to certify whether they are fit to begin secondary education or to seek employment. Madeus and Greaney recounted in detail the Irish experience, which persisted for twenty-four years.

After years of discussion in the Irish parliament of "orthodox bureaucratic concerns"—a perceived decline in standards, a determination to get educational value for tax contributions, and a belief in concentration on the "basics"—an examination that all sixth standard (Grade 6) students were required to take was set by the Department of Education. The inevitable consequences, which led to the eventual abandonment of the system in 1967, were teacher resistance, exclusion or holding back of children likely to fail, teaching to the test at the expense of other areas of the curriculum, and "remediation" geared to the content of the tests. Madeus and Greaney report that all strategies adopted by teachers and schools to demonstrate improved results on the examinations in fact undermined what the examination was supposed to achieve.

The Smokescreen of "Excellence"

Educational managers appear to be most adept at whistling in the wind. The worse the situation gets in schools, the more the word "excellence" is used. The federal commission whose report on U.S. education entitled *A Nation at Risk* was published in 1983 was designated the "National Commission on Excellence in Education." The word "excellence" makes frequent appearances in contemporary advertisements for instructional materials and software. The 1985 Holt, Rinehart and Winston programs promise "quality and excellence in education," and Radio Shack's TRS-80 color computer offers "The Blueprint for Academic Excellence." The Silver Burdett Company advertises its kindergarten-through-eighth-grade English series as "The new standard of excellence that's sweeping the nation."

A number of recent studies and investigations, like those of the National Commission on Secondary Education for Hispanics and the National Board of Inquiry Into Schools, have seen the pursuit of excellence as a not-too-subtle means of discriminating against disadvantaged populations. Children who do not do well on tests receive less attention in school and in educational programs. Beverly P. Cole, principal of an alternative school in New York, believes that standardized tests, with their "narrow and rigid" definition of how children should be able to exhibit their knowledge, determine whether schools see children as "okay" or not. "In the process we damage all children—we devalue the variety of strengths they bring with them to school. All differences become handicaps." James Vasquez, superintendent of schools in the Edgewood School District of San Antonio, declares, "The prevailing attitude in the school system is that you develop excellence through exclusivity. In the past, when poor and minority kids were kept out of the school, test scores were high. Now people are saying, 'Let's exclude them again and the scores will go up and we can all boast that American education is in great shape.'" The two statements were reported in a 1985 article in *Carnegie Quarterly*. The unnamed Carnegie Corporation author reviews a number of studies and inquiries, and concludes "the relative inattention to changes required for educating minority, low-income, female and handicapped youngsters is a critical flaw in the current drive for educational excellence."

In the two years following publication of the Commission on Excellence's 1983 report, the author continues, there were at least thirty other national studies of education, 290 state commission and blue-ribbon task force reports, two network television documentaries, and widespread newspaper and magazine coverage of the problems of public schools. "The vast majority of these studies and commentaries have called for raised academic standards, tighter discipline, a return to the 'basics' in school curricula, and incentives to improve teaching"—as if there were a conspiracy among students and teachers not to learn.

In October 1985, the Hawaii Department of Education announced twelve state goals to "raise the quality of public education to excellence." None of these goals said anything about how improvement, let alone "excellence," would be achieved, except that students would be expected to achieve higher scores in seven different kinds of tests, participate more in co-curricular and adult education activities, reduce daily absences from school, and engage in fewer criminal offenses. Superintendent of education Francis Hatanaka and Ken Froelich, president of Frito-Lay of Hawaii, held a joint press conference to announce that the fast-food company would award prizes to schools that attained outstanding achievements in the drive toward excellence.

Excellence in Place of Teachers

It is widely assumed that schools can get by with many fewer teachers if they become more efficient. And while many teachers are struggling to cope with additional loads, they are being exhorted to aim for excellence.

Dave Pitre, principal of Central Junior Secondary School in Victoria, British Columbia, was faced with the prospect of losing eight teachers for his 609 students in the wake of educational "restraint" in the province. "Two years ago I used to cringe at the idea of thirty-two students in a class, but now I'm looking at thirty-eight and thirty-nine," he said in an interview with the local newspaper in September 1984. "It's pretty scary." What could he do about the situation? He said that every student had been given a button bearing the school name and emblem and the proclamation "In Pursuit of Excellence." "We paid for them out of nonschool funds . . . profits from the cafeteria, tickets, raffles, that sort of thing," he said. In neighboring Lambrick Park secondary school, principal Gary Taylor said, "We're trying to do the very best we can for each student in this school," where some science classes had jumped from twenty-eight to thirty-seven students. He pointed to the motto on the front of the school's course booklet: "Pursuing Excellence."

The district superintendent of these two principals, Bernie Chandler, offered his own solution in the same newspaper five days later. He said he was putting finishing touches on a plan that would emphasize a range of proven, effective teaching techniques which would lead to improved instruction in the district's schools. "Providing immediate feedback to students to make clear to them whether their answers are right or wrong is one important technique," he said. He did not elaborate on why he thought teachers might at present be dilatory in providing information to their students about whether answers were right or wrong, or why he believed that being told that answers were wrong as fast as possible would transform children into more efficient learners.

British Columbia, where I live, is unfortunately typical of much of North America, where in recent years the provincial or state government has vigorously slashed educational budgets, reducing the number of teachers and increasing class sizes, while at the same time claiming that the result would be a better education for children. In an article in the British Columbia Government publication *Provincial Report* in November 1985, under the headline "Proposals Will Improve Schools," the then education minister Jack Heinrich summarized how he planned to "improve the quality of education" while cutting funds. His aims were: (1) to increase the instructional use of computers, (2) to improve the quality of the curriculum, texts, and support materials (all of which are mandated or "recommended" by his ministry personnel), and (3) to emphasize the need for sound basic education. The final aim was to "upgrade teacher training and education"—presumably in the instructional use of computers, in following the improved curriculum, and in emphasizing basics. The minister concluded that the government would take a "planned and strategic approach to ensure that the quality of education in the province is improved." In other words, tighter control and more tests.

The constraints and the pressures are growing everywhere; not even small and remote schools are immune. In Santa Barbara county in 1985, I talked with teachers from a 250-student kindergarten-through-seventh-grade school, with only one class and one teacher at each grade level. The heavy hand of the California State Department at Sacramento could still be felt. "It's done through selective funding," one teacher told me. "We have to make commitments to get teacher aides and other facilities. There's less money going into general funding, where the school can make decisions, and more into categorical funding and enhancement funding, into special projects. In order to get this money, teachers have to write proposals, specify objectives, and say precisely what they intend to do and hope to achieve. And even then, we don't always get the money. We get pressure from the principal to write the kind of proposals that are most likely to be funded, the ones with lots of detail and evaluation in them, and if we succeed then we get pressure to conform to the terms of the proposals." And however small and remote the school, no public educational institution in the state can escape administering the California Aptitude Tests for all students at the end of third, sixth, and eighth grade. Nor can they escape the results. "School scores"—the average for each school of the scores of all students who took the test—are published in local newspapers, with schools compared against each other and against state averages. "In a small school, we only need two kids to do badly and we look as if we're not doing our job properly," another teacher said.

In Texas, teachers in El Paso told me why their morale was low: "We're still recovering from last year's reform, and now we're going to be reformed again." They had just learned that the state, which had competency tests at Grade 3, 5, 7, and 9, was now to have them at Grade 11—another obstacle for the same students, more harrassment for the teachers.

In Britain, too, there is growing concern about government determination to extend centralized control of instruction. Nanette Whitbread, a teacher at Leicester Polytechnic, has detected a new directive, confrontative style in pamphlets and policy statements from the Department of Education and Science. There is the typical combination of determination to cut costs and expectation of raising quality and standards. The language is changing, Whitbread notes. Teachers have become "agents" whose role is to "deliver instruction" to students. Instead of talking of children who learn by engaging in activities and gaining experience, the departmental publications talk of "pupils" who must "acquire knowledge and skills." The minister, Sir Keith Joseph, asserts that schools should be "teaching units with syllabuses and specific standards of attainment."

A common rationale is that the focus on "basics" and on "minimum compentencies" will ensure that, at the least, children have the experience required for any subsequent employment they might be able to find. But when Larry Mikulecky of Indiana University compared the reading done by forty-eight high school juniors and fifty-one adult technical school students with 150 workers from a variety of occupations "ranging from blue collar to professional/technical." he found little similarity. He reported: "Results suggest that students read less often in school than most workers do on the job, that they read less competently, face easier material which they read to less depth, and that the strategies students employ may be less effective than those employed by workers." So much for training students for the workplace.

In March 1978, Kenneth Goodman wrote an open letter to the president appealing for more support—in terms of teacher assistance—for children who were being taught English. Commenting on the back-to-basics movement, Goodman said: "with revenues increasingly tied to Washington, and following federal program guidelines, educators have acquiesced as schools are treated as factories in which children are measured, treated, manipulated, modified and measured again."

Testing in the Future

The lunatic heights to which educational testing had already risen were spelled out with a certain pride in March 1982 in an article on "The Next Stage in Educational Assessment" by three specialists in statistics, testing, and computer-based instruction. R. Darrell Bock, Robert Mislevy, and Charles Woodson begin by asserting that "Now approaching its 20th year, educational assessment in the United States is on the threshold of maturity. It shows every sign of fulfilling its early promise and becoming a permanent and vital part of American education."

They trace "the inception of the assessment idea to the accountability movement of the 1960s. At that time, legislators and educators were arguing for some form of cost-benefit accounting in education by which state governments could defend and direct the expenditures of tax revenues for their school systems." It was not difficult to calculate costs, but benefits were not so easy to assess, they continue. Following up students to see how they fared after leaving school would be prohibitively expensive. Measuring student performance while they were still in school, on the other hand, was straightforward and economically practical. The technology of educational testing could readily be applied in evaluating the "productivity" of schools in terms of scholastic accomplishment. Teachers were already equipped to carry out the data collection. Student achievement could be sampled and assessed, and school performance evaluated.

Bock, Mislevy, and Woodson view the California Assessment Program—"the largest and most developed of the state programs" —as a model of state assessment. Statewide testing of all students in one form or another has been required by law in California since 1961. By 1980, the third-grade instrument in the California Assessment Program assessed more than sixty "skill elements" in reading, writing, and mathematics, with more than a thousand test items. Other specifications were written for "instructional objectives" in content area courses at Grades 3, 6, and 12. Summaries of student performance on these tests enabled 4,500 schools to be compared.

An example of a third-grade score report for a "typical California school" is provided by the authors. They call the school Vista Grande Elementary. Each skill element is reported together with estimates of its statistical error. An average is calculated, and a computer automatically signals those items which are above or below average, characterizing them as "relative strengths" and "relative weaknesses." For Vista Grande Elementary, relative strengths in reading were "vowels; recognizing word meanings; details from two or three sentences; and alphabetizing." Relative weaknesses in reading included "analysis of prefixes, suffixes and roots, . . . details from single sentences, . . . drawing conclusions about details."

How students were able to comprehend details from two or three sentences but not from single sentences was not explored. The authors simply present the report and comment: "Local authorities can use diagnostic information of this type to adjust curricular emphasis if it is deemed necessary." The third-grade teachers at Vista Grande Elementary, in other words, had better start concentrating on consonants, prefixes, and single sentences, and can relax a little in their concern with vowels. It is not difficult to imagine the kinds of exercises and drills in store for the students as teachers focus on their relative weaknesses: "Put away those books you're reading, children, it's time to work on your prefixes."

It is by such elaborate statistical methods that distant administrators can blindly control what any child must do in any classroom. Work is continuing on ways to analyze even more test scores on a "probability-sampling" basis as inexpensively as possible. As Bock, Mislevy, and Woodson say, "New methods of collecting and reporting data will make assessment results more useful in educational research, evaluation and management."

Things are not going to get better. The testers are even more ambitious for the future. In October 1985, over 900 educators, psychologists, and test constructors attended an invitational conference in New York City organized by the Educational Testing Service of Princeton, New Jersey, the largest producer of educational tests in the world. The president of Educational Testing Service, Gregory R. Anrig, and Professor Theodore Sizer of Brown University, together announced a $30 million plan to produce a battery of high school tests called the "Secondary School Leaving Exhibition" which will demand written tests, oral interviews, and a portfolio of work done in high school for all students. One aim is to provide a standard against which home-schooled students can be compared. Another is to assess more completely "higher order thinking skills." Many of the participants talked of the inadequacies of current achievement tests, especially their multiple-choice items. But few suggested that the solution might be fewer tests. Most were looking for better tests, which would examine in more depth and more detail, more rigorously and consistently.

Robert Glaser, of the University of Pittsburgh, a pioneer of systematized instruction, spoke of a "continuing need" to produce tests to guide instruction, focusing on areas that have never been tested before like "cognitive structure" (or the way the individual mind is organized). Richard Wallace, the Pittsburgh Superintendent of Schools, described a "Syllabus Driven Examination Project" designed specifically "to raise expectations and standards." There would be testing at all grade levels, in all subjects, between four and six times a year, with a major emphasis on critical thinking (which means that thinking, like reading and writing, will be broken down into meaningless fragments and ritualized drills). The three levels of thought distilled from Bloom's taxonomy—literal, inferential, and evaluative—will be respected, of course. Teachers will be given individual student profiles on test performance seventy-two hours after test administration, like a physician receiving an urgent report from a medical laboratory. Is the aim to have students wired up like patients in intensive care, constantly monitored to ensure that their vital learning functions are working at the desired minimal level?

Boston College's George Madeus—the researcher who disclosed the Irish experience in minimum competency testing—attended the New York conference and expressed concern that performance on tests is becoming what is most valued in education, that tests may come to dominate curriculum (which is, of course, what the test-makers intend), and that tests manipulate learners. He was in the minority.

CHAPTER 7

Good Teaching:
The Practical Alternative

I have never seen an ideal school, but I have met many exemplary teachers, the opposite of mindless programmatic control. Ideal schools may be unattainable, but teachers sometimes do remarkably well. The r-bbit's hold is not yet universal. Good teachers are not difficult to identify. There are plenty of them, engaged in the kind of teaching that is a practical alternative to tests and systematic instruction. They create environments in which everyone has a chance of learning.

All societies need schools, and not simply as places where students of all ages are expected to acquire a basic education in academic subjects, or even for the mundane but important reason of daytime child-care. Schools should represent learning, inquiry, and open-mindedness; they reflect the intellectual vigor of a community. I would not abandon schools. But schools could be much better than they are. Students could learn much more in the schools we have today, if the teachers and students were trusted. Better schools need not look very different from the schools we now have—improvement is not a matter of fixtures and fittings. Problems do not melt when they are blanketed with money. What matters is attitudes and understanding about the kind of places schools ought to be—and can be, with a more intelligent use of human and financial resources. The issue inevitably comes back to the teacher, to the teacher's competence and autonomy.

The Good Teacher

I often ask writers what first made them write. Relatively few people claim to be competent or even keen writers, but there is nothing particularly distinctive about people who regard writing as a worthwhile activity, in their personal lives as well as in their occupations. Writers are not necessarily more intelligent than people who don't write, nor are they inevitably more sensitive, more dedicated or disciplined, more introverted or extroverted, more austere or more self-indulgent. Writers come from large families and from small families, rich families and poor, families where everyone writes and families where no one else ever writes. In other words, the only apparent difference between writers and people who do not write is that writers write. So I am interested in what made them start writing, and what kept them at it. Many writers mentioned school.

But none of the writers who mentioned school said anything about programs or tests, about exercises or drills. Not one of them cited inspiring grammar lessons or unforgettable spelling lists. They all mentioned a person; they mentioned a teacher. And the teachers whom the writers mentioned were not necessarily tender and permissive. Some of these teachers were difficult and demanding curmudgeons. But they were all teachers who respected students and who respected the subject that they taught. They thought that writing was worthwhile. They were members of the writers' club.

When I question other people with a vocation—artists, artisans, scientists, athletes—they invariably tell me the same story. They were influenced by someone who was already a member of the club they joined, who admitted them as novice members. The influential individuals demonstrated that certain things were worth doing, they collaborated with the novices, and they inspired them to do those things themselves. (It is true that we can sometimes be admitted into clubs through the works of authors, musicians, or artists whom we have never met, but then someone must have earlier initiated us into the club of people who are responsive to books, music, or art.)

Good teachers respond instinctively to the way in which children—and adults—learn, without direction from outside authorities. Good teachers never rely on programs or tests, and they resist external control when it is thrust upon them. They do not allow themselves or their "apprentices" to engage in pointless ritualistic activities. Instead, these teachers manifest attitudes and behaviors that learners become interested in manifesting themselves, and then these teachers help learners to manifest such attitudes and behaviors for themselves. Such teachers attract and indenture apprentices without knowing they are doing so; they initiate learners into clubs. The two essential characteristics of all the good teachers I have met is that they are interested in what they teach and they enjoy working with learners. Indeed, they are learners themselves.

Teachers and Clubs

Good teachers give the impression that they would be engaging in the activity they teach even if they were not teachers. To such people, being able to teach their subject is a privilege. Unfortunately, not all classroom teachers practice what they preach. Some could not do so if they wanted to, since they have never joined the club they teach about. There are reading teachers who only open a book if they are required to do so in the classroom, and writing teachers who hate to write. There are teachers who make students read and write poetry but would never do those things themselves, who teach mathematics that they do not themselves understand, or who assign science projects that they themselves find boring. What do these teachers teach their students?

A very upset primary grade teacher once told me that yes, she hated writing—but she always showed an interest in what her chil-

dren wrote. When I asked what she thought the children learned
from her, she reflected for a moment, then quietly suggested, "Hy-
pocrisy?" A high school teacher was more aggressive. He had to
teach seven different subjects in the course of a week—and couldn't
be expected to be interested in all of them, could he? He had a
point, of course. It is often said that good teachers can teach anything, provided they keep one lesson ahead of their students. When
I first found myself expected to teach a subject I knew nothing
about, my university colleagues assured me that there was nothing
unusual or intimidating about the prospect—I could "teach" from
a book in the library. Teachers who consistently operate in this way
are doubtlessly "professional," even dedicated, but what do they
really teach?

There is a solution for all teachers required to teach a subject
in which they are not expert. Provided they are interested, they can
become learners themselves, turning a handicap into an advantage.
Teachers have sometimes told me they have decided to improve
their teaching by taking a university course in creative writing,
algebra, physics, computer programming, or whatever else they
feel inadequate about. But they could do better—they could collaborate in learning with their students, writing with them, exploring
with them, advancing in the relevant club together. The realization
that even a teacher might have to struggle to understand something, making mistakes or producing less than satisfactory work in
the process, is a valuable lesson denied to most students at school.

A few years ago I met a vigorous, white-haired teacher from
Denmark named Chris Messell who had been touring Canada by
train, visiting schools and educators. In previous years she had
traveled, usually by train because it is easier to see the country and
to talk with people, through China and South America. During her
long career she had taught every level from kindergarten to graduate school. And she told me that she had never taught a class where
she thought she had nothing to learn herself. She did not think she
could be an effective teacher if she just sat or stood in front of the
students and fed to them what she thought she knew.

Chris Messell does not fit the conventional image of what a
teacher should be—although I have met plenty of teachers with a
similar philosophy. But the common view is that the teacher is

supposed to have knowledge to pass onto people who lack it. I was always glad when I could be relieved of that enormous responsibility when I was a university professor, charged with "transmitting information" about education and learning to graduate students who were usually far more experienced teachers than I was. (This book is a product of much that I learned from the "students" I was supposed to be teaching.)

I once mentioned to a colleague, a distinguished professor of experimental psychology at the University of Toronto, that I frequently told my students that each one of them knew some things that the others in the class did not know, including the instructor, and that we all had something to contribute and something to learn. My colleague was astounded. If I admitted to students that they might know more than I did, what defense could I have against them? Again, I think I see his point. But what sort of teaching is it that considers it "unsafe" to admit or display ignorance—or rather, learning? Why do there always have to be answers in teacher manuals for all the questions that students must be asked? The teachers who get "burned out" are not the ones who are constantly learning, which can be exhilarating, but those who feel they must stay in control and ahead of the students at all times.

Schools should be learning emporia, places where people congregate to learn, and no one should be there if they do not want to participate in learning—whether their role is to be a student, a teacher, or an administrator. I know that most children are required to attend a school of one kind or another, but children who don't want to learn what we try to teach them will not learn, and "staff" who do not display learning will not teach children anything worthwhile. Teachers have to ensure that children are in meaningful situations where they want to learn what we want to teach them.

Good teachers demonstrate learning. But this is not what most teachers are taught to do. They are trained to administer programs and tests rather than to engage in collaborative learning. Teachers were once dedicated learners themselves, and they would be more effective if they were free and competent to "teach" in the collaborative clubs that could be the essence of every learning institution. There is no shortage of good examples to follow.

Clubs in the Classroom

I claim no originality for any of the ideas or suggestions that follow. I have taken them all from teachers. I have seen many examples of clubs and of clublike enterprises in schools, though the students and teachers involved in them did not always realize their nature and their educational desirability. Some were monumental —like the opera that was written, scored, choreographed, directed, produced, and performed by kindergarten children in Victoria, British Columbia. Music and drama groups exist in many schools, of course. They are not usually regarded as part of the curriculum, and in fact they should not be put in the curriculum. But they should not be crowded out by formal curriculum activities—they are not the dispensable "frills" they are often perceived to be. Such enterprises are central opportunities for students and teachers to achieve constructive ends by planning, organizing, cooperating, thinking. But many clubs are small and informal, and their importance is likely to be overlooked.

There are reading clubs in many primary classrooms, sometimes rather artificially organized under the acronym USSR (which stands for Uninterrupted Sustained Silent Reading), where everyone in the room—and sometimes in the school—spends at least fifteen minutes at a fixed time every day reading. But this kind of reading is better when there is some movement, with learners (teachers and students) helping each other and talking about what they have read recently, the way readers normally behave in the world outside school.

Jim Sullivan is a first-grade teacher in Boston. Almost every day he sits in a rocking chair in his classroom and reads to the twenty children in his class. The children listen, chime in occasionally when they predict what will happen next, and talk afterward with each other and their teacher about the stories. They comment on the characters, the plots, the themes, even the authors' writing styles. Occasionally they act out some of the dialog. Often, one or another of the children volunteers to occupy the rocking chair and to read a story. At other times they read by themselves or with a friend.

The children are also authors themselves. Help is available from their friends or from the teacher if they need it. They do not write like schoolchildren completing an assignment, but like authors—making drafts, revising, editing, discussing ideas. They illustrate their own stories which, if the child chooses, are typed for them, are bound, and then become part of the classroom library. Naturally, the children's writing often reflects the styles of the stories they have been reading and hearing. But they also develop their own styles, their own voices, as they feel the power of writing and reflect their individual interests and experiences. The children have joined the writers' club, learning with a fluency to which programmatic instruction could not aspire.

Sometimes principals do not recognize the value of just simply *reading* in the classroom. A few have been known to make comments like "Why is everyone reading in this room? Hasn't anyone got any work to do?" Teachers also do not always appreciate the importance of reading to children. They may regularly say to their pupils, "Work at your workbooks for the next half hour (put a ring around the duck that faces the wrong way), and before you go home I'll read a story to you." At the end of the year all the children are enthusiastic and experienced members of the reading club, and the teacher says, "Weren't those workbooks marvelous?" Some teachers know better.

Jeannette Veatch, of Mesa, Arizona, is a retired university professor with many professional scholarly publications to her credit. She was also a classroom teacher who could engage children in reading. She knows from experience that the implementation of her ideas does not require unusual skill or expensive facilities and equipment. She says they are for the majority of American classroom teachers, with typical classes, ordinary equipment, and average skill, experience, and training. First, she says, get lots of books, of all kinds—from the librarian, the PTA, supervisors, principals—even the school board, at least a hundred for a class of thirty. Second, "fix up a nice place for the books," a quiet and comfortable corner. Instead of teaching children rules of reading show them how to get books and use them without disturbing others. Instead of teaching them dictionary skills, show them how to look up things they want to know when they have the need themselves. It is enough to show one or two children in the class. They in turn will show others what to do at an appropriate time, in the natural way children help each other when mutually engaged in interesting activities.

Shirlee Morris knows Veatch is correct. Morris is a fourth-grade teacher at Castlemount School in Sherman Oaks, California. With the support of a teacher in another school, Helene Sabel, and professor Victoria Miller of the University of California, Los Angeles, Morris removed all the skills programs from her classroom and set out with a very simple objective. "Most of us know what it is to find a book so compelling that we can hardly put it down," Morris told a workshop at the 1983 Reading Convention in Anaheim. She thought children should have the same experience in school. Instead of drilling her fourth-grade children, she began reading novels to them until she found one that they liked. Instead of testing them afterward on what they had read, she helped them in enterprises related to anything that had caught their interest. Children who had been reading about a visit to an art museum constructed a two-story model of the museum and took the class through a tour of it through the eyes of two characters in the book. Children who had been reading about a character who liked chocolate conducted a survey of consumer preferences and arranged taste tests of four different kinds of chocolate, organizing and analyzing the data themselves. Others made models of characters in the books or acted out incidents, engaged in collaborative activities involving imagination, planning, and initiative. The children wanted to read more, by themselves and with their friends. They wrote more, including their own books, which they then proofread, illustrated, and bound. They *talked* about their reading and writing, not in groups organized by the teacher but among themselves. They argued about the meaning of words, the motivation of characters, and the credibility of plots.

Margaret Reinhard and June Domke have arranged to take turns in teaching kindergarten and first grade at Fairburn school in Victoria, British Columbia. The provincial ministry of education prescribes that teachers should use the Ginn 720 series of basal readers, containing such prose as:

Ted said, "Go, Nan, go."
Bill said, "Ben, get Lad."
Ben said, "Lad can not run."
Jill said, "Nan can go."

Reinhard and Domke are among the fifteen percent of primary grade teachers in the province who reject the government prescription, though as one Victoria children's librarian said, "If you go into a school and see that everyone is using the basal reader, you've got to have a lot of moxie to say, 'I'm not going to do it anymore.'" Reinhard and Domke practice whole-language learning; "We don't teach reading. We let it happen." They have decided that reading is traditionally taught back-to-front, starting with letters and the pronunciation of individual words and ending with the enjoyment of books. Their first-grade classroom has a sandbox in the middle filled to the brim with children's books. "You trust a kid to learn to read," Domke says.

Ann Bayer, now a professor of education at the University of Hawaii, trusted children to learn to read when she was a classroom teacher at Abbott Middle School in San Mateo, California. In the early 1970s, she and her colleagues Eileen Gearhart and Barbara Warner saw where segregation of students according to reading "levels," remedial instruction, no time for reading, money spent on drill kits instead of books, were leading. So they turned their world upside down. Supported by their administrators Anthony Rose and John Belforte, they brought students together in groups of twenty-five to thirty that were as diverse as possible in terms of abilities and interests. Students were free to read what they wanted to read—and lots of alternatives were provided to keep them interested and learning. Students who were initially "turned off" were provided with comics, magazines, books on tape—and abundant help from their classmates. No one had to read aloud unless they had volunteered to prepare a part for a play or unless they accepted invitations to read to students at a nearby elementary school.

School counselors were soon reporting that students wanted to be transferred into the reading program rather than out of it. Teachers from other disciplines began showing an interest and reporting improved reading in *their* classes. A citywide evaluation showed that during an eight-month period, ninety percent of the students categorized as "remedial" made gains on standard tests ranging from 1.6 to 1.8 years.

At Atkinson Academy, the public school where Donald Graves works in rural New Hampshire, researcher Lucy McCormick Calkins compared two adjacent third-grade classrooms. In one classroom, the teacher "took a gamble" and moved out all the regular instruction materials, and instead helped and encouraged the children to write and allowed them to invent and employ their own punctuation. In the other classroom, the teacher taught punctuation conventionally, with daily drills, workbooks, frequent tests —and rare opportunities for writing. At the end of the school year the children who received no formal instruction could explain or define an average of 8.66 different kinds of punctuation marks, compared with only 3.85 for those in the group who had the drills and tests. In their writing, the students in the class of the teacher who took a chance were using more than twice as much punctuation —with more than twice as much variety—as those in the other class.

Different teachers create different scenarios, whatever they and their students feel most comfortable with. A British teacher, Moira McKenzie, has described a classroom where a cafe has been set up in a corner and children aged from five to seven, from a variety of cultural backgrounds, share their experiences of being taken shopping and to restaurants as they run their own business. They select materials, construct menus, calculate prices, take orders, and compute bills. While some children decorate paper plates with jokes and riddles, others produce newspapers for customers to read while waiting, including advertisements for their own enterprises. At Parkway School in East Meadow, New York, teacher Barbara Fox and visiting artist Karen DeMauro help children in the "remedial reading room" to improvise short plays of dramatic conflict using characters from stories or articles. The children edit scripts made from transcriptions of their performances. In the Montebello school district of Los Angeles, Mitzi Cholewinski helps children set up post offices that actually deliver and receive correspondence of all kinds which the students write and read.

Writing clubs can flourish in many guises. All that is needed is a sensible reason for using written language and a few experienced club members (who can be other children) to help newcomers who want to engage in club activities. Unfortunately, many teachers have forgotten what written language is for. They have become so involved in what is done in formal literacy instruction in the classroom that if anyone asks them what reading or writing are for, they will recite the programmatic classroom activities they engage in. So also, as a matter of fact, will children. Ask a few. Children learn in school, and what they learn is what is demonstrated to them. For many teachers and children, reading is what is done from 9:15 to 9:50 every weekday morning.

So what is written language for? What are the kinds of meaningful enterprises in which written language can be used, in school or out? Written language is stories to be read, books to be published, poems to be recited, newspapers to be circulated, letters to be mailed, jokes to be repeated, notes to be passed, cards to be sent, cartons to be labeled, instructions to be followed, designs to be made, recipes to be cooked, messages to be exchanged, performances to be organized, excursions to be planned, catalogs to be compared, entertainment guides to be consulted, memos to be distributed, announcements to be posted, bills to be collected, posters to be displayed, cribs to be hidden, and diaries to be concealed. Written language is for ideas, action, reflection, and experience. It is not for having your ignorance exposed, your sensitivity bruised, or your ability assessed.

I am not happy about giving teachers *specific* recommendations, because they may expect a panacea. I argue against the notion that outside "experts" should tell teachers what to do—or that teachers should expect to be told. Club activities should always be a contract among a group of learners (including the teacher). However, if pushed for a suggestion, I am inclined to propose the publication of a newspaper or magazine; not the formal school undertaking that might, in a desultory manner, come out once or twice a year, but a regular weekly (or even daily) journal that is produced with serious deadlines in a professional manner. Nancy Weisner does this with students in the fifth and sixth grades at Puohala School in Hawaii. Her paper is now in its eighth volume. She is the "advisor" to a staff of reporters, editors, artists, poets, and "Dear Aunt Blabby." There is usually no difficulty in finding local journalists willing to serve occasionally as experienced club members to provide any guidance that is needed.

My newspaper suggestion no doubt reflects my own journalistic interests. If I belonged to the club of musicians, horticulturists, or astronomers I might propose forming a symphony orchestra, starting a market garden, or building an observatory. But newspapers do offer wonderful opportunities for enthusiastic people with a variety of interests to learn in many ways, not limited to reading and writing. Individuals are needed to look after news and sports reporting, summarizing current events, copyediting, headline writing, editorials, letters to the editor, advice to correspondents, all the different kinds of features, photography and graphics, captions, layouts and paste ups, printing, advertising, promotion, circulation, and accounting. And no one ever has to say, "Why am I doing this? What is the purpose of this activity?" Every activity involved in the production of the newspaper makes sense.

Exactly the same possibilities arise in building a shed, another enterprise I occasionally suggest to teachers who want a specific example of a club activity. To build a shed, club members need to consider purposes and functions, decide on locations and dimensions, calculate quantities, compare costs, order materials, read and write correspondence, handle money, plan work schedules, as well as do all the digging, sawing, gluing, nailing, and painting. The enterprise involves literacy, mathematics, economics, science, planning, and social relations. And once again, no one need ever say, "What am I doing here? Why are we doing this?"

John Willinsky, who teaches in the curriculum and instruction department at the University of Calgary, recently spent a year relieving classroom teachers by working with their students in surrounding grade schools, two weeks in each of twenty classrooms. Understanding that one of the greatest reasons for any writer to write—and to continue writing—is to be published, Willinsky contrived a unique way to help students get themselves into print. He demonstrated half-a-dozen ways in which students could publish their own work, at the same time involving them in a history of publishing in Western civilization. He guided students from the orally-communicated poetry of Homer and public festivals, through the first scribes, early paper, illuminated manuscripts in medieval monasteries, and Renaissance technology, to computerized production and printing. Students in Grades 4 to 7 were inspired to write, to polish to professional standards, and to publish what they wrote. Were these writing classes or classes in history, sociology, civics, or technology? Where exactly in the curriculum would such activities fit? The answer of course is that the activities did not fall into any sterile school category at all. Every enterprise was a real-world undertaking, engaged in by the students for the same reasons that writers have striven throughout history, for the satisfaction of sharing an imaginative and carefully produced piece of writing with others.

In the Des Moines Public School District of Iowa, veteran teacher Maxine Robinson, who is now superintendent of reading, has established a novel scheme to bring about changes in the fifty-five schools for which she and her four assistants are responsible. She has persuaded the principals in fifty of her schools to form "partnerships" with one of their own teachers to demonstrate to other teachers in their school how students become literate through being engaged in literate activities. The teacher-principal pairs spend at least an hour a week studying and talking together, they attend monthly meetings where their experiences in different schools can be shared, and they are achieving remarkable results.

Dennis Deardorff is a language arts teacher at the Watrous-Traditional School in Des Moines and a member of one of Robinson's principal-teacher partnerships. Deardorff has a simple recipe for helping any student with reading or writing problems in his class, and for all the other students as well. Forget the dreary worksheets, discouraging grades, and academic drills. Get them to write poetry.

One of Deardorff's seventh-grade students in 1983/84 was Jeffrey Chiodo, who had been diagnosed as reading more than two years below his age level and writing no better than children four years younger. His scores on the Iowa Test of Basic Skills put him near the bottom third of the population. He had already been committed to a "learning disabilities" program for an hour a day. Deardorff introduced Jeff to the classics, reading Homer to him until the student could read the epics for himself. The teacher helped the student to write poetry about the gods of mythology and the world of man until Jeff was writing poems by himself—six worthy of inclusion in the literary magazine that Deardorff's students publish annually for the school. Within a month the youth was scoring near the top third on the Iowa test. In his one year in Deardorff's classroom, the former reading failure read everything in his sixth-, seventh- and eighth-grade readers, achieved the honor roll (which he has never since left), became the class leader, class poet, and collaborator with the teacher in helping other students with difficulties out of the pit of the instructional treadmill. When I last heard of Jeff, the former "learning disabled" student was student council president, a member of the Iowa Governor's Youth Conference, and the author of a first novel.

The exemplary teachers I have been discussing are characterized not so much by what they do as by what they do without. Their classrooms are all different, but none of them relies on commercial programs, prescribed tests, inflexible procedures, or tedious drills to ensure that students learn. Instead they establish clubs in which they trust their students to learn and themselves to teach. I want to distill their experience into a summary of the criteria for establishing clubs in schools. I should perhaps say in advance that these criteria are not always easy to achieve. But any club enterprise that does not meet the following four criteria runs the risk of being just another school activity and of missing its aim.

The Criteria of Learning Clubs

(1) No Grades

It may sound extreme to suggest that marks and grades—even *good* marks and grades—are counterproductive in school. But I have deliberately made the absence of grades the first criterion for establishing whether an activity qualifies as a club activity from which children will learn. Grades are the kiss of death; they stigmatize an activity as a pointless educational ritual, worth doing only for the sake of the grade itself.

Any activity with a mark or a grade attached to it is tainted and cannot qualify as a genuine club activity. And if a child is reluctant to engage in an enterprise because there is no grade, then the teacher is obviously confronted with a remedial situation. The teacher's role is to initiate children into clubs that naturally employ abilities we strive to develop at school. A child who has learned that something is worth doing only for a grade has learned the wrong thing. Abilities are frequently evaluated in real-life clubs, but only in terms of efficacy or appropriateness, for fitness of function, never for anything as vapid as a "mark." Scores are important only in games and contests entered into voluntarily by individuals who are already secure in their membership in the club. The genuine club activities from which children learn worthwhile things can never carry a grade.

(2) No Coercion

Engagement in club activities is a straightforward matter in the world outside school. Members are not forced to engage in activities in which they do not want to engage, and they are not excluded from those in which they wish to participate. There is no coercion. Teachers cannot dragoon a child into an activity just because they think it will be good for the child—at least not without clearly informing the child once again that the activity is an otherwise-pointless educational ritual. It is the essence of clubs that their activities are entered into freely.

Teachers cannot impose club activities on children, no matter how desirable the teachers may think the activities are. The teachers must themselves demonstrate, as experienced club members, that the activities are worth doing. What about children who would just refuse to participate in any activity if given a choice? That is the teacher's problem, not the child's. Children will not willingly remain bored and unoccupied, at least not unless they are irretrievably out of sympathy with the teacher. Either way, the teacher must show that clubs are worth joining and that there is a place in one club or another for every child. Coercion tells a child one thing only: that this is another school activity, which people in their right minds would never want to do at any other time.

(3) No Restrictions

Schools (and universities) are strange places. They put up walls (or parking lots) between themselves and the world outside so that it is difficult for any normal kind of activity to get into the institution itself. And then they build other walls inside the institution to restrict people who wish to engage in any kind of useful interaction with each other. Parents and friends are not allowed in, even when they are needed most. Students are allocated to "classes" in which they stay together most of the day for months at a time. They are grouped according to "age and ability" as though that will facilitate their learning in some way. But on the contrary, grouping in this way prevents learning. The students are grouped according to mutual ignorance and incompetence, as if the aim is that not one member of a class can possibly be helped by any other. Students are grouped that way—according to size, like vegetables and fish—solely for administrative convenience.

Once again, this is not the way of the world outside school. There, children who can do things help children who can't. Younger children expect to get assistance from older children and to assist even younger ones in their turn. Some of the most successful instruction occurs in school when children help each other. Many teachers know that with younger children especially, if you have taught one child you have taught the lot. Many children know that if they really have a problem of understanding—especially with computers these days—they should ask another child, not the teacher. When children of different ages—and more mature students of differing degrees of ability—work together, everybody learns.

There is another kind of constraint that restricts genuine club activities in school—the constraint of the timetable. Perhaps I need not elaborate upon how unnatural it is to restrict children to "reading" during one specific "period" of the day and to writing, arithmetic, social studies, and other subjects at other specific times.

Clubs should extend across and beyond the timetable, just as they should permeate the physical boundaries.

(4) No Status

Perhaps the hardest requirement of all for teachers is to stop acting the role of teacher. Teachers belong in clubs with their students. They may be the most experienced members of the clubs they belong to. But within their clubs, they should not necessarily be obviously in charge. Their task is to help when help is needed.

Clubs need initiators. They often need organizers. And they certainly will always have some members who are more experienced than others. But for a teacher to be automatically in charge is an inevitable giveaway that the club is just another school activity, part of a program in disguise. A teacher should not necessarily be the editor of the newspaper. A teacher may be the architect of the shed, but by virtue of being the most experienced club member, not because of an irrelevant job classification. Children will not spontaneously apprentice themselves to members of a club who claim to be different.

Psychologists Rita S. Brause, of Fordham University, and John S. Mayher, of New York University, distinguish two kinds of language interactions, which they term *empowering* and *controlling*. Teachers' language in school, they have discovered, is frequently controlling—authoritarian, impersonal, evaluative, time-pressured. They *tell* students what they are expected to do, and the result, however unintentional, is intimidation, insecurity, and dependency. Out of school, especially at home and between friends, language is usually empowering—it is collaborative, personal, cooperative, comfortably-paced, and responsive. Suggestions and offers are made, and the result is growth, assurance, and independence. No one is implying that teachers are naturally or invariably authoritarian, impersonal, and so forth. Out of school they talk much like anyone else. The language goes with the job; it is a consequence of the constraints of formal education. The fact that the language goes with the job is the reason why teachers must drop the role of controller when they enter the activities of the club.

Combatting a Common Enemy

In February 1978 I was invited to address a meeting of special education teachers in Norman, Oklahoma. I was not sure I wanted to accept. "Special education" is a field notorious for rigidly structured, often authoritarian approaches to children who experience difficulty in making sense of what goes on in regular classrooms. Even the language with which special educators frequently work reveals biased, pseudomedical assumptions that any child who cannot make sense of the classroom must have a mental disability. Why should such a group want to hear what I had to say? I decided to go when I learned that another speaker had been invited, Kenneth Goodman of the University of Arizona, whose long campaign for sense and humanity in education I have already mentioned. No one could have invited the two of us to a meeting by mistake; this must be an unusual group.

The meeting *was* unusual. The thirty-four participants came from nine states, and most of our discussions took place in the kitchen of the home of Gaye McNutt, an instructor at the University of Oklahoma. I quickly learned that this was a mutual support group, struggling to bring about a change in direction of the traditionally-oriented Council for Learning Disabilities to which they belonged. They were radicals in their own profession, trying to bring sense and sensibility into special education in place of diagnostics and treatments. Their leaders came from a variety of backgrounds—McNutt had been a first-grade teacher in Austin, Texas; Virginia Brown, who was currently teaching in Kansas City, Missouri, had been a teacher and reading specialist at several grade levels in several states; Donald Hamill was a speech therapist in a high school in Corpus Christi, Texas; Lee Wiederholt was teaching "educable mentally handicapped" adolescents in Philadelphia. None of the people present expected Goodman and me to tell them anything they did not know; they were looking for encouragement.

During a break I mentioned to Goodman that I had just returned from visits to Britain and to Australia where I had met many individual teachers who thought in exactly the same way as the people in this kitchen in Norman, Oklahoma. Whenever I spoke at conferences in Canada and the United States I found teachers who understood everything I talked about. Teachers frequently asserted that what I told them about children and learning would be difficult to implement in the particular districts in which they worked—I should be talking to their administrators—but few argued that my views were wrong or based on unsound research. And I knew Goodman had experienced the same supportive phenomenon on his own extensive travels. How was it, I asked him, that so many teachers all over the world, including those in Norman, Oklahoma, and in every other part of the United States that we had visited, understood the criticisms we made of schools, tests, and systematic instruction? Was there perhaps an underground network that disseminated subversive information, linking questioning teachers in different geographic regions so that they tended to think in the same way?

There was no underground network, Goodman told me. No positive force or organization existed to bring scattered teachers to a consensus of opinion. Instead, there was a common enemy. Thoughtful teachers tended to think in the same way about education because they all confronted the same difficulties: the obstacles and oppression of programmatic instruction. There is a resistance movement, but it is not organized in the way the enemy is organized.

Separated as they sometimes are by distance—and by the barriers that the educational system itself sets up within schools—resisting teachers need more than good intentions to change what is taking place in classrooms. They need sound theories with which to confront the barrage of pressure to follow prescribed programs and to engage in meaningless test-based teaching, and they need support and encouragement to make a stand against the continual eroding of their independence and autonomy in the classroom.

Fortunately there are a number of individuals who are providing such support in the struggle against the common enemy, some at national and even worldwide levels, many others locally. They offer influence and support by engaging in meaningful and collaborative learning activities with individuals they have inspired to learn, by providing examples of how all teachers should teach. I can't name all of these leaders in the many clubs of resistance to mindless education—I'm not trying to inaugurate an educational Hall of Fame—but I shall refer to a few as illustrations.

Expanding Ripples of Resistance

The influence of a few individuals can be enormous. For twenty years Yetta and Kenneth Goodman have been the center of a growing movement among classroom teachers to resist the incursion of programs and tests in reading and language education, particularly for bilingual and minority group students. For almost as long as the r-bbit has been around, the Goodmans have inspired and guided teachers directly and through the efforts and examples of their students and the students of their students—first at Wayne State University in Detroit, where Kenneth Goodman taught, and later when they both joined the faculty at the University of Arizona at Tucson. These associates of the Goodmans, scattered across the continent, formed a nonprofit group to which they contributed lecture and workshop fees in order to finance their own research, hold annual "renewal meetings," and work with groups of teachers who requested their help. Early members included Carolyn Burke and Jerry Harste in Indiana; Dorothy Watson in Columbia, Missouri; Dorothy Menosky in Jersey City; Louise Jensen in Chico, California; Jayne DeLawter in Sonoma, California; Rudine Sims in Amherst, Massachusetts; and Judith Newman in Halifax, Nova Scotia, who all became the focus of hope for otherwise despairing teachers in their own areas. They called themselves "the CELT group," for Center for the Expansion of Language and Thinking, and their driving philosophy was that all children could become literate if they were treated with respect in a supportive educational environment where written language was used meaningfully. They were vehemently opposed to prescribed instructional programs.

The philosophy has had a number of labels. At first it was called "psycholinguistic," because many of the insights about how children learn about language, whether spoken or written, first or second, came from the collaborative investigations of psychologists and linguists. Back in 1972, Kenneth Goodman and I published an article called "The Psycholinguistic Method of Teaching Reading." The title was intended to be satirical. Our argument was that a such a method of teaching reading could never exist, because the essence of the psycholinguistic point of view was that children learned to read from people, not from programs. Our irony was misplaced. Publishers rapidly created a bandwagon of "psycholinguistic" reading programs, tarnishing the term so much that it lost its original utility as an educational attitude.

The latest term for the philosophy that most antiprogram educators share is "whole language." Inevitably, the new term is being exploited by publishers to promote their materials, but it is still used widely among knowledgeable teachers in reading and writing instruction. Several of the CELT group pioneers I have already mentioned, and many others, have now organized informal "Teachers Applying Whole Language" (TAWL) groups in many parts of the United States and Canada, while similar groups have sprung up in Britain and Australasia. I have met groups in Columbia, Missouri, in Tempe, Arizona, and in California whose numbers, at regular informal meetings, are in the hundreds.

Sharon J. Rich, a reading consultant for the London, Ontario, Board of Education, began a whole language newsletter through which whole language teachers could encourage and inform each other. Her idea was to give busy teachers things that were *short* to read and think about. One copy of the newsletter was sent to each of the sixty-five schools in her district. She explained how whole language was not a formula for teaching but a shift in the way teachers should think about their art, and practice it. Children in whole language classrooms read and write daily—anything that is of interest to them. Talk is important, and the children have many opportunities to discuss their reading and writing with each other. There are lots of children's books and quiet corners for reading. Teachers and children together keep journals.

Rich says whole language is "an attitude of mind which provides a shape for a classroom." Accomplishment is rarely easy because of the external pressure of tests and lockstep instruction to which teachers are often required to conform, and because of the conventional expectations that surround them. She describes a typical reaction to a teacher who decided that the only way to survive with a first-grade class of twenty boys and six girls was to abandon the basal reading program and to engage the children in activities that interested them—activities involving water, sand, and lots of books. Not everyone understood. The teacher in the next classroom offered dittoed worksheets to help the teacher get back to her phonics drills. The principal wanted the door kept closed because visitors were disturbed by all the activity. A parent was concerned that her son was not reading the same book as children in other classes. Only when the children demonstrated to the principal and a superintendent how well they were reading, and how much they enjoyed it, did the principal express an interest in learning more himself. The teacher invited him to join the local whole language support group, whose existence he presumably had not suspected. Rich's ideas and efforts quickly drew widespread attention. After two years a publisher—Adrian Peetoom of Scholastic Canada— appointed her editor of a whole language newsletter which reached thousands of schools in Canada and the United States. It is now required course material in several schools of education.

Other ripples spread. When a young Canadian named Orin Cochrane got his first job teaching fifth graders in Winnipeg, he was dismayed to discover that children weren't learning very much and that no one was enjoying school very much, either the students or the teachers. Then he went away to teach at a junior high school in another district. Eleven years later he returned to the primary grades in his old school district as an assistant principal, and he found that nothing had changed. Children still were not learning, and school remained the drab part of the day for students and teachers alike. They were even using the same materials that he remembered. Two reading series were in mandatory use for all students—one for the "top" group, and another for the "bottom." One test was given every year to determine which group every student went into. The tests were marked mechanically outside the classrooms, and there could be no appeal from teachers, parents, or students against the results. From a range of several hundreds of points on the test, just one point difference could determine which group a child was committed to for an entire year, no matter what group the child was in the year before or what the opinion of the teacher might be. To prevent teachers from surreptitiously moving students into the higher group, only a fixed number of books in each series was allocated.

Cochrane rebelled and found a small group of Winnipeg teachers who felt the same way—Ethel Buchanan, Donna Cochrane, Sharen Scalena, Karen Reynolds, Janet Potter, and Joan Gemmell. In 1972, the seven formed a nonprofit professional development group which they called CEL (for Child-centered Experience-based Learning). At first, they met to clarify their own ideas and to give each other mutual support as they strove to replace the nonsensical materials and damaging tests in their own schools. Within a few years, other teachers in the Winnipeg area were asking the group to visit their schools and talk with them. By the end of the 1970s, members of the group were giving workshops all over Canada and in parts of the United States. They began to organize annual conferences in different Canadian cities. Their fifth conference, held in 1986 in their home city of Winnipeg, attracted 2,500 teachers and administrators from all over Canada and the United States, some traveling thousands of miles and many at their own expense. The Cochranes, Scalena, and Buchanan have put their ideas together in a book called *Reading, Writing and Caring,* which they initially published themselves and which is now a best-seller among teachers in many parts of the United States, a required course book at thirty colleges of education on the West Coast alone. They also have a newsletter called "Connections" which they publish three times a year. And the CEL group still has only thirty members, all working teachers.

One teacher who thought the CEL group had the right approach was Margaret Stevenson, now Coordinator of Consultants for the Edmonton School Board in Alberta. Through the joint efforts of Stevenson and CEL members, seven independent and voluntary support groups were set up in the Edmonton region, each with at least twenty-five teachers. Eleven schools in the region are now totally committed to "whole language" education.

A few dedicated people can achieve remarkable results, not by proselytizing but by example, so that others become interested in what they are doing and want to be involved. In October 1983, I participated in an international conference in San Francisco attended by 1,500 special education teachers. This was an exceptional conference for special educators because the themes, addresses, and workshops were focused primarily on meaningful learning and teaching rather than on the usual diagnostic tests and remedial exercises. The conference was organized by the Council for Learning Disabilities, (executive secretary Gaye McNutt), a direct consequence of the meeting I had attended in McNutt's kitchen in Norman, Oklahoma, ten years previously.

Donald Graves is having an influence on writing instruction similar to that of the Goodmans on reading, as Graves's students and associates, and his own writing, carry their humanitarian message across the continent and overseas. More and more teachers are encouraging and helping their students to write rather than plaguing them with exercises and drills. The teachers understand writing better because they have started to write themselves and have observed their own pleasures, problems, and frustrations.

Mary-Ellen Giacobbe was one of the teachers Graves first worked with at Atkinson College in New Hampshire. She ignored the workbooks and drills in her first-grade classroom and made it a policy that children had opportunities to write every day. In most schools, writing instruction does not begin until after the children can read. Giacobbe helped her students to write and edit the stories they wanted to write, and she helped them to help each other. She typed and bound the results of their efforts and put them on the bookshelves with commercially published books. By third grade some children were spontaneously revising their writing more than a dozen times because they wanted to "get it right." They were writing like professionals. Giacobbe is now in high demand as a speaker at conferences and workshops for other teachers, who want to learn what she has learned.

One of the teachers Giacobbe directly encouraged was Lucy Calkins, who with Susan Sowerby was one of Graves's earliest students and collaborators. Calkins says that the greatest insight Graves gave her was that teachers should always listen to children, responding to what children indicate about their learning rather than depending on what a program or test directs should be the next move. Now director of a writing project at Teachers College, Columbia University, Calkins has written a book about how children learn to become authors without having their confidence and interest destroyed; its title is *Lessons from a Child*. She also is busy responding to requests from teachers across the continent to come and talk at their professional meetings.

Another teacher in great demand at professional meetings is Nancie Atwell. She was one of fifteen teachers at the regional school at Boothbay Harbor, Maine, who came to the radical conclusion that the best way to prepare a new writing curriculum for kindergarten through eighth grade at their school was not to swap teaching recipes and to review commercial programs, but to investigate the nature of writing. They thought they should learn how writers actually wrote, and even how they, the teachers, learned to write. Their third-grade students now read thirty-five books a year —and read *and critique* the articles in professional teaching journals like *Language Arts* and *College English*.

"When we looked long and hard at ourselves as writers . . . we could no longer think in the terms of the fine old tradition," says Atwell. "Scope-and-sequence programs based on rules, forms, and isolated 'skills' had nothing to do with how we wrote or how we had learned to write. In truth, our own teachers' methods had had little positive effect—and much negative effect—on our writing. And, the hardest truth of all, we were perpetuating their methods in our own classrooms. The most surprising revelation came from the four teachers who simply couldn't recall writing in either elementary or high school. Their time in language arts classes was devoted to drill and skill: memorizing parts of speech, handwriting, punctuating workbook pages, and copying spelling lists."

One of her fifth-grade colleagues, Connie Bataller, said, "Either no one was interested in what I had to say, or it was assumed I'd put together all the bits and pieces learned from English workbooks and diagramming sentences and some day—magically, on my own—I'd write." Third-grade teacher Debra Matthews remembered "the boring task of opening up the *World Book Encyclopedia* and plagiarizing the lives of composers"—making sure to change one word per sentence." Nancy Atwell summarized: "For us, writing was either a fast reformulation of the teacher's ideas, or a demonstration on demand of correct mechanics and form."

Fortunately, the teachers also had more positive memories.

They remembered teachers, relatives, and friends who helped them to write and encouraged them to write, who submitted their work to local newspapers, who showed them how to write "letters of all kinds, journals and diaries, logs and scrapbooks, autobiographies, lyrics, poetry, essays, greetings, short stories, skits and plays, parodies, caricatures, cartoons, genealogies, notes passed to friends—even a eulogy for a deceased pet dog." None of the teachers gave much credit to the formal instruction they received at school. "How did we learn to write?" asked Atwell. "Were we in fact taught? As a group, we couldn't attribute our growth as writers to our teachers' explicit instruction. Our expertise grew through a combination of experiences—some outside school and some inside, when we were encouraged to think we had something to say and knew someone was interested in helping us say it."

In her discussions with thousands of teachers throughout the country, Atwell found that they, too, "reveal school experiences with writing bereft of meaning, logic, or satisfaction. The angry teachers isolated at the end of the Boothbay peninsula were joined by thousands of angry colleagues." Atwell and her own colleagues have not been able to change their world. They do things they would rather not, assigning topics for the whole class to write about, assigning deadlines, jotting comments in the margin—but trying always to bring their new understanding to bear. They are trying to change their own attitude toward their students' efforts to write. "The writing program that emerged at Boothbay Region Elementary School is today less a program than a way of life," she reports. "Our new curriculum isn't attractively packaged—it's messy, as thinking often is, and it changes, as thoughts often do."

Similar experiences of insight and self-discovery have been made possible for many other teachers through the "Bay Area Writing Project"—a group of summer institutes where teachers learn how to teach writing by observing themselves as they write and by discussing their experiences with each other. The project was begun in 1974 by high school teacher James Gray, with support he managed to gain from the University of California, Berkeley, and a grant from the National Institute of Health. Gray is still director of the Bay Area Project, the California Writing Project, and the National Writing Project. Project "sites" have been established in forty-nine states (New Hampshire is the exception—but it has Donald Graves). Other sites have been established in Britain, Australia, and Scandinavia. With luck—if the programmers and computers do not take over writing instruction completely—it may become rare to find a teacher teaching writing who is not a writer, sensitive to the struggles and demands of writing.

One angry and particularly outspoken teacher is Susan Ohanian, now an editor and frequent contributor to educational magazines. She makes her feelings heard by scores of thousands of educators. In the November/December 1984 issue of *Classroom Computer Learning*, for example, she warned, "Most reading software is foolish and impudent, an odious endeavor. . . . Today's software certainly drills with pizzazz. But what I find foolish is the basic premise—that reading can be achieved by drilling students on discrete skills. . . . Folks who play the educational numbers game never ask what a collection of 1,392 of these skills is good *for*, what the kid should do with them. Acquisition is the only goal. Computers, which allow isolated skills to multiply faster than the biblical tribes, merely encourage the foul bureaucratic impulse for collection, storage and retrieval." She went on to express her gratitude that when she taught reading she was unaware that the New York State Education Department had over 1,800 reading objectives stored in its computer bank. "Bureaucrats seem ever able to find thousands of dollars for up-to-date ways of delivering the same old skills at the very time they cite budget deficits as the reason for laying off librarians. . . . One good book is worth a thousand floppy disks." Ohanian's alternative: "I hope to nurture my students in an environment that convinces them they might want to read a book someday. I see too many proficient decoders, kids who perform extremely well on standardized tests but never willingly pick up a book. They have mastered an incomplete system, one they find lacking in marvel or mystery."

There is a constant battle for the control of classrooms between educational programmers and testers who want to hold teachers accountable for delivering instruction in the misguided manner they think children are best taught, and teachers who know there is a better way. Teachers like those I have named have become major figures in a struggle to turn the tide before the programmers, and the computers, take over completely in the instruction—or destruction—of literacy. Others, often more isolated and beleaguered, engage in individual resistance in their own classrooms. They are not always aware that they are part of a widespread revolutionary movement. There is no guarantee that they will win—all the political power is with the forces ranged against them—but they know that if they do not succeed in making their students interested and competent readers and writers, nothing else will.

The strength of all these influential individuals and groups in the struggle against the tyranny of drills and tests is their *collaboration*—with their students and with each other. Collaboration is not the easiest relationship for teachers to establish with students, or even among students, in conventional school settings, yet it is essential if they are to succeed. Programmatic instruction is the antithesis of collaborative learning. Good teachers almost instinctively ensure that collaboration pervades the atmosphere that learners breathe. There must be collaboration in three ways: among students, between students and teachers, and among teachers.

Collaboration Among Students

Once again it may sound perverse to suggest that schools actually teach children not to collaborate, but evidence that this is the case is not hard to find. In my days as a professor of education I tried to free my students from some of the worst consequences of the treadmill of coursework to which they were committed. There were times when I had no choice but to give them a grade for their work, and they had no choice but to complete an assignment for which they would be given a grade. So I told them they could work on their assignments collaboratively, in groups of two or three which they would select, and that all members of the group would share the grade. And the students hated it.

They gave me three objections. The first objection was a logical impossibility: Every student seemed to think that he or she would be the person in the group who would do the most work. The second objection was more familiar—students were afraid that they would not get personal credit for any good ideas they might have. I had experienced similar cautions from my own faculty colleagues, who occasionally thought that I was profligate with ideas in discussions and conversations. Wasn't I afraid that someone might steal an idea and publish it first? Of course, the notion of a scoop was not unfamiliar to a former journalist, but another of my naive expectations had been that universities promoted the collegial production and testing of ideas, in which one could hardly expect to have proprietorial rights. The third student objection to my proposal was simply that any enterprise on which two or three people collaborate would result in a lower quality product than if they all worked independently.

These students were all experienced and intelligent teachers, the people who were supposed to be showing children how to learn. Where could they have learned that collaboration is essentially unfair, unprofitable, and unproductive? Only in one place, of course: in school. To test the hypothesis that antipathy to collaboration is taught, I went back to my helpful second-grade teachers and asked them to make the same offer to their pupils; work together and share the mark.

The six-year-olds rejected the opportunity—for exactly the same reasons that the graduate students gave. In fact, the children had an additional objection of their own: collaboration was cheating. The children's attitudes are so fixed on these matters that once again some teachers were persuaded that unwillingness to do things together is natural, and that children are born unwilling to learn unless they can do so competitively and in isolation. Schools tend to make their mark on children early, deeply, and permanently.

How do teachers foster collaboration among their students despite the pressures of school? There is only one way, and that is by demonstration, by teachers engaging collaboratively with children themselves. But being a collaborator with students is not the easiest thing for teachers to do.

Collaboration Between Students and Teachers

It is a popular and romantic notion, especially among teachers, that teachers are collaborators with children in the learning enterprise. They are usually not. Teachers are usually the dispensers of grades, and at critical times such people become antagonists to the children receiving the grades. Ironically, it is to the children who most need a collaborator, the children who are most confused or least interested, that the teacher is the greatest antagonist, the dispenser of the *low* grades. This is one reason I make the elimination of grades the first criterion of clubs. Grades put children and teachers into conflict.

Many teachers do not find it easy to collaborate with students in any case. It is much safer to detach oneself and work behind a barrier of distance. I have suggested to many teachers that the way to improve their own writing is to write with children, not only sharing the product of their writing but actually joining in the activity, composing stories or articles together. But some teachers resist this notion—especially in matters where they might be a little self-conscious.

Several teachers have told me vehemently that they could never share a poem they have written with children. But when I asked why, I got two different answers. Some teachers said their poetry was so good it would intimidate students to see it; students would feel they could never aspire to the model. But other teachers said their poetry was so bad they would be ashamed to reveal it to students. Both types of response miss the point of collaboration. With a true collaboration, no one can say, "This is what I did, and that is what you did." A true collaboration is like two people carrying a heavy object that neither of them could carry alone. When children apprentice themselves to people who are building sheds, fixing the plumbing, reading books, or writing shopping lists, there is never a question of "I did this bit; you did that." Collaboration occurs when individualities are merged—which is the reason why the elimination of status is one of the essential criteria of clubs in schools.

Several advantages accrue when a teacher who is less than perfect at an activity collaborates with students. It is very hard to learn anything by trying to emulate a perfect model. Not only is the model far beyond current expectations of attainment, but the learner is also denied the opportunity to see the kinds of things that go wrong. It is not always true that we learn most effectively from our own mistakes; it may be better to observe the mistakes of others. When children see a teacher struggling with a task, they can learn that it is normal and predictable to struggle with a task. Unless children collaborate with an artisan or scientist who is using mathematics, children will never discover how mathematics is used by artisans or scientists. Because most children (and many teachers) have never actually seen a writer writing, they can be afflicted by the misconception that writing springs fully formed from the author's head. They are unaware of the drafts, and the blocks, and the alternating frustration and exhilaration. They do not really know what goes on in writing. Without the actual collaboration of a writer, it is difficult to learn about those essential tools of the trade— the paper clip, the scratch pad, and the wastepaper basket.

Unless teachers collaborate with students, how will students learn to collaborate? Children learn *exactly* what is demonstrated to them by their teachers. A lecture or a set of exercises is not an alternative to an apprenticeship. Collaboration empowers students; instruction leaves them dependent. But paradoxically, a good deal of collaboration between teachers and students will not be possible unless there is more collaboration among teachers themselves.

Collaboration Among Teachers

The peculiar educational habit of isolating groups of twenty, thirty, or more students of roughly the same ability in the same room is compounded by the additional custom of confronting them with just one teacher. Schools would be much better if classes were twice as big (with preferably a mixture of ages) and there were two teachers in every room. I am not arguing for larger classes, but I am asserting that there should often be more than one teacher present. When just one teacher confronts a group of individuals, especially if they are slightly bemused by what is going on, the teacher talks in a very peculiar way. And this does not help students to learn to talk about the things the teacher is trying to talk about.

There is nothing unusual about this phenomenon. We all talk in a peculiar way when we are confronted by someone who does not understand everything we say—a visitor to our country, for example. Parents talk in a peculiar way when they talk to babies. Parents talk to babies in baby talk, and babies are not interested in baby talk. Babies only talk baby talk to please parents. Babies are interested in grown-up talk, and they usually hear grown-up talk only when grown-ups are talking to each other.

Many teachers complain that students do not know how to have a discussion. Some even complain that this is because children have not been taught "discussion skills." The teachers do not realize that they never demonstrate how discussions are conducted.

A teacher once invited me to visit a "discussion" she and her third-grade students would be having on stories the children had written. The teacher and I sat on chairs, and the children sat on the floor. Children who wanted to say something were expected to raise their hands. Those who never raised their hands were firmly invited to contribute, and we all waited while they searched for something to say. Who ever has a normal discussion like that?

One child was desperate to say something. "What do you have to say about Freddy's story?" asked the teacher. The child said, "I liked it." The teacher beamed at me. "Tell us why you liked Freddy's story," she prompted. "Because it was full of detail." The teacher was delighted. But later, when I suggested that this was nothing like a real discussion, she was most upset. The child was talking teacher talk. When does anyone recommend a book to someone else because it is full of detail? Do we ever say how much we enjoyed the heap of detail in a novel? If detail is the essence of an interesting book, then telephone directories would top the best-seller lists.

I am not blaming the teacher, who did not have a chance to demonstrate how normal discussions take place. To do that, she would have had to invite the children into the staff room, or at least have another adult in the room so that the two could talk about stories to each other. Having a discussion was impossible when just one teacher was in the classroom.

I can tell a similar story against myself. I used to complain that my graduate students would never argue with me. I offered them plenty of time and opportunity; I would even provoke them to challenge what I had been saying. My students were ready enough to say whether they agreed or disagreed with me, but they did not know how to engage in a debate on the topic. I told a friend, who then put me right. He said they had no experience of seeing anyone argue with me; that was the reason they did not know how to. He suggested I invite him to my next class.

I accepted the suggestion. Within a few minutes he had challenged a point I was making. I attempted to make him see where he misunderstood. He tried to show that I had overlooked an alternative explanation. Very soon my friend and I had a full-bodied argument taking place in the classroom. We started to recruit students to help with our points of view. The students started arguments among themselves. Quite suddenly I found we had started a club of people who argue with me. I had forgotten—or I had not learned—that people learn in the clubs to which they are admitted. Whenever I taught after that, I tried to ensure that someone who could argue with me was in the classroom. (After all, I wanted my students to be able to argue my point of view with other people.) I learned, and the students learned. But the learning would have been impossible for us all if I had been the only "teacher" in the situation, with ideas or "information" flowing in one direction only.

This handicap of having only one teacher in the classroom is particularly acute in the situation in which nearly fifty percent of the children in many parts of the United States and Canada find themselves: They are expected to learn a language that is not the language they speak at home. Trying to teach a student how to use English (or any other language) is virtually impossible for just one teacher alone; the demonstrations are all wrong.

I am not arguing for "team-teaching" as it is practiced in many schools and colleges. With team-teaching, one teacher usually works with one group and the other with the rest. Or the teachers take turns with the entire group. I am talking about teachers working more with each other than with the students, establishing a club that the students are free to join. This is not easy for teachers, because teachers customarily do not work together. They do not visit each other's classrooms. They divide responsibilities rather than share them. They are caught up in the rituals and traditions of school.

Furthermore, teachers are rarely taught about collaboration themselves. I have been critical of "schools," but I am using the term generically. My comments apply to colleges and universities as well. Some of the most rigid and unimaginative teaching practices I have seen have been in the daily routine of teacher preparation in colleges of education. There is a vicious circle here. Teachers are taught to perpetuate in grade schools the way they usually are. The teachers are taught so effectively that many never learn that there is an alternative—and the college professors' justification is that they are preparing teachers for the schools that already exist.

I find this situation particularly ironic because one aspect of university education—unfortunately rapidly dying—comes close to my idea of what a good school would be like. I am referring to the tutorial system, where groups of individuals with common interests gather around a "professor"—who literally *professes* dedication to a certain subject or discipline—to explore collaboratively that subject's possibilities and implications. A tutorial is a club. I am not talking about something that is impossible. Tutorial situations exist in many public schools today, but generally only at the kindergarten level. To see individuals of different degrees of experience entering wholeheartedly into common enterprises in which there is very little grading, restriction, coercion, or status, go to a kindergarten. By first grade things often start to go wrong. R-bbits begin to take over. As students ascend through the grades, the programs and the tests become more conspicuous and compelling. And at the university level, often, the situation is worst: courses almost totally preplanned, classes of a hundred or more, and constant preoccupation with grading, restrictions, coercion, and status.

Fortunately, there are exceptions. Schools and colleges may be infested with r-bbits, with junk-learning programs, and with respect-demolishing tests. But there are individual teachers who strive to maintain the kind of environment in which they know, intuitively at least, that learning occurs most effectively.

It is easy to describe good teaching and the ways in which schools should change. Bringing desirable change about is another matter, to be raised in the final chapter. But whether we like it or not, schools are changing in any case. Computers are entering classrooms, even if teachers try to bar the door against them. The possible roles of computers in education must be considered next, because in the conflict between teachers and r-bbits, the side that controls the computers will be the victors.

CHAPTER 8

The Promise and Threat of Computers

Computers are ubiquitous in the world beyond school. In government, commerce, and industry, in every profession and every art, computers can be found in productive and creative use, facilitating present aims and expanding future possibilities. But anyone looking for a similarly rich and imaginative employment of computers in education will be disappointed. Unless used for administration, for teaching "computer science," or for instructional programs at properly scheduled times, computers in education are regarded as frills, as "extras"—like electric typewriters.

Student teachers are still graduating without ever having laid hands on a computer, let alone knowing anything of the productive ways in which the technology can be used in classrooms. Many practicing teachers will not have computers in their classrooms or will accept them only if they are also given instructional software so that they will not have to make decisions. It is because so many teachers are ignorant about computers that they are vulnerable to the quick fix of the r-bbit's seductive drills and tests, and employ the computer resources they have in such unimaginative and unproductive ways. Yet there are many exciting ways in which computers can facilitate and expand learning.

Games and Simulations

Computer games can be more than entertainment; they can be compelling exercises for the mind (like "Dungeons and Dragons" and "Rocky's Boots") or for hand and eye (like "Pacman"). While waiting at an airport recently, I watched a four-ring airline pilot play "Pacman" with total absorption for over twenty minutes. I remember hoping that he would exhibit the same concentration and dexterity if he was to fly the plane I was about to board.

Computers are superb game-playing devices. They can constitute a stage for the enactment of dramas and tragedies, adventures and escapades, by people alone and by people in groups. They can provide excitement, interest, and relaxation, a convenient way of passing the time or an outlet for many human drives and emotions.

I am not urging more game playing on computers in school, however. Quite the reverse. Game playing is a conspicuous use of computers, but not the most interesting. It is like the fact that pots of flowers can be put on grand pianos; true, but not the most productive use of the instrument. Computer games can command a particular compulsion on the attention of children, rather like the Saturday morning television cartoon shows with which many games have such a family resemblance, sharing animation techniques, scenarios, and even plots. This cartoon aspect of computers is often exploited in the major instructional software. And most children will tolerate twenty minutes of the r-bbit if they know they will get ten minutes of "Pacman" afterward.

But show children that something is worth doing only for the fun or the reward, and they will learn to do it only for the fun or the reward. If children will not learn without irrelevant incentives, that is an indictment of the way they are taught. If computers are employed in the classroom to make it fun for children to engage in an otherwise pointless activity (like filling in the missing letter of r-bbit innumerable times a day), it will be at the expense of meaningful learning that could otherwise be accomplished. Education critic Neil Postman has made a similar argument about the way the technology of television has distorted education. In a book pointedly entitled *Amusing Ourselves to Death,* Postman argues that "Sesame Street" may be a good television show, but it does not encourage children to love school or anything about school. It encourages them to watch television. Computers can make the things we already do badly in schools even worse, just as they can make many of the things we already do well infinitely better.

A particular kind of computer game that has attracted interest in education is the *simulation,* in which the computer replicates events or situations that might occur in real life. Perhaps the best known examples are the many varieties of flight simulation, in which all the motions and calculations of landing a small plane at a real airport can be experienced at the keyboard of a computer.

Many kinds of computer simulation are available for educational purposes, from the exploration of a newly discovered island or a region of outer space to investment on the stock exchange. Many educational simulations are available in various forms from a number of publishers under different titles. One popular scenario involves the operation of a soft-drinks stand. Children engage in planning the purchase of materials and location of the site, make all the necessary calculations for the buying and selling, and even obtain weather forecasts to help anticipate the demand for the product. Many activities of this kind are collaborative, with children working together. Others are competitive, and children compare their profit and loss accounts among themselves or against a preset standard. A simulated soft-drinks business may help children learn a few things, but so would a real one, and teachers and children may treat the simulation differently, as a school activity with "skills" that must be mastered and tested. The desirability of simulations depends on how they are used.

A computer simulation that has been extremely popular in England concerns the discovery and raising of the hulk of the Mary Rose, a British warship that capsized in Portsmouth harbor in the 1600s. Efforts to raise the real vessel attracted national interest over a long period, and the drama of the actual recovery was widely viewed on television. In the simulation, children have to take weather and tide conditions into consideration both in searching for the wreck and in recovering it. One false calculation and the fragile structure crumbles in the water or in the air.

Hundreds of computer simulations are now available for use in schools. Many cost about forty dollars or less, and one copy usually suffices for an entire class. For an individual teacher, especially one inexperienced with computers, the choice is bewildering. There are genetic simulations, where generations of birds, kittens, and dogs can be bred, to study the inheritance of dominant and recessive characteristics. Oceans and forests can be formed, flourish, and die as thousands or millions of years are condensed into minutes. Nuclear power plants can be constructed and operated—and the consequences observed as an accident melts them down. Surgery can be conducted on humans and animals, and mechanical repairs can be conducted on automobiles. Physical systems and organs can be represented and experimented with in clear color and compelling action. Frogs can be dissected and put back together again. Computers can allow learners of all ages and degrees of expertise to explore and experiment in situations that would be too dangerous, too expensive, or simply impossible to experience in any other way.

There are educational simulations or working demonstrations for—to give a partial list—astronomy, ecology, electronics, archaeology, nutrition, population growth, evolution and adaptation, predator and prey systems, cell theory, plants and trees, animal management, meteorology, fish, insects, hives, reproduction of every kind, forms and transformations of energy, entropy and randomness, drama, aviation, town-planning, dress designing, the stock exchange, parliamentary systems, life after disasters, statistics, calculus, virtually every occupation and sport, and travel through time, space, and the human body.

I do not want to argue whether particular simulations are good or bad. I have no testimonials. Everything depends on how teachers make use of the tools that come to hand. If simulations are ignored, students and teachers will be deprived of compelling learning opportunities, a chance to do many things they might want to do but not otherwise be able to do. But used indiscriminately, simulations can bore students, deprive them of more meaningful experience, and either discourage them from using computers or seduce them to concentrate only on games. Always, one must ask what will happen to the students who can't or won't do whatever is expected. I have already heard in England of children who lack essential "Mary Rose" skills.

Simulating Language

An incidental by-product of some flight simulations has been an opportunity for students to learn aspects of particular kinds of language, for example, the jargon of air traffic controllers. Language instruction has in fact been one area of education in which there have been great hopes for computer simulation, and also great misconceptions about it. These expectations are notably high in special education and in second language instruction, especially where there are problems related to bilingual education and teaching English to children who are native speakers of other languages. Many people who reject the drill-and-test approach of the r-bbit to language education feel that computers can make a major contribution through simulations. Whether such people believe this because the computer is seen as filling a need or simply because they see it as a way of using the computer is not always clear.

The argument for language simulation is simple enough. Children learn best in situations that are meaningful to them, and they learn about language best when the language makes sense and is used in meaningful ways. A child is much more likely to learn "May I have another donut?" in a donut store than in a regular classroom. A computer can simulate a donut store. It can present an image of a counter, the figure of the salesperson behind it, and in written or spoken language the computer can say something like, "Good morning. What can I do for you today?" Depending on the learner's response (usually typed on the keyboard), the computer can appear to conduct fragments of a sensible conversation. The computer can say, "I'm sorry, I don't understand you. Please repeat what you have said in another way." And it can even correct some of the typical errors that learners make. Thus, it is sometimes argued, computers can provide reasonable facsimiles of real-life language situations, especially in circumstances where the language experience would not otherwise be available. Not every child can be flown to France to hear French being spoken, but a simulation of French language use can be made available to all children by computer. While recordings and movies can reproduce illustrations and even actual samples of the foreign language in use, they cannot provide "interactive" opportunities for the learner to participate, the way computers can.

The ability of most computers to simulate language is often a large part of what is claimed to be "user-friendly" materials. Next to "fun," user-friendliness is perhaps the most frequently touted competitive virtue of educational software.

"Individualized" conversational gimmickry is trivially easy for anyone familiar with computer programming to accomplish—in fact, *writing* such simulations themselves may be one of the few useful activities for children to engage in if computers are to be used for language instruction. Even the professional effects become less impressive when you know how easily they are achieved, and in any case, the effects do not usually impress children. When a computer asks their name, knowledgeable children are quite likely to respond with something like, "George Washington slept here," observing with satisfaction the computer's automatized response: "Good morning, George Washington slept here. Can you tell me the second letter of the word r-bbit, George Washington slept here?"

Nevertheless, sophisticated attempts to program computers to engage in realistic conversation have produced some remarkable results. A classic example named "ELIZA" was written nearly twenty years ago by Joseph Weizenbaum as a research simulation of a consultation with a psychotherapist. After obtaining the client's name, the computer would ask something like, "And how do you feel today, Harold?" And if Harold responded that he felt particularly lousy, the computer might say, "That's too bad, Harold. Why do you think you feel that way?" If Harold said that his wife had just left him, or he'd been fired, or he'd crumpled his fender, the computer might respond, "What do you think brought that about, Harold?" Most of the time the computer turned questions back on the client, asked for the client's opinion about something, or simply said, "Hmm, hmm." or "Tell me more about that." Of course, the computer didn't *understand* what the client was talking about, but it managed to hold up its side of the conversation quite well. In fact, I have been assured that clients frequently felt better after a chat with "ELIZA." Simulations like "ELIZA" are the nearest computers have come to passing the "Turing test," devised by British mathematician Alan Turing, who proposed that a machine could be said to behave *intelligently* if a questioner could not distinguish between language produced on a teletype from an unseen computer in one room and an unseen human in another.

So should computer simulations be used to teach about language? My own conclusion is a qualified "No." With a few limited exceptions, computers are both unnecessary and inadequate devices for language instruction. Simulations are generally unnecessary because there is rarely a shortage of language that children could observe and become involved in. People are talking, reading, and writing all the time in the world outside school. It is rarely difficult to find people who could engage children in meaningful spoken or written language enterprises. The difficulty usually is to fit meaningful language into the school curriculum in an instructional setting with the appropriate drills, exercises, and tests. Computers are better at doing this.

But computer simulations of language are inadequate because children learn language from the way it is used, from the manner in which language fulfills intentions, and computers do not have intentions. Few children have a compelling desire to emulate a computer. It is infinitely more useful for a child to hear a story told by a person than by a computer (or by a tape recording), because the greatest part of the learning experience lies not in the particular words of the story but in the involvement with the individual reading it. Children must learn that people read, otherwise they will never be interested in reading for themselves.

The qualification I wanted to make about the use of simulation in language instruction concerns situations when direct experience of a language is not possible, for example in providing a French-speaking environment for every child learning French. But simulated language situations can be helpful only in a limited sense—

to teach special uses of language rather than language itself. The air traffic control situation is a case in point. Flight simulation will help student pilots learn the particular jargon and terminology of what might be called "air traffic control English"—but only if students already have a substantial knowledge of English. Learning a specialized jargon is not the same as learning a natural language like English, Spanish, or Chinese. The simulation must engage the learner in an activity that is meaningful. What makes air traffic control English even partially learnable from a computer is not the desire to learn the language but the desire to fly. The potential pilot has intentions for which the controllers' language is relevant, even if he is only flying in a computer simulation. Simulations of language itself are not likely to result in much useful learning, but simulations of situations in which the learner can meaningfully participate can have more productive results.

The Misuse of Games and Simulations

No form of education is a problem for children who can already do what they are required to do, who can make sense of the situation even if they do not already know the "right answer." Even r-bbity drills raise no difficulties (apart from tedium) for the child who knows or can work out that A is the letter required to fill the blank. The problem is always for the child who cannot do the exercise or who does not understand what is going on.

A child who does not know enough English to converse with an ELIZA-type simulation would have difficulty with it. A child who does not know enough French to engage in a simulated French-language discussion will not learn French in this way. The activity becomes another handicap, and teachers unfortunately have been trained to believe that their role is to focus on children's difficulties, not on what they can do comfortably. So the tendency is for children to be kept struggling in situations that they do not understand, from which they gain only discouragement, where there is little possibility of learning. This is especially the case when the activity is permeated with grades and marks, as instructional situations usu-

ally are in school contexts. Then, all that many children are likely
to learn is that that particular kind of activity is difficult and discouraging.

With every computer simulation, two questions should be
asked: What other kind of experience is being displaced by the time
taken up with this activity? And what happens to the child who
cannot do it, or who is bored or threatened by the activity?

Computers as Information Systems

The mass of human knowledge, important and trivial, that is
now maintained and managed in the memories of computers can
lead one to wonder how industrial society coped before electronics.
The answer is: relatively inefficiently, and only because armies of
clerks spent lifetimes trying to impose order on mountains of paper.
The storage and retrieval of information—to use the contemporary
jargon—had to be accomplished by painstaking record-keeping in
notes, files, journals, ledgers, registers, daybooks, and memoranda.
Only a few people might know their way around the archives of a
company or an institution, and when they moved on or died, access
to records were often permanently lost.

Today, for better or for worse, every item of information can
be stored and every item can be retrieved. Not only can individuals
and organizations file in their own computer systems every fact that
might conceivably be of interest at some remote time in the future,
but systems can be interconnected so that what is on one computer
can be made available to all.

Of course, massive computerization has led to serious social
problems, ranging from unemployment to loss of privacy, not to
mention such occasional monumental errors as a pension recipient
being mailed a check for millions of dollars or an aircraft being
flown into a mountainside. But computers also make manageable
the complexities of modern transportation, medicine, banking, in-
surance, the stock market, large industrial corporations and their
operations, and of government itself at every level. All of this *order*
has been achieved because computers can store immense quantities

of information in a relatively small space almost instantaneously, and can usually retrieve quickly whatever is required.

There is little sophistication about much of this handling of information. Computers do not usually store their facts in an organized way, like the alphabetical order of directories and encyclopedias or the logical or topical classificatory systems of the library catalog or the yellow pages. Computers tend to file facts in their magnetic furrows the way most of us store old photographs, tennis rackets, and check stubs in a hall closet; the last thing in goes on top. And computers generally conduct their searches in an equally haphazard manner, examining whatever comes to hand to see if it is what is sought. Endlessly patient computers conduct their "random searches" so fast, and usually so successfully, that they get credit for more sense than they have. If computers had existed before printing, there might have been no alphabetical order.

Knowledge gained by many individuals through years of experience can be pooled into "expert systems" on computers that can not only analyze problems but also suggest solutions. Physicians, for example, can readily examine as many relevant case histories as they wish. They can use the computer to identify possible diagnoses and treatments for particular patterns of symptoms, thus drawing upon the accumulated expertise of colleagues they might otherwise never be able to consult, except perhaps through prohibitive hours of searching in the stacks of specialized libraries. There is probably no profession or pastime today that does not have relevant software and "on-line" current information available on computers. The world is brought to everyone's doorstep.

Consider some of the advantages that computers offer writers, not just in facilitating the mechanical acts of writing and of editing, but in making information available just when it is needed. Spelling is an example. Neither experienced writers nor beginners need be delayed in the course of writing by uncertainty about a spelling. When I have finished typing the present chapter on my own computer, I shall routinely pass it through a spelling checker to test for errors and mistypes. If I want to confirm a spelling at any time— say the word "encyclopedia"—I can type an approximation of the word on the keyboard and my computer will provide the correct spelling. But it is not necessary for me to stop for every unfamiliar word. I do not even have to struggle for an approximation. I can write any unique combination of letters, such as *enxx,* and at the end of the day instruct the computer to change every occurrence of *enxx* to *encyclopedia* for me. I can employ this shortcut for any word that I use frequently. Writers, in other words, no longer need worry about spelling as they write, nor need children who are learning to write. They can get on with the more important business of getting thoughts on paper.

None of this means that I think children should not learn to spell. There is a fear that children will not bother to learn if a computer can do their spelling for them. But children who are anxious about the consequences of spelling errors as they write do not stop to learn the spellings that they do not know; they just avoid the difficult words. Forcing children to worry about spelling during composition—especially during early drafts—simply makes them write less. So not only do they still not learn to spell, but they get less general experience as writers. Wise teachers avoid any kind of "instruction" that reduces the amount of writing children do. These teachers want children to learn to spell, punctuate, capitalize, and so forth, but they recognize that this learning occurs in other circumstances (and primarily through reading) rather than through obstacles in the process of writing.

Computers can do much more for writers—and learners—than provide correct spellings. They can provide words and meanings. Dictionaries are available in computer software to allow us to check the meanings of words as we write, without the disruption of having to go to a bookshelf or to find space for the open pages of a bulky volume on the desk in front of us. And the cost is rarely much more than the cost of the printed alternative. We need no longer inter-rupt our thoughts with trips to the thesaurus for those words that hover on the tip of the tongue; the computer will provide a set of synonyms or of antonyms. With the right kind of telephone connec-tion, authors can get answers to just about any kind of question they might have. If I am in doubt while I am writing, I can type some-thing like "PERU, CAPITAL?" or "CHILE, MAIN INDUS-TRY?" and receive the answer before I have lost my train of thought. Reference books may be fascinating for the occasional browser, but computer access is a boon for anyone in constant need of specific facts of all kinds (and a different kind of browsing becomes possible). In 1985, schools in New Jersey began to link their students' personal computers with the twenty-one-volume, 9 million-word *Academic American Encyclopedia,* putting a world of facts at learners' fingertips.

The facilitation of writing or research in this way again makes some teachers and parents anxious. They seem to believe that learning is worthwhile only if it is effortful. But even experts are inclined to engage less in an activity if they find it frustrating. Nobody forces children to talk the way their family and friends talk, but their learning does not suffer. I have never met adolescents who failed to learn to drive because no one made driving difficult for them. The moment the child has a real need to go to a dictionary or encyclopedia, the child will learn to do so, but this will probably not happen in the middle of a complicated composition. Frequent trips to a dictionary or encyclopedia never made anyone a writer, but *writing* opens the door to spelling and punctuation.

It is not just physicians and writers who benefit from the memory resources of computers. Architects can call for plans of particular buildings or for illustrations of standard design techniques, planners and explorers can examine any chart or map, mathematicians can remind themselves of any formula, and scientists can have all the data they might need—and so can every child learning any aspect of these activities. Any information that is in any of the world's libraries or archives—or in our own filing systems and closets—is now within reach of the computer keyboard.

At Lexington High School in Massachusetts, Alan November has a class called "Computers and Society." It is a course with scarcely any coursework or academic pressure, and no homework, although students often stay after school voluntarily. The students use the computers to work on projects that benefit the community or to pursue their own interests. They have listed all the services available for children in the town of Lexington, the scholarships available to Lexington students, and the services of more than a hundred agencies for handicapped people in the greater Boston area. They have compiled a file of after-school job opportunities, and they have surveyed wheelchair access to help the town apply for funds to build sidewalk ramps. Students have designed a com-

puterized order form for an after-school business and created a
system for ranking professional football players. They use the same
kinds of word processing, spreadsheet, database and graphics software that are used in the world outside school, and they have also
designed their own software. The instructor says he feels more like
a traffic cop than a teacher as he tries to ensure that the students get
access to the equipment that they want, but that doesn't matter. The
important thing is that the students help each other. "One student
is our graphing expert. Another specializes in form letters. Each
student is expected to lend his or her expertise to anyone who needs
it," says November. "This course builds students' self-esteem. Success comes to every individual, regardless of academic ability."

It is a great convenience to have masses of facts and figures
stored away in a computer, instantly accessible when a learner
might need them. But it can be disastrous when the computer is
employed in the reverse direction, to try to cram facts and figures
into a child's head. Instead of being a source of support and knowledge, a computer that dispenses programmatic instruction becomes
an instrument of manipulation and control, as I described in Chapter 5.

There is no need for teachers to turn their backs on technology. Awareness of the damage that computers can do—and have
begun to do—when used blindly or ignorantly should not result in
computers being banned from classrooms. Every child should have
access to computers for the information management resources I
talked about earlier, and for the way they facilitate writing and all
forms of drawing and design. Anything that facilitates worthwhile
activities should be welcomed, especially when much of the technology is relatively inexpensive and is falling in price. Computers
can be used as creative tools and as collaborative devices.

Computers and Creativity

Writing is second only to games as the most frequent domestic
use to which computers have been put, and the most enlightened
general use of computers by children in schools has probably also

been in conjunction with writing. Computers have become so influential in every aspect of writing that they are even changing the way we talk about making visible representations of language. Computers (and computer software) used by authors and secretaries alike are called "word processors," an ugly, unnecessary and misleading term that has nevertheless come to stay. The fact that a phrase like "word processing" could become synonymous with "writing" illustrates how technology frequently comes into our lives through the agency of people who have little sensitivity to what they are actually doing.

The term "word processing" is inappropriate because computers do much more for writers than manipulate words. They frequently perform operations on sentences, paragraphs, or entire chunks of text. Recently there has been a trend toward calling word processing software "text editors," a slightly more felicitous term but still inexact. In addition to editing functions, most word processing software facilitates the original composition of texts—the getting of ideas and putting them in concrete form—as well as their subsequent modification and revision. Computers have many of the separate advantages of paper, pencils, electric typewriters, and filing cabinets, and a few additional advantages of their own.

The simple and enormous advantage of electric typewriters over pens and pencils is that typewriters are faster. The sluggishness of writing with pen or pencil is probably one of the greatest handicaps confronting most writers and all children learning to write. An average "normal" speed for talking, for listening to speech, and for reading is about 200 words a minute. Try deliberately to slow this rate, and there are immediate problems—thoughts race ahead faster than words, the beginnings of sentences are forgotten before the ends are reached, and distraction takes place. Most people find it impossible to talk, listen, or read if they are forced to slow down to a third of their usual rate, say to one word a second, sixty words a minute. Yet most people writing with a pen or pencil cannot produce words faster than twenty a minute, a reduction to a tenth of the rate at which the brain is comfortable dealing with language. This is the main reason that writing by hand is such hard work for most people—it is a strain upon hand, memory, and patience; it demands *effort*. And for small children struggling to control large unfamiliar letters on printed lines, perhaps producing only one or two words a minute, the marvel is that they are ever able to write anything at all.

It is no coincidence that there is often an inverse relationship between the quality of written ideas and their neatness of production, especially in original composition. When ideas flow, the hand must race to keep up with the mind, and handwriting, spelling, and grammar all tend to suffer. On the other hand, college teachers know that neat and laboriously handwritten papers often consist of immaculate nonsense. Most of the author's attention has been spent on the superficial characteristics of the text, leaving ideas to fend for themselves all along the way.

Electric typewriters offer both speed and neatness, giving ideas a better chance to get on paper in a legible form—an advantage for writers as well as readers. Electric typewriters (and word processing computers) are a special blessing for children because they take care of the two biggest problems all children have in learning to write: directionality and neatness. Letters are perfectly formed every time, on an absolutely straight line, and they always appear in the right direction.

It may once again be objected that children ought to learn to write neatly and from left to right. And isn't there an advantage sometimes in slowing down and not writing so fast? Doesn't the effort of handwriting force you to reflect more on the words you are producing?

The first question may be getting tiresomely familiar. The objection was raised with respect to spelling and punctuation and can be raised with respect to music and art, and anything else. I can only reiterate that children learn what is facilitated for them. Difficulty only slows them down and may eventually discourage them completely. The word processor shows children constantly that our written language is produced from left to right, without their having to get anxious about it. As for deliberately slowing down, writers need to have their thoughts very much under control to be able to write slowly. Writing slowly is a special skill that comes only with experience; it is not a prerequisite for writing.

However, the advantage of electric typewriters over pens and pencils was purchased at a price. What they gain in speed, they lose in flexibility. Inserting additional words into a line is relatively simple with pen and paper but difficult with a standard typewriter, and it is almost impossible to draw the arrows that indicate the transposition of words and phrases, especially when the movement is from one line to another or from the bottom of a page to the top. Marginal comments on typewriters are usually out of the question, especially if you want to insert something sideways. But with word processing computers, groups of words can be moved all over the place with ease, not just from one line to another but from one part of the text to another. Word processors have made writing a plastic art again. They combine the speed of the typewriter with the flexibility of pencil and paper. That is why computers are such ideal editing devices; they bring an entire text under control.

This facility for editing actually encourages better writing. Authors are more inclined to make changes, to work through additional drafts until they get exactly what they want. Most children given access to a word processing computer begin by revising stories they have already written. Not only is revision more rewarding, but it doesn't have to be retyped. Any human is likely to protest when changes to a few words at the beginning of a piece mean that an entire manuscript has to be retyped, especially if it has already been carefully typed and proofread several times. But the ever-patient never-complaining computer can be left to print out yet another final draft while the author goes off to celebrate the completion of a better job.

Not that I think computers will ever take the place of paper. Everyone who uses a computer keeps notebooks and writes on scratchpads. There are always times when computers are not available or convenient. No one *needs* a computer to write or to learn to write. Computers may not take care of every aspect of writing, but they can do a great deal to help all kinds of people to see themselves as writers and to perform more like professionals.

Another advantage that word processors have over both typewriters and pencils and pens is that they can keep our correspondence and other writing in order. It is often much easier to store a piece of text on a computer disk and to retrieve it from the disk than it is to put it in a drawer or file cabinet—which means, of course, that computers are a heaven-sent gift to bureaucrats. But this asset provides much more than simply a superior form of paper shuffling. For the writer—and for children learning to write—the filing capability of computers is another way in which they offer control over *ideas;* they can act as an extension of the human mind.

If I want to find where I might have written about adolescents and spelling in this book, or anywhere in my previous writing by computer, I no longer need thrash around through hundreds of pages hoping to get on the trail of the notion I have in the back of my mind. I can ask the computer to *search* through the manuscript for sentences or paragraphs where the words "adolescent" and "spelling" both appear, and it will do so with speed and efficiency.

It is an oversimplification to assume that computers can only help writers and learners to manipulate words. Computers offer power in the control of ideas—a much more dramatic possibility. Software programs are becoming available that claim to function as "ideas managers," or—of course—"knowledge processors," or "outline processors." These programs essentially offer alternatives to scraps of paper or scratchpads; they facilitate the organizing of specific ideas or notions under particular headings or in a structured form, and the recovering or amending of those ideas very quickly.

Computers enhance creativity. They are productive devices at the service of our imagination. They permit the exploration of new possibilities—the generation of alternatives and the exercise of choice, surely the basis of all art. Students who use computers for writing in school, even the very youngest ones, write more and write better. They are more enthusiastic about writing, and the writing they produce reflects their confidence. They *see themselves* as authors, and as any experienced writer knows, that is the basis of becoming one. Compared with how computers can be used creatively to liberate student writing, the r-bbit is very feeble and inappropriate indeed. Computers can help in the construction of worlds of words.

And writing is only part of the picture. Computers offer advantages in every form of expression and creative learning that should be at the heart of education.

Composer, Conductor, and Orchestra

Mozart and Bach never had the musical resources commanded by anyone today who attaches an inexpensive keyboard to a personal computer. Play three notes on the keyboard and the computer will play them for you, whenever you want. You prefer three other notes? The computer will play the new set instead. You'd like the first three back? Both sets together? Combined with yesterday's composition? Played forward, backward, transposed up a tone, down an octave, counterpointed, harmonized, in waltz time, in march time, syncopated, bring in the brass, mute the percussion? The computer will do it all for you. It will perform your concerto on your digital stereo as often as you wish, modifying whatever you desire. And when you are satisfied, you can give an instruction and the computer will print out the score.

A common objection at this point is that creativity cannot result from such a mechanical process. But the essence of creativity is the generation of new possibilities, and the essence of art is choice. The computer facilitates the exploration of as many alternatives as the individual can produce, and it faciliates selection among those alternatives. Both the originality and the discrimination have to come from the user. Nothing is done mechanically unless you want it to be. The freedom of the user is absolute. There is no soul in the computer, but it can be an instrument of our deepest human desires. Computers can give everyone a chance to be a composer, and many composers have made excellent use of them.

The class computer will not replace the student orchestra, but it can open the door to music for many children who might otherwise never find themselves on the stage or in the audience. The computer will not take the place of piano lessons, but it could encourage more children to take them.

Computers have made possible new forms of art and expanded the possibilities of conventional media. Look at the special effects in films (and in television commercials), for example. Computer graphics permit us to travel through new worlds of the imagination. Exciting art generated through the imaginative use of computers can be found today not only on the walls of galleries but in advertising and in the folios of primary schoolchildren.

Just think of what an inexpensive "graphics tablet" linked to a computer can do at the service of a creative mind. You want to draw a cow under a tree? With the computer you need never run out of paper as you work. You can erase and modify to give your cow exactly the shape and expression you want. You would like your cow to browse under the tree you drew yesterday? The computer will get the tree for you. You wish the cow had been facing the other way? The computer will turn it round. You would prefer the cow to be a little bigger? The computer will enlarge it for you. You would like a family of cows, in descending order of size, under a sun that is a perfect circle, in a frame that is an accurate rectangle? Just command the computer and modify or reject what you don't want. You can color your entire picture at one sitting without worrying that the paints will run, and you can remove or overpaint the colors without jeopardizing the original sketch. You can display your landscape in the silvers and gray of dawn or the gold and orange of sunset; you can lead your tree through the cycle of the seasons. You can animate your cows to dance around the tree—or you can make an acorn fall and show it growing into another oak.

Computer graphics are used by professionals in many ways—and anything that helps a professional can help a learner or a child exploring possibilities. Architects can use computer technology and software to move walls and doors and windows around in the buildings they design, presenting immediate alternatives for themselves as well as for their clients—and children can do the same in constructing maps and layouts of their school. Designers can contemplate a variety of arrangements for the furniture in a room, and so can children in their classroom. Patterns can be constructed, reflected, and repeated in ranges of size and color to create harmonies for wallpaper, fabrics, or carpeting. New shapes and styles can be devised for clothing and cars, for jet planes and book jackets, even for plants and animals. Computers can convert columns of figures into graphs, charts, and blueprints. No child need be condemned to an imprisoned imagination because of an inability to draw a straight line or because of the risk of "wasting paper."

Old Worlds and New

There are endless possibilities for imaginative teachers and for all students. History can be recreated—expeditions planned, alliances examined, documents signed. The game—or critical thinking exercise—of "What if?" can always be played, and events can be reconstructed to explore what might have happened if the expedition had foundered, the alliance had fallen through, or the document had been discarded. The geographical features of land and sea can not only be presented, they can be manipulated. What will happen to this valley if we build a dam? What will happen to the tides if the ice caps begin to melt? How will the climate change if the Amazonian jungles are denuded of trees? Learners can *participate* in cosmic events.

The panoply of life can be unrolled—from egg to chicken to egg, from seed to seed. Population genetics becomes more than a subject to study; it evolves into a giant glass bead game that can actually be played out. Students can try to breed a superchicken, or a marmalade cat with one blue eye. They can investigate the consequences for other populations and life systems when a species becomes extinct, or if its numbers rapidly increase. They can take excursions through their own respiratory system, wander through the chambers of the heart, and if they wish, perform their own operations—all on the screen of the computer. Many of the thousands of educational versions of such systems cost less than fifty dollars. Students who enjoy computer programming can create their own systems.

There could never be enough time in the day in any classroom for students or teachers to exhaust the creative possibilities of computers, even if all the deadening and distorting routines of drills and tests were totally abolished. The technology already exists, and is in place in many classrooms, to make every school an El Dorado of productive enterprises in which everyone can learn, students and teachers alike. It is a tragedy, then, when the same technology is used only to trivialize and stultify learning, boring children and burning out teachers.

Acknowledging the Danger

In the present chapter I have focused primarily on the tremendous opportunities that computers promise to classrooms. Every teacher and every student should have access to computers to enable them to do better what they would want to do in any case and to engage in some of the new things that can only be done with computers. But I do not want to minimize the dangers. Computers are a natural habitat for the r-bbit. In earlier chapters I gave examples of the massive development and promotion of nonsensical computer-based drills and tests until I feared wearying the reader. Computerized instructional systems—electronic learning—could destroy learning, except in the eyes of those who believe that learning is the mechanical assimilation of information. And there is no reluctance on the part of educational administrators to take advantage of everything that is offered.

By the end of 1986, all students at Carnegie-Mellon University in Pittsburgh were expected to buy a personal computer in order to receive their instruction. In the November 1, 1982 issue of *Newsweek,* Richard Cyert, president of Carnegie-Mellon University, talked of the system set up by his faculty and IBM in the following words: "This network of personal computers will have the same role in student learning that the development of the assembly line had for the production of automobiles. . . . The network personal computer system will enable students to increase significantly the amount of learning they do in university."

Stephan L. Chorover, a neuropsychologist and professor of psychology at M.I.T., calls himself a "student of psychotechnology." In an article in the June 1984 issue of the computer magazine *BYTE,* he discusses how technology changes the way individuals behave and think, and especially how computer-based instruction is affecting education. He believes that whether or not the computerization of education will revolutionize the way people teach and learn, it will undoubtedly affect how students and teachers relate to each other. One of Chorover's interests has been how the application of the factory metaphor to education—as in the quotation by President Cyert of Carnegie-Mellon I have just cited—

has been expanded with the increased use of computers. Chorover quotes Dr. Arthur Melmed, an official in the U.S. Department of Education, writing on "how to improve productivity in education." Melmed said, "The key to productivity improvement in every other economic sector has been through technological innovation. Applications of modern information and communication technologies . . . may soon offer education policy makers . . . a unique opportunity for productivity management." My own translation of that statement is that technology has led to labor saving and work efficiency in business and industry, and will be a powerful weapon in the hands of anyone trying to manage the efficiency of classrooms.

Chorover points out that the introduction of technology has always affected the people who used it, but not always in a salutary manner. "All too often automation has led to worker displacement, deskilling, and alienation. What reasons do we have to believe that technological innovation will follow a different course and lead to a different outcome in the field of education?" He tries to take the point of view of educational policymakers in an underfinanced city public school system where the teachers feel they are underpaid and overworked. The officials are concerned with "improving their productivity" and keeping track of the current system's "inputs and outputs" through the use of standardized tests. A group of computer experts, possibly with university support, promises to improve classroom efficiency with "a courseware package of both hardware and software, with which a student who has no prior computer experience can work in a self-paced manner. Any information a student needs can be encapsulated into a computer program. . . . The system will be extremely cost-effective. Instead of teachers who are subject-area specialists, the school can hire relatively unskilled people to be 'resource managers' and 'system monitors'. . . . The university (or company) will provide all the expert assistance the school will need, including curricular material, lesson plans and examinations." The school will be able to say good riddance to their skyrocketing professional payroll, says Chorover.

The solution that Chorover suggests is stated in computer jargon: "Computer-based systems should not be introduced from the top down." He means that planners and bureaucrats should not impose computers on schools and then require them to be used in particular ways. "Too many schools still follow a well-established recipe for disaster: first, policy makers choose the hardware, then decide on the software. They then teach teachers and other staff how to use the system, and finally, everybody tries to figure out what the goals of system utilization are to be. . . . Instead, teachers and students should be involved at all stages of the process, including the initial and difficult (often neglected) one of defining the educational values and goals that any such system is intended to serve." Chorover's very simple recipe for the intelligent use of computers in education is: "We must take it as our goal to draw people into an intimate and creative human context."

Professor of computer science Joseph Weizenbaum, a colleague of Chorover's at M.I.T. (and the author of the influential "ELIZA" computer language simulation program) believes that the introduction of computers into primary and secondary schools has been basically a mistake. Looking at only the dark side, he also wrote in the June 1984 issue of *BYTE:* "Our schools are already in desperate trouble, and the introduction of the computer at this time is, at very best, a diversion—possibly a dangerous diversion. Too often the computer is used . . . as a quick technological fix. It is used to paper over fundamental problems to create the illusion that they are being attacked. If Johnny can't read and somebody writes computer software that will improve Johnny's reading score a little bit for the present, then the easiest thing to do is to bring in the computer and sit Johnny down at it. This makes it unnecessary to ask why Johnny can't read. In other words, it makes it unnecessary to reform the school system, or for that matter the society that tolerates the breakdown of its schools."

Administrations often lead school districts into "innovation" with the best of intentions but no idea about what they might reasonably expect to achieve or of what the consequences of their action might be. The Shoreham–Wading River school district on Long Island, New York, is one of the richest in the United States, thanks in part to the presence in its school tax area of a nuclear power station. In 1985 the district board was planning to give every family in the district a computer so that their schoolchildren could have a computer to work on at home as well as in school. The biggest problem was to select what the children were to do with the computer, which was not expected to be simply a homework machine. The district did not plan to look critically at its own educational aims and expectations. Instead, the district was planning to invite a group of national "computer experts" to a conference to give their opinion about ways to use computers for instruction. No one in the district that I talked to had wondered what need there would be for teachers, or indeed for schools, if children could learn at home from computers that had been programmed by outside experts.

A system called *"telesoftware downloading"* already in place in the United Kingdom shows how tenuous the classroom teacher's hold could become. In fulfillment of a government plan, every school in the country has at least one Acorn computer that can be plugged into the television set already in most classrooms. During the night, when there is no public broadcasting, the British Broadcasting Corporation can "download" from the television into the computer the software for the next day's instruction *(tele-software-downloading.)* The only reasons education has not already been destroyed in Britain, I think, are that there are not enough computers and computer programs. But both shortages are being rectified. How long will it be before someone realizes that teachers aren't needed to switch on the computers in the morning? Computers can switch themselves on. When will someone realize that if education is to be delivered to computers through television, there is already a television set in every home?

One of the experts the Shoreham–Wading River school district hoped to invite to say what should be done with the computers to be put in every child's hands was another M.I.T. professor, Seymour Papert. Papert's computer software program "LOGO" is known in most schools where there is a computer, partly because the program contains some drawing elements that are extremely simple for teachers and students to operate and partly because Papert makes impressive claims for what the program as a whole can achieve.

In his book *Mindstorms,* which has become something of a cult document among computer enthusiasts, Papert states that LOGO, which he designed to help children become their own computer programmers, will foster the production of "powerful ideas" and advance intellectual and mathematical development. Criticism of such claims has come from both sides of the Atlantic. Nova Scotian educator Judith Newman, an expert on "whole language" in reading and writing instruction and also on the school use of computers, says that children using LOGO frequently learn only to replicate elementary demonstrations in the manual, like the construction of a simple symmetrical flower. John Davy, of Emerson College in Sussex, England, is afraid that children will finish up playing with LOGO flowers instead of real ones.

Davy is concerned with what he terms the program's "tendency to experiential impoverishment." He questions just how powerful will be the ideas of children who learn to think too much or too often in accordance with the way computers are programmed. He fears a "loss of a real connection with childhood." He asks: "What kind of a culture are we developing if people have to meet its most powerful ideas through machines rather than through people? If people—that is, teachers—consistently work in such a way that they block access to these ideas, should we not be looking at how teachers work rather than selling them a prosthesis?"

Davy was writing in Columbia University's *Teachers College Record*. In another article in the same issue, Robert J. Sardello, of the Dallas Institute of Humanities and Culture, enlarges on the threat of computers to culture and education. Paradoxically, he does not regard computer-assisted instruction as a threat. "Teaching machines or programmed instruction have already shown themselves to be dismal failures, precisely because they turn the learner into a mechanism, who duly responds with frustration and boredom." He also sees no threat from word processors and similar functional programs, which, he says, are like pocket calculators in that they are technical devices that can free the imagination for the consideration of matters involving mathematics, accounting, economics, or business, or . . . the craft of writing itself." Sardello sees danger in the claims that teaching children to program computers will teach them processes of thinking itself. He argues that "There is a huge inflation to the suggestion that the artificial terminology of computer programming constitutes a language at all. It assumes that language no longer emanates from the life of a community, from geographical place, from heritage, ritual, from the living body of a people, from the voice of things in the world. The new origins of culture, so the inflated claim would state, are IBM, Apple, Xerox, and Texas Instruments. Computer terminology is certainly not a living language, but rather the enslaving of language by turning every form of speech into an object to be manipulated by the totalitarian grammar of computational logic."

Unfortunately, teachers' own professional organizations sometimes approach computers in the most simplistic and unimaginative ways. The National Council of Teachers of English has published a "primer" for teachers called *Computers in the English Classroom,* edited by Sally N. Standiford, Kathleen Jaycox, and Anne Auten. Readers are told that "the computer can provide one-to-one instruction—if necessary, repeating information or offering examples for hours without losing patience or varying moods." The reference is presumably to the computer's patience and moods, not the student's. "It can incorporate a student's responses into this instruction, branching into a reiteration if necessary—or advancing to a higher level of instruction if the learner seems competent to handle such progression. . . . Most important, it can store vast amounts of data and manipulate that data with incredible speed. This is what allows the flexibility of instruction. It is also what provides the potential for evaluative applications." The enthusiasm for mechanical and dehumanized drill and test does not abate. "For the student who lags behind in ability to generate 'standard usage' or who constantly confuses apostrophes with semicolons, [the computer] provides opportunities for endless tutoring or drill and practice— free time from the embarrassment of 'being wrong' in the eyes of classmates or of stretching a teacher's patience to the limit when asking for a repeated explanation. . . . And beyond instruction, computers can provide instructional management: keeping records of 'who has done what,' testing, maintaining performance statistics, or even generating letters to students or parents offering records of students' academic activities."

The assumptions underlying such statements are astounding from an association dedicated to the humanities. "Lagging behind in the ability to generate 'standard usage' " is standard educational jargon to denigrate anyone who does not speak the idealized prestige dialect of the classroom. I have known experienced writers occasionally to confuse apostrophes and possessives, or colons, semicolons and periods, but I have never met a student, even a child, who confounded apostrophes and semicolons; it would take a remarkably inept kind of instruction to produce one. The authors of the NCTE document appear to see endless drill and tests as an ideal of English instruction, with "errors" constituting embarrassments for the learner and a strain on the patience of teachers. Little wonder the authors assume that English teachers would be happy to have computers write letters for them to parents to report on student academic activities. In short, the approving catalog of what computers "can do" in the classroom is primarily a list of what the computer ought not to be used to do, a list of the dangerous and futile ways to be avoided.

Yet none of these dreary, threatening, or unimaginative ways of using computers need be imposed on students or teachers, as I have shown in this chapter. Computers can be productive, creative, facilitatory devices for experts and beginners alike. What is wrong is not the computer but the thinking of many of the people who want to flood schools with electronic teaching technology. Computers can help students apprentice themselves to more experienced writers, artists, engineers, explorers, and scientists; computers can dissolve the classroom walls.

Bringing People Together

Computers are often perceived as solitary devices that isolate their users from other people and from social activities. This is a misconception. Computers can bring people together who might otherwise never have an opportunity to meet. They can enable people to work together in ways that were never before possible.

Computers can easily be interlinked by direct cable connections within a room or building to make new forms of collaboration possible. Reconsider the painting of the cow under the tree that I described. Students can see on the screens of their computers what is happening on the screen of the *teacher's* computer; they can see how the teacher goes about drawing a cow under a tree. Any child who wants to take over the teacher's picture at any time can do so —provided the teacher agrees—without disturbing the teacher or any other child. The teacher can look at what is on the screen of any child and give any help or instruction that is necessary, without marring the work of the child. If the child does not like the modification the teacher has suggested, the computer can be made to reject the modification and retrieve the original.

For the first time, two people can work together on the same picture, the same plan, the same design, without one having to take the work from the hands of the other, and without the risk that proposed changes will damage or destroy the original (or damage or destroy the collaboration). Teachers can help children without leaning over their shoulders, taking their pens or brushes from their hands, or antagonizing them by making irreversible changes or comments on their work.

At last, two people can collaborate on writing the same text. I can now cooperate in writing an article or book without the frustrating wait while my manuscript is in the mail, without the annoyance of having my immaculate manuscript defaced. Suggested amendments can be made directly on the screen in full view of both collaborators, and if one objects, then the other cannot insist. Instead of one person exploring his or her ideas in a lonely exercise of authorship, two people can explore their mutual ideas, without delay or getting in each other's way.

Systems are already on the market that permit a number of computers in a classroom to be interlinked. In essence, such systems work as follows. There are three buttons (or, more formally, "function keys"). Press one button, and you can look at what is on anyone's screen in the room. You can examine the picture that anyone is drawing or the poem anyone is composing. Press another button, and you can change what is on anyone's screen; you can make your own contribution to the picture or the poem. The third button is perhaps the most important—it is the "override," the privacy button. Press that button, and you can prevent anyone from looking at your screen or making alterations to your work. Unfortunately, the only times I have seen such systems in use, only one person in the room had the three buttons. That person of course was the teacher. What could have been a productive system of collaboration became another technology of control. Computers are not a threat to education or liberty, but the ways in which people might use them are.

Collaboration need no longer be confined to the classroom. In many schools in Canada, English-speaking students are drilled for three laborious years or more in the hope that they will acquire sufficient expertise in the French language to write a rudimentary letter to a French-speaking student in another part of the country. But already the technology is in place for an English-speaking student on the West Coast and a French-speaking student on the East Coast to write the letter *together*. Students need no longer be confined to the expertise of the people who happen to be in their own school or to the collaboration of their own classmates. Through computers connected over the telephone system, students can extend their immediate experience over thousands of miles. There is no need for simulation. The cost of this technology and of the use of communication links is rapidly falling, especially for large-scale users, and is minor compared with the cost of years of failed instruction.

Interested students of all ages can apprentice themselves directly to experts and learn through personal involvement in activities requiring skill. Soon, for example, it may not be necessary for you to wait for the next book from your favorite novelist to arrive in the bookstores before you read it. If the author agrees, you'll be able to read the book as it is being written. Many authors may not find such a possibility appealing, but I am sure others will make a specialty of it.

Many authors already write on a word processor, transferring their manuscript to disk files which they then send to their publishers. Alternatively, text can be sent directly to the publisher over telephone lines. Either way, the editor at the publishing house can arrange for the manuscript to be reviewed and revised, copyedited and set in type, ready for printing, without the text once having been put on paper. In the same way, many newspaper reporters type their stories directly into newsroom computer networks to be discussed, modified, edited, laid out, composed, and made ready for print, all once again without going on paper. And neither the book nor the newspaper story need in fact ever go on paper. Instead of being sent to the printshop, the final computerized product can be sent directly to your computer screen. Some journalists are already writing for the new media of computer data bases, electronic "bulletin boards," and information services where their stories and reports go only to computer screens.

I do not think computers will take the place of books, at least not until a computer screen can be as compact, convenient, and aesthetically pleasing as a book. But once again, I am not talking about computers replacing anything, but of offering something new, an alternative which in some circumstances can be desirable and even infinitely more appealing. There is much more to be learned about how a book is written by looking over the author's shoulder than by seeing only the final version of the book, when all the false starts, the errors, and the rough edges have been smoothed away. Art lovers may prefer to see only the finished products of a sculptor's work, but students will learn much more if they can also see the sculptor at work, observing how the artist begins and ends—and also seeing the pieces that are spoiled or thrown away. Authors are frequently affronted by the reader's assumption that anything that is easy to read must have been easy to write. At last, the effort and craft that go into writing can be made evident to readers without marring the final product.

Computers can extend opportunities for learners to share in the creative act of the expert in many ways. Students of engineering can observe the calculation and design of the structures of a bridge as intimately as medical students can observe an operation. Music students can eavesdrop on a composer at work in the way they have so far only been able to hear an instrumentalist at rehearsal. The architect can design a house in direct and immediate consultation with the client, and again under the observation of students.

Many experts and artists will not want to share their most intimate moments of crisis and creativity, but some will specialize in the new possibilities for collaboration, teaching, and performance. Computers can make schools the focal point of society, where the wisdom of the elders and the aspirations of the young meet in mutual benefit.

Not all teachers and students need be computer experts, but

turning one's back on the computer is like rejecting radio, television, automobiles, and electronic calculators—ignoring the good for fear of the bad. Everyone in the educational system must get on top of computer technology, so that they know when they are being bamboozled and when they are being helped.

The Future

I do not think anyone can predict how the future will be if we—I mean our children—learn to use computers intelligently and creatively. Not even computers could make such a prediction for us. But I can offer an analogy.

I remember vividly a story told to me by Shirley Richardson, the director of a Toronto center for young people with cerebral palsy who had total physical handicaps—who could not attend to any of their own needs and who could not even communicate what those needs might be. Workers at the center experimented with giving some of the youngsters electronic keyboards with half-a-dozen large symbols on them representing messages like: "I'm hungry," "I'm tired," and "I'd like to look out of the window." The symbols could be operated by the elbow, or by a toe, or by a "unicorn's horn" strapped to the forehead. The technology exists today to activate the symbols simply by the line of sight, by a glance, almost by an act of will.

Very rapidly the youngsters mastered the original keyboard and demanded more symbols—ten, twenty, a hundred, even thousands, until some of them were surrounded by symbols. They invented new combinations of symbols to construct and communicate meanings of their own. They spent hours every day and night *talking* to each other and to anyone else who took the trouble to enter the world they had created.

And, Richardson told me, the staff at the center suddenly *knew* that inside each of these mute and immobile individuals was an intelligent, sensitive, creative, artistic, language-using personality—waiting to get out.

Everyone is handicapped. We are all muted and immobilized to some degree by the limitations of our perceptual systems, the speed at which we can look and listen, and the ease with which we can memorize and recall. I have no idea what a future will be like when technology enables us to transcend constraints of the mind the way it allows us to magnify the powers of the body. But what the jet plane has done for jumping, computers can do for thought—if we do not allow the instructional exploitation of computers to shackle thought itself.

CHAPTER 9

Protecting Children and Schools

Evidence that people learn constantly from what they see others do, and from what they are helped to do for themselves, is everywhere around us, except where it is obscured by the miserable technology of modern education. Out of school, we learn to talk and to comport ourselves the way we do, we learn about the world as we know it in all its complexity and detail, without the need for fragmented instruction and the perpetual harassment of tests and grades. But in schools and colleges, students are not taught in the way in which they naturally learn. Their "instruction" insults their natural intelligence. Teachers are required to be agents of unseen authorities who determine what teachers and students must do—and who design and impose the tests to ensure that the misguided centralized will is obeyed. Students are plagued with drills, grades, and tests. Children and older students have few opportunities to learn what they are supposed to learn in school, in any subject—unless they are lucky in the teachers they get. Instead, students are taught a good deal that is false and unproductive about themselves, about what they are expected to learn, and about learning itself. Teachers and parents must act to reverse this disastrous trend.

It should be impossible to keep students *out* of schools. Learning is a basic human activity and need. A school that is boring and mind-deadening should be a contradiction in terms.

But the r-bbit of ritualistic drills and tests has driven most possibilities of meaningful apprenticeships out of classrooms. Teachers have lost the opportunity to be teachers, and students of all ages, especially children, learn that learning is difficult, pointless, and dull. Apathy, cynicism, and resentment pervade educational systems. And the situation is getting worse. New crises are being created as the omniscient outsiders expand their influence.

Creating an Educational Crisis

New York State is about to experience an epidemic of previously unknown intellectual disabilities among children. The problem is largely imaginary, but decisions have already been made about how many children will be afflicted, and even who these children will be.

I first heard about the impending disabilities early in 1984 in a telephone call from a professor on the education faculty of a university in New York City. He thought I might be interested in a major educational endeavor in the state. The office of the New York State Commissioner of Education was launching a coordinated attack on the problem of critical thinking.

I asked whether the new direction meant that the literacy problem, which was the center of attention ten years ago, had been solved. "Priorities have been reordered," the professor told me. "Funds have been reallocated. The focus has shifted to teaching critical thinking skills."

I asked what evidence there was that children lacked ability to think critically and that deficiencies could be remedied by specific instruction at school. Children are perfectly capable of thinking—in thinking environments. How exactly was critical thinking being defined? My caller had no patience with these questions. This wasn't the time for theoretical speculation. The commissioner's office wanted action. "We have to find a test and a program as soon as possible."

I had been told much the same thing in Canada a few months earlier, when I had a call from a friend in the provincial ministry of education in British Columbia. It had been decided that children's "listening skills" required urgent attention but none of the ministry experts knew exactly what listening skills were. And they did not have the resources to find out. They needed a test and a program, so they could get on with their jobs.

Tests are always required when administrations decide to take charge of some aspect of education. There can be no educational problems without tests. And instructional programs are required to help children take the tests. The programs and tests are expected to ensure "quality education" and to solve educational problems. Instead, the programs and tests are blind instruments of external control that deprive children of the opportunities for learning and teachers of the possibilities of teaching. The control creates the crises.

I told the New York professor that no one knew enough about critical thinking to construct a test to reveal what skills children might lack or to construct a program that might teach those skills.

"We can't wait," he said. "We've got to get started. Any test will be better than none." The professor was talking about a test that would label thousands of children for life as intellectually disabled. There is no shortage of tests of that nature, on every conceivable topic. If a test doesn't exist, there are specialists who will quickly construct one, on any subject an administrator cares to propose.

I asked if the professor would like a test that every child could pass. Easy tests are popular in school districts that want to demonstrate success.

"Don't be ridiculous. What's the good of a test like that? We'd have nothing to do."

What about a test that every child would fail? Difficult tests are in demand among school districts hoping to demonstrate a need for supplementary grants. Again I was told not to be absurd. "We need a test that will discriminate," the professor said. Discriminate—that was his word.

So I asked what proportion of children would be an appropriate number to fail.

And the professor told me: Twenty-seven percent.

Before the end of the 1980s, if this plan goes through, twenty-seven percent of New York State children who take the test will be diagnosed as deficient in essential critical thinking skills. New York City and four other cities have already formed a consortium to engage in pilot studies of possible programs and tests. If too many children pass the test, or if too many fail, the criteria for passing will be revised.

Not only have officials decided exactly how many children will be afflicted by new and exotic intellectual deficiencies, they know precisely who those children will be. If too many children who do well on other tests start to fail the critical thinking test, then the test will be changed. To be "valid," the test will have to fail those children who fail the other tests, the children already stigmatized as educationally deprived and disadvantaged.

Ingenious explanations will then be found to explain why these children fail the thinking tests and why they do not profit from the instructional programs that are supposed to help all children to acquire the thinking skills to pass the tests. Areas of "high-risk" children's brains will be discovered that are malfunctioning. The children will be found to come from homes where critical thinking or listening is not practiced. The defect will be found to run in families and to affect particular ethnic and economic groups. Experts will explain that the children have inherited a genetic deficiency or suffered an irreversible birth defect that makes normal mental activities impossible for them. Something will be wrong with their brains. Special treatment will be prescribed, expectations will be lowered, and the children will be segregated into groups where they can make even less sense of what is done to them in the name of education. And it is all unnecessary—a wasteful and ignorant misuse of children's minds.

The destructive mania for imposing detailed external control through tests and programs on the classroom activities of teachers and students is widespread and growing, with older students as well as with young children, all the way from kindergarten to graduate school. Education has become bureaucratized, and intelligence is being strangled, one inexorable blank and test item at a time.

Laying the Blame

Often when I talk with teachers about the myth that "quality-controlled education" can be achieved through the reduction of instruction to systematic nonsense, they tell me that I should address my remarks to the principals of their schools. But when I discuss the same matters with principals, they say I should talk to teachers. I have tried working with principals and teachers together, only to be told that parents insist on grades and the knowledge of how well their children are keeping up with the rest of the class. I am also advised to impress the message upon superintendents and other senior administrators, but they in their turn refer me back to teachers and principals. School personnel at all levels blame publishers and the professors of education who are supposed to be responsible for teacher preparation. But publishers retort that they only sell what schools are anxious to buy, and college instructors say they are training teachers for schools as they exist today.

I do not think that any of these conflicting responses can be dismissed simply as passing the buck. Rather they reflect an entire system that is in the grip of myths about how individuals learn and how the delusions of omniscient outsiders can ensure learning. No one person or category of person is responsible for the current condition of education, not even the politicians. Most of the people involved in education, from the classroom level to the national cabinet office, would like to do well by students. They may feel that their jobs allow them little freedom to do what they think might be best for students; and they may often be ignorant. Changing a few people will not change the face of education. What is needed is more education; not so much *by* educators as *for* them. Everyone who influences educational policies and everyone who implements these policies must learn about learning, and about the r-bbit and its delusions of teaching through programs and tests.

In June 1984, a panel appointed by the National Education Association, which has a membership of nearly 2 million teachers, reported to the association's representative assembly in Minneapolis that the nation's schools would have to be totally restructured if education was to improve. The panel, which consisted of teachers, not surprisingly called for higher salaries for teachers. It also called for a rigorous evaluation of teachers and the better training of teachers. The panel wanted teachers to do a better job. But it added that this better job could not be done unless teachers rather than centralized school districts made the decisions that affect instruction.

Victor Weisskopf, emeritus professor of physics at M.I.T., has said "It will take a long time before the whole governmental structure changes its attitude towards education. But much can be done. . . . We can have interchanges between schools and industry, schools and colleges. High school teachers should be able to spend some time in universities and in industrial laboratories. This is also important for their social status. . . ." Weisskopf talks of the importance of teachers having more time to spend together, to discuss among themselves better ways of teaching. "But one thing is important," he adds. "The control of all these activities should be in teachers' hands. Teachers themselves must and will, if they are given the opportunity, take part in planning these activities or it will again be a case of pressing things into their brains instead of bringing things into being on their own initiative."

The Transformation of Teachers

There are three stages in the transformation of teachers from classroom managers to effective leaders in the learning situations that I have metaphorically called clubs. The first is for teachers to learn to distinguish between the r-bbit and worthwhile learning activities, the second is to eradicate the r-bbit as much as possible, and the third is for teachers to protect themselves and their students against the nonsense that remains.

(1) Learning to Tell the Difference

For many teachers, programs and tests have become such a part of classroom life that they cannot imagine teaching without them. Rote learning, question answering, and fill-in-the-blank exercises take up so much of the day in school that they are accepted, in most teachers' minds, as being worthwhile. More than one teacher has said to me, "Why would we be required to do these things if they don't help students learn?"—as if the very presence of programs and tests is a guarantee that they work.

Such teachers are exhibiting what psychologists refer to as "the reduction of cognitive dissonance." If we think or behave in ways that are logically incompatible or mutually exclusive, then we persuade ourselves of something else to eliminate the dissonance in our minds. If, for example, we aspire to better health yet eat primarily junk food, we may convince ourselves that an occasional square meal counteracts the poor nutrition and that in any case a more sensible diet would be so stressful that our indulgence is actually better for us. Teachers dedicated to helping students learn persuade themselves that the programs and tests they use cannot be harmful and can actually help students learn. If there were no programs, how *would* students learn?

Once, when I was trying to acquaint some teachers in North Carolina with the dangers of prepackaged instructional materials, I pointed out that some of the programs now being developed are labeled "teacher-proof" because they are deliberately designed to make it impossible for teachers to tamper with them. One of the teachers came to me afterward and asked where the teacher-proof materials could be obtained; they were just what she needed in her own classroom.

One consequence of this irrational faith in educational technology is that teachers give programs the credit when students learn, and blame students and themselves when programs fail. The meaningful club-type activities that so many teachers engage in when they can find the time—when there is no "work" left to be done —are dismissed as "enrichment" or as "rewards" rather than being recognized as the basis of learning. Worthless time-wasting worksheets get the credit that is due to teachers and students. Teachers say to children, "Get on with the worksheets for the next half an hour, and then I'll read a story to you." At the end of the year the children can read, and the teacher thinks the worksheets were marvelous. The demands of programmatic instruction become the yardsticks of progress. Anything that cannot be marked and graded becomes incidental or a distraction.

Teachers must learn to tell the difference. They must learn that when students do well it is despite programmatic instruction, not because of it, and that when students are confused or "falling behind" they need less programmatic instruction, not more of it. Meaningful experience is the key to all learning; boredom and bewilderment are urgent signals that the teacher should turn to something else more relevant.

Teachers can do each other inestimable damage. The work of one enlightened teacher at an Oregon school was demolished in 1983 by a substitute teacher who put the students back to working on the set drills—and then reported the original teacher to the school board for not following prescribed procedures. The original teacher eventually won her case, but only after a painful public hearing into her competence. Another teacher at the school told me, "It's scary for teachers to work without workbooks."

Teachers can win, to some extent at least. In Seattle in 1984 a new assistant superintendent brought in a "Prescriptive Reading Inventory," which teachers objected was permeated with tests of "basic reading skills." Teachers complained that they were supposed to take students from one test to another and that no one would have any time for reading in the classroom. They boycotted the test and were successful. But when the teachers told me of the case the following year, they said they were still overworked, isolated, and could be moved around without notice. They were expected to be able to teach anything, even totally new subjects, with no time to prepare. None of this was a consideration for an administrator who believed that teaching was a matter of getting the appropriate programs and tests from a storeroom shelf.

There is a heavy responsibility on faculty in colleges of education to master sound contemporary educational theory and to question conventional practices. They must instill confidence in student teachers, based on knowledge and experience, so that they can evaluate the appropriateness of the programs and techniques urged upon them and resist the blandishments of salespersons who are frequent visitors to schools.

Since teachers themselves are rarely taught to distinguish programmatic instruction from meaningful learning, how can they learn to tell the difference, especially since so many programs are grandiosely promoted and insidiously packaged to look like genuine learning opportunities? The distinction is not, in fact, hard to make; there are inevitable giveaways. The most obvious clues are the grade or score that must always be given, the blanks that must be filled with letters or words, and the batteries of questions with multiple-choice answers. Programmatic instruction always has right and wrong answers; there is always a means of numerical evaluation so that scores can be assigned, "progress" assessed, and comparisons made. My first essential criterion for club activities was the absence of grades, and any activity imposed upon or recommended to teachers and students that includes a scoring procedure can be identified immediately as programmatic. There are other clues: repetitive drills, questions where teachers themselves have to be told the answers, sequenced activities, "loops" whereby students who do not succeed have to start over again, and behaviors that people in their right minds would never want to engage in out of school. The materials themselves may be disguised as meaningful activities, certainly as "fun," in their labeling and promotion and in the way their procedures are dressed up as games and simulations. But they will inevitably be accompanied by the pervasive tests and scores.

(2) Changing What Can Be Changed

Teachers must change themselves and change others. Changing themselves is not always the easiest thing to do. Whatever a teacher is like on arrival at a school, at the end of the year that teacher is probably teaching like the teacher in the next classroom. There is enormous inertia in educational institutions, not all of it imposed from outside the classroom. The solution is for teachers to try to achieve change together. Teachers need mutual support, even if they cannot work together in the same classroom.

The aim must be to abolish programmatic routines from the classroom or to confine them to as small a part of the day as possible, to allow room for club enterprises that make meaningful use of written language, arithmetic, science, and whatever else students are supposed to be learning. The enterprises should not be expected to fit neatly into the categories of the curriculum; in fact anything that looks too obviously like a conventional classroom activity in "reading," "writing," or "arithmetic" is likely to have a programmatic effect. The enterprise—whether it is writing the menu for the school cafeteria or organizing the logistics and finances of a school lunch service—becomes a wedge to open a crack in the monolithic mass of programmatic instruction. Teachers must first demonstrate to themselves that the world will not fall apart if they devote time to ungraded activities that do not follow a predetermined sequence. They must learn that students will become neither riotous nor apathetic if control is relaxed.

Programs are used primarily for control. When teachers rely on programs, it is because they do not trust students to learn. Teachers may be afraid that if they do not teach students facts or skills directly related to items on the examination that students must take at the end of the year, the students will not do well on the examination. But by focusing on items in the examination, teachers deprive students of the best opportunities to learn what the examination is supposed to test. Meaningful involvement in the activity, on the other hand, promotes competent and confident examination performance. Teachers must learn to trust students to learn, which they can best do by working with students in a more open manner and by experiencing the results. Teachers must educate themselves with the collaboration of the students in their classes. Teachers and students can learn together that the most efficient way to learn is through collaborative participation in meaningful activities, even if at the beginning only a small part of the day can be allocated to those meaningful activities.

Teachers must also educate people outside their classrooms, starting with the teachers of neighboring classrooms and the administration of the school. Once again the best way to educate is through demonstration. If there is one thing that persuades teachers and administrators, it is *success.* Colleagues and principals who resist divergence from "traditional" ways of doing things, even when those ways have themselves been found lacking, are afraid that matters will get worse, and even out of control, if something radically new is tried. What reassures them is direct experience of something that is manageable and that achieves results.

Teachers should not rely on outsiders to change the minds of reluctant or disbelieving colleagues, principals, parents, politicians, or anyone else. What is needed is *education,* and it is teachers themselves who must be the educators. Teachers are—or should be —the experts. They should not expect others to be better qualified and more authoritative in changing the teaching world for them. Even if others live up to this heavy expectation, which I think is improbable, it will serve only to underline how ineffectual teachers can be.

It is more important for many teachers to educate outside the classroom than within. The learning of their students could go a long way to taking care of itself if teachers could deflect the influences converging upon the classroom from outside. Teachers must teach the rest of the world that they know best, at least as far as classroom *practice* is concerned. Society should tell teachers what they are to teach, but not how. What, otherwise, is the point of having teachers? School boards should specify what goes into the curriculum, but not the details of how it should be taught. They should not expect teachers to have lesson plans laid out weeks or even months ahead to show that they are following the program systematically, regardless of where their students might happen to be. (Some teachers are even *proud* of how well they plan their classroom activities in this straitjacketed way, their minds already made up about what exactly will occupy their students' attention.)

Outside authorities impose detailed programs upon teachers because they do not trust teachers to teach. If programs were taken away from teachers, I am often told, chaos would result. If this is true, then it is the programs that are responsible. Programs are destroying teachers.

Teachers are required to teach by program because they are not trusted to make teaching decisions themselves. In other words, the issue is political. And this means that the solution must be political. Teachers will have to make themselves heard politically if they are to drive the bureaucratic interference from their class-rooms and regain control themselves. They must refuse to be told how to teach by outsiders, reject the tests and programs, and force administrators to change their purchasing policies for instructional materials. An enormous diversity of materials is available that could improve the learning climate of classrooms—provided the choice is made by teachers to suit their own needs and aims rather than imposed upon them months and even years in advance. The money saved could be much better spent on teacher training and smaller classes.

Members of other professions do not expect outsiders to protect them from harassment, even by governmental authorities. If members of the public wrote letters to newspapers or passed restrictive laws demanding that engineers build bridges in a standard way, or that surgeons perform operations in a particular manner, the engineers and surgeons would not wait for someone not in their profession to rescue them from the intrusion. It is because their own members would respond immediately themselves that these professions are largely free of the kind of ignorant interference—at least as far as their general procedures are concerned—to which teachers are subject.

Teachers must be confident in their knowledge of how students learn and of how best to teach them if they are to engage in the necessary educational and political activity to regain autonomy in their own classrooms. They must be ready to act by themselves if need be—but they will be far more successful if they have the collaboration of parents, and of students too.

(3) Being Honest With Students

Changing the world will not be easy for many teachers, nor will it happen rapidly. Teachers should introduce meaningful activities into schools whenever possible, but not everyone will change at once. In most schools a large part of the day will still be dominated by programmatic activities. How can teachers who strive to change protect their students from the r-bbits that remain? The answer is by taking students into their confidence.

It is remarkable how little time is spent at school discussing school, the rationale for its curriculum, or learning. The routines and rituals of school are taken for granted, the way that fish must assume an entire universe composed of water. Perhaps most students, even the very youngest, think that everything in school must be important for learning because most teachers think the same thing.

Yet there is nothing that I have talked about in this book that I have not talked about with school children, even in the primary grades. Children understand ritual, and can empathize with teachers who do certain things "because they are told to." Discussions of this kind can do a great deal to help young children come to terms with the confusions they can encounter in school. I have held quite academic conversations with groups of six-year-olds on how they learned to talk and the circumstances that help and hinder learning to read. I have talked with high school students on topics that I considered too technical for this book, on differences between long-term memory and short-term memory or on the precise manner in which the eyes move as we read. The students grasped the technicalities without difficulty and spontaneously related them to their own learning difficulties.

Teachers may not be able to shield their students completely from programs and tests, but they can help students to know programs and tests for what they are, to recognize why they are imposed, and to cope with them as effectively as possible. This was all I could do for many of my graduate students at the university, whose work I had to grade (the students themselves would not have allowed me to do otherwise) even though I lectured against grading. So collaboratively we tried to make graded assignments only a small part of the work we did together, discussed reasons why grading might be required despite the damage it can do, and tried not to let the grading interfere with learning or dominate the direction of the course.

A Nova Scotia teacher told me of a novel strategy with first-grade children, which I have passed on to other teachers. If a teacher feels there is no alternative to requiring a child to spend half an hour on a set of r-bbity worksheets, putting a ring around the duck facing the wrong way, and so forth, the child should be given the reason. "Do you know why I want you to do this? It's to keep you quiet. I could tip a jar of buttons over the table, ask you to sort out the different colors, and mix them all up again when you've done. I just want to keep you out of my hair for a while." Children have no problem with this kind of request. People tell them to keep quiet all the time out of school. They understand why. The trouble arises when they are given a nonsensical activity in the classroom to keep them quiet and told that it is reading, writing, or some other critical academic subject. They are told that the activity is important and that their performance reflects whether they are smart or stupid.

When teachers are honest with their students, teachers and students become allies rather than antagonists. They understand each other better. They learn together. And among informed students, teachers can find some of the support and much of the confidence they need to try to change the world of education.

I have one other set of suggestions for teachers, and that is that they educate parents, be honest with parents, and collaborate with parents.

The Right of Parents to Be Involved

There is one simple, basic, and essential rule for parents who want to protect their children from the inanities of drills, grades, and tests. The rule is: *Get into your children's classrooms.* There is no other way for parents to find out what is happening or to influence what is happening. A fifteen-minute interview with a teacher is not enough. An occasional telephone conversation is not enough. An earnest discussion in the principal's office or the staff lounge is not enough. Parents have to see the threat for themselves, and they must become involved.

To many parents, their child's classroom is as remote as the oval office of the White House. The classroom is the teacher's sanctum, even though the child spends five hours a day there. If parents are permitted to penetrate into the chamber of mysteries, it is likely to be when no children are present (on the evening of the parent-teacher conferences, for example) or when something unusual is taking place (like the display of children and their work on visitors' days).

But parents must know what is going on. A perfunctory rundown of a child's "strengths" and "weaknesses" on an evening when the teacher is reporting to a dozen parents or more tells nothing about what is happening in the classroom. A guided tour through a selected workbook or a timetable of the week's activities says nothing about what a child is learning. Homework and examples of schoolwork brought home provide clues to what a teacher thinks is important, but they say nothing of the environment in the classroom. Parents *must* discover how the school looks to their children, and the only way they can do so is by entering the classroom when the teacher is teaching.

Children are rarely distracted for more than a few moments by visitors, especially when they are accustomed to them. Children engaged in engrossing activities with the teacher and each other pay no more attention to a visitor than they would if they were watching a favorite program on television at home. If they are more interested in a visitor than in what is going on in the classroom, something is said about the classroom. In any case, an interlude with an interesting visitor may be a far more profitable occupation and less disruptive to the rest of the class, than having nothing to engage the attention.

Parents are not always welcomed in schools, especially if they want to cross the line that takes them into the "learning areas." David Winkler, headmaster of Grove Junior School in Birmingham, England, cites a primary school colleague who would announce at parents meetings twenty years ago that all he asked was that they "should bring 'it' to school clean and well-dressed. I shall do the rest." The situation is not much different today, according to Winkler, who says parents are often welcomed if they make appointments with the secretary, subtly underlining that they have no role in the institution.

Many teachers will object to the presence of parents, of course. Some will be reluctant because they lack confidence in what they are doing; it is usually not impossible to change their minds with reassurances about the nature of the parents' desire to observe and collaborate rather than to intrude. A few teachers may resent any possibility of interference because of a conviction that they could not be wrong—an attitude that does not automatically deprive parents of their right to sample what is happening to their children in the name of education. Generally, the likelihood that casual visitors will be discouraged from entering classrooms will be directly proportionate to the rigidity of the structure in the classroom. *Anything* is a distraction when children are slogging their way through a routine of programs and tests. R-bbits cannot tolerate competition for attention.

Parents should nonetheless strive to get into the classroom, not as antagonists but as collaborators, or at least as interested observers. It is the right and the responsibility of parents to find out what is happening to their children. Parents should trust teachers—but only if they know what the teachers are doing.

What Parents Should Look For

Parents must strive to put themselves in their children's place. It is not necessary to disturb the class in order to do this; it is enough to play the role of an additional student. If the children are working from particular books or with particular worksheets, arrange for the books and worksheets to be available to you. Do the work that is assigned to the children. Engage in the activities that are opened to them. Then ask yourself some questions.

(1) What exactly are the students doing? Does it make sense? Don't look at the title of the book or the printed heading on the worksheet—the fact that an activity is labeled "reading," "comprehension," or "social studies" does not entail that this is what it means to the student doing it. If the activity is underlining all the adjectives in a passage of text or doing twenty consecutive multiplication problems, ask what the exercise tells the student. Remember that practice in itself does not guarantee learning. Repeated error simply practices error. Repeated failure teaches despair.

Don't ask what the drill is supposed to help the student to learn; ask simply what the student is *doing*. What kind of activity is the student engaged in?

(2) Why are the students doing what they are doing? Are they doing it because the teacher insists, because they have no alternative? Are they engaging in the activity voluntarily? Do they regard it as a routine and boring necessity? Are they doing it for scores and grades or simply to accommodate the teacher? Some students will say they like repetitive activities, and even tests, especially if they "do well" and receive praise for their performance. Could students ever be persuaded to engage in such activities outside school? What would be the point of doing so? Why is the teacher asking them to engage in the activity? Is it because it is obviously worthwhile and meaningful, to keep them quiet, or because it is the next item on the curriculum or the lesson plan? Is everyone concerned only with the "right answer"?

(3) What happens to students who aren't doing very well? Mind-deadening and nonsensical activities are damaging enough for students who do well; they learn that the activity is a boring waste of time. But for students who have difficulty "achieving" on any non-sensical activity, the consequence can be disastrous. Students can be confronted all day with activities that are repetitively pointless— and these activities are the ones most likely to be the causes of failure. Does the teacher—or do other students—come to the aid of students having difficulty? Or is failure simply the occasion for such students to be even further reminded that an activity is difficult, punishing, and pointless?

(4) What are the students' relationships with each other? Do they collaborate or are they competitive? Do they cooperate with each other only to obstruct or antagonize the teacher, or to help each other to accomplish what the teacher is trying to achieve? Is the classroom a *community?*

(5) What are the students' relationships with the teacher? Do they regard the teacher as a collaborator or as someone to be mollified?

Do they believe the teacher *learns?* Do they willingly go to the teacher for help (and if so, is that because the teacher is the only one with an answer sheet)? Do the students know why the teacher requires them to engage in their classroom activities? Note, occasionally, how teachers *achieve* their effects: Are they authoritarian, seductive, cajoling, wheedling, or collegial or companionable? I have heard many teachers over the years saying proudly that their students love them and would do anything for them. But students should want to engage in an activity for the sake of the activity, not to please, placate, or pamper the teacher.

(6) How does the teacher decide what to do? Does the teacher "follow the book," adhering closely to a lesson plan or proceeding unswervingly through a published sequence of activities? Or does the teacher respond sensitively to the students, clarifying matters for those who are confused and finding something else for those who are stymied, despairing, or just plain bored? Does the teacher engage in activities in front of the students for his or her own sake —reading a newspaper, writing a personal letter, or balancing a checkbook? Parents can not always be relied upon for these demonstrations, and in any case, teachers must show that school activities are sense, not nonsense.

(7) What is the relationship of teacher and students to the rest of the school? Is the principal a disembodied presence—an unpredictable interruption over the public address system—or a frequent visitor? Does everything stop when the principal walks in? Do students visit the assistant principal only for punishment? Do students know the teachers and the students in other classes? Do they engage in collaborative enterprises?

(8) What is the general atmosphere of the school? Are the halls generally cheerless and deserted? Is the entrance reminiscent of the main gate of a prohibited area? Are the office staff welcoming or forbidding, and do they ever participate in activities with students? Are *students* tolerated in public domains? Is the library a welcoming retreat, where students can find adults making use of the books and other materials? Does the school look like the kind of place where

anyone might engage in an interesting activity? Does the school
play an active role in the life of the community (so that, for example, students and the elderly can find time to talk)?

Perfection should not be expected. Nothing is ideal. I am
talking of possibilities and attitudes, whether a "work" or a "learning" atmosphere prevails. Children do not enter school with a
checklist on which they evaluate good points and bad, and parents
should try to see the school through the eyes of children, not of
school inspectors. If everything has to be boiled down to one
question, it should be whether the students are likely to engage
voluntarily outside the school in the activities they have been engaged in inside. A more detailed checklist is provided at the conclusion of this chapter.

There is a particular temptation for parents to contrast their
children's teachers and classroom activities with their own experiences as schoolchildren. But there were no good old days in education. The relics of our own past are always romanticized, and we
are always likely to give undue importance to what we remember
best. Learning is generally inconspicuous, and any occasion when
we can particularly recall striving to learn is probably an occasion
when very little learning took place at all.

Talking With the Teacher

The next step, after the classroom visits, is a conversation with
the teacher. The aim should be for parents to understand what the
teacher is trying to do and to communicate their own observations
and reactions. And there is no reason why children should not be
participants in these discussions. The conversation should not be
confrontational.

The language of teachers has to be watched. Parents should be
aware that words like "needs," "progress," "skills," "disabilities,"
and "weaknesses" are used in rather special ways in school. Students are frequently said to *need* improvement or development, as
in, for example, "Johnny needs to pay more attention to the semico-

lon." Teachers use "needs" the way the word is used in the sentence "John needs to pay his income tax" rather than the way it is used in "John needs an income." The need, disability, weakness, or progress relates to the demands of a system, not to anything intrinsically lacking in the individual. Ann Adams, of the Duke University reading center, has recommended that instead of discussing additional skills practice, parents should ask how many library books their child has read, how much creative writing the child has done, and what knowledge of current events the child has acquired from newspapers.

The topics of discussion between teacher and parent should not be "the child" and all of his or her supposed virtues and failings according to a system of arbitrary standards and procedures, but the climate of the classroom, what in general the teacher is trying to achieve, and why, and how the teacher is trying to achieve it.

When conditions are favorable, this is the point at which parents and teachers could become allies, working together to consolidate what each is trying to achieve. Clublike activities and enterprises should be a bridge between school and home, not in the form of homework but because people normally engage in meaningful enterprises out of school. Parents who wish to protect their children should talk about school with them, in the way I recommend teachers to talk to students, and should ensure that programmatic activities do not insinuate themselves into the home. Just as teachers should not "teach to the test" in school, so parents should not engage children in drills at home in the belief that this will facilitate "success" at school. Parents must reject the plethora of "instructional" games and other materials in the bookstores—and even the supermarkets—designed to cash in on parental guilt or anxieties. Parents who are able to become involved in school should take care they are not simply used as auxiliary classroom managers to distribute, collect, and occasionally correct worksheets. They should be participants in worthwhile activities in which teachers are trying to engage students.

When parents and teachers are in accord about changes they believe desirable in a school, then they can work together, educationally and politically, to try to bring the changes about. A delegation of parents and teachers to a principal or a politician is much more effective than either party trying to make a point alone.

Sometimes, however, parents will have to try to make their points alone because they cannot find out what teachers are actually doing or because they disagree with what they are doing. The next step should be to go to the principal.

To the Principal, and Beyond

The principal is the most influential person in a school. Persuade a principal, and you have probably gone a long way toward persuading many of the teachers. The principal frequently is also the most sensitive person in a school. Principals are inclined to be more responsive to external pressures and to individual suggestions than many teachers. And persistent telephone calls are likely to have more effect on a principal than on an unforthcoming teacher, even when the principal is protected by a secretary. Principals are concerned with public relations.

Whatever the circumstances, parents—like teachers—must be prepared to act politically if they want to bring about such major changes as developing the autonomy of the teacher in the classroom or reducing the pernicious influences of programs and tests. Parents should be alert to public pronouncements that there is a new campaign to achieve "excellence" or "quality in education" in their schools. Such campaigns usually mean nothing more than additional pressure on teachers and students, the opposite of improving their learning conditions. Parent-teacher associations must lobby in state departments of education and with state and federal legislators against the bureaucratic stranglehold on life in classrooms. Representatives, mayors, and governors must be made aware that parents and teachers know what is going on and that they resent it. Every letter or editorial in a newspaper calling for further control of teachers and teaching must have a response. If the trend is to be resisted and reversed, a total collaborative effort will be required from parents, teachers, and school administrators alike.

Meeting the Objections

Objections are inevitable. Proponents of programs and tests, and of the status quo, predict calamities ranging from unfathomable ignorance to educational chaos when confronted with arguments of the kind I have presented. If this book is to be useful as ammunition against the r-bbit, it may be helpful to exchange a few practice shots in advance.

The changes won't work; they'll lead to anarchy in the classroom.

It is a common superstition that if rigid instructional procedures are taken out of the classroom, chaos will result. This is just not true. Students who are interested and involved in what they are doing are always more tractable. It is the students who are constantly engaged in mindless activities who become rebellious and vengeful. There is no suggestion that teachers should do nothing. Nor are "permissiveness" and "sloppy classrooms" proposed. The argument is simply that teachers must take charge of education, organizing meaningful learning opportunities for students instead of leaving them in the hands of unseen and unresponsive programmers.

Teachers don't have the time to give all students individual attention.

There is no suggestion that students must be given more individual attention. When students are primarily dealing with nonsense, there is little they can do to help themselves or to help each other. When students are engaged in meaningful club-type enterprises, it is much easier for them to get on by themselves, even the youngest ones, and it is much less demanding on the teachers. The assumption that students will not learn unless they are goaded and rewarded by programmatic instruction underrates their brains and libels teachers.

Don't students have to learn basic skills?

The term "basic skills," as it is used in education, is a misnomer. Basic skills are regarded as essential components of what learners need to know if ever they are to become experts. In practice the situation is the opposite. Take spelling and punctuation, for example. Until one is a writer, spelling and punctuation are meaningless activities and extremely difficult to learn. It is only when writing makes sense, when it is done for a purpose, that spelling and punctuation are needed and learned. In other words, children must first join the appropriate club in order to learn; "basic skills" training delays all children's entry into the appropriate club and keeps many of them out.

The word "skills" should always be closely watched. In the mouths of many people it is synonymous with "drills," and what they are talking about is heavy doses of rote learning.

People who oppose continual testing have no standards.

Of course they do. It is typical educational obfuscation to suggest that anyone who doesn't adhere to programs and tests doesn't care how much students learn. My concern is that students should learn much more than they do. It is a disgrace that so many students "graduate" from high school with scarcely any ability to read or to write, and with even less interest in doing either. Programmatic instruction trivializes what it teaches and lowers its aims in order to be able to claim that it teaches anything.

Students learn at their own pace with programmatic instruction.

"Learning at their own pace" is a misleading slogan, like "individualized instruction." Students are not learning at their own pace when they are required to proceed as fast as they can along a predetermined path that is essentially meaningless to them—and when a slow pace is automatically rewarded with the invidious discrimination of a low grade. "Individualized instruction," when applied to programmatic instruction, is a euphemism for being forced to spend more time on activities that are not understood. The two terms are empty justifications for unnecessary and unproductive activities. Neither term is in common use outside schools, where it is taken for granted that different people will learn different things at different rates, and that everyone helps everyone else.

How can teachers tell that students are learning without grades and tests?

A teacher who cannot tell without a test whether a student is learning should not be in the classroom. Faces reveal when students are not learning. They are learning unless they are bored or confused, and boredom and confusion leave unmistakable traces. It is not always possible to tell whether a student is learning a particular thing at a particular time, but that should not be a significant consideration for anyone who is not a paranoid bureaucrat. Most parents should be able to tell whether a child has learned anything about reading, writing, or arithmetic over a period of a month just by seeing how well the child reads, writes, or calculates compared with the previous month. If parents cannot do this, then teachers should be able to show them how. A problem only arises when someone wants to put *numbers* on learning, to compare how much is learned this week with last week, which makes about as much sense as trying to distinguish apples from oranges by weighing their colors. Parents who insist upon test scores to know "how well" their child is doing in class must be educated by teachers or other parents that the marks are unnecessary and misleading.

Grading is not required to demonstrate that something is well done. If I write a story or paint a picture, if I repair a flat tire or put a shelf up in the kitchen, I may want to know if I have done it adequately or well. I may seek the opinion of others—but not in the form of a grade. It doesn't help me to know that the shelf I have put up in the kitchen ranks seven on a scale of ten or a B-plus. Scores and grades are only needed (outside of competitive sports) for bureaucratic record-keeping or when there is no functional way for evaluating something.

Grades and tests are supposed to be "objective," free of the bias or variability to which the "subjective" evaluations of people are susceptible. But this objectivity is bought at a price. Many subtleties that people can take into account in their evaluations, like effort and attitude, are ignored by tests. Tests are more appropriate for superficial indications than for general impressions. Tests do not know students the way teachers do. And the acknowledged variability of people can be a safeguard. If teachers make a mistake in an evaluation, there can always be an appeal. There is no appeal against tests, and their judgments are rarely challenged.

This is a competitive world, so students should get used to grades and tests.

Whether the world is always competitive, and ought to be, is debatable. So is the question of whether school is a consequence of societal competition or a cause of it. But it is false to suggest that students learn more easily when they are anxious, aggressive, or under stress. If we want to teach students to compete, it should be a separate subject, justified in its own right, not part of everything that students are expected to learn. Examinations may occasionally be desirable or unavoidable, as a part of college or professional entry requirements, for example, or as a ritual of "graduation." But these examinations are not the same as constant tests imposed for bureaucratic purposes to monitor "learning" or to ensure that teachers are following the designated pathway through a predetermined program of instruction.

It has been interesting to observe the outraged response of teachers in Texas and other states recently to find themselves subjected to "competency" tests in reading, writing, and simple arithmetic. They rightly feel their self-esteem is challenged by the kind of tests their students must constantly face. Since teachers have been trained to teach activities that they are not expected to practice themselves, it is not suprising that thousands are unable to pass the tests. The teachers themselves are products and victims of the programmatic instruction they are expected to impose on their students.

Isn't there any place for drills? What about learning mathematical formulas and the multiplication tables, or historical dates and irregular verbs?

People are drilled in the services, but that is for unquestioning obedience. People often drill for aspects of physical activities, from playing the piano to athletics, but that is for muscular strength and coordination. There are no muscles in the brain. Learning by rote is the hardest and most pointless way to learn. Mathematical formulas are quickly forgotten when they are crammed in order to pass a test, and they are useless unless embedded in understanding. They are like telephone numbers—we easily remember the ones we use regularly and rapidly forget the rest. Students who use memorized formulas without understanding commit monumental mistakes without suspecting their errors. Students who *understand* math, on the other hand, learn important formulas much more easily; they can generate new formulas for themselves when required and usually know when they have made a mistake.

Most of us know multiplication tables because we make small calculations so frequently—and because the tables were memorized initially more as songs or chants rather than as facts (much the way most people recall how many days there are in each month by reciting "Thirty days hath September" rather than by recalling items from a memorized list). Similarly, committing historical dates to memory does not help us to understand history; understanding periods of history facilitates not only learning dates but also making sense of them. Few adults remember more than half a dozen historical dates before the present century, and those dates are often lodged in our minds for the most bizarre of reasons. (I seem destined never to forget that King Charles I of England was executed in 1649, for the sole reason that I once noticed that 16 was 4 squared and 49 was 7 squared.) Children have no problems learning irregular verbs in their first language—at least in the way their friends produce them. Frequent drills and tests usually fail to change the way they talk. Most people can remember only a few things drilled into them in school—like *amo, amas, amat.* Such shards of rote learning should never be used as justification for an unproductive instructional method.

Teachers are already free to decide what they want to do. They can close the classroom door and do what they like.

Pressures upon teachers easily permeate closed doors. The fact that students will be examined on specific items at the end of the year is a very strong impetus for teachers to feel they must concentrate upon those specific items, rather than engage more generally in the activities the examination is supposed to sample. And it takes a strong-willed teacher to ignore the expectations of the teacher in the next grade or a principal who insists that "work" be focused on what the tests will contain. Besides, the argument is not that any teacher should have to teach behind closed doors (which is not in itself a particularly desirable lesson for students to learn) but that it should be possible to learn with the doors open.

Students can't be left to decide what they will learn.

That is not the suggestion. Experienced people should decide not only what students should learn but how they will best learn it. Students should not be left adrift to learn whatever happens to cross their paths or whatever is determined by instructional technologists who cannot even see them. Experienced and sensitive teachers should be able to ensure that learning proceeds in all the areas that we want.

Shouldn't teachers be held accountable?

Of course they should. To give teachers control over how they teach is not to license them for any kind of arbitrary behavior. Society has an absolute right to assert that teachers should teach reading, writing, and whatever else—but not how they should teach these things. Instead of constantly testing students to monitor how *well* they read and write, it would make more sense to check on how *frequently* they engage in these activities or on what students think about them.

Students who leave school interested enough in the subjects they have been taught to engage independently in activities related to those subjects always have a chance of learning more. But there is no hope for students, no matter how well they have "achieved," who graduate thinking that all school activities are a bore. If students were polled on how often they engage in activities that society thinks they should learn, the direction in which change should be made would be obvious. A student who does not read very much, or who reads only a limited range of materials, needs more opportunities to read not more instruction.

Teachers aren't competent enough to teach without programs and tests.

If that is the case, it is programs and tests that are largely to blame. And if teachers are inadequate, the solution is better teachers, not more programs. Recognition that mechanical or electronic drills and tests can never take the place of people must be the first step in the improvement of teachers.

Putting control of education into the hands of individual parents and teachers would be too great a risk.

I have more confidence in the ability of experienced teachers and responsible parents to educate each other and act in the general best interests of children than in distant administrators, technologists, and systems analysts. No one has ever voted for the remote control that central agencies have over education today, or for the trivial and ritualistic means by which that control is exercised. Children learn best and most intelligently under conditions of sense and collaboration. Doubtless, every aspect of child-rearing could be improved. The issue is always whether improvement should be brought about by education and personal example or by centralized control.

Many parents work and cannot get time off to visit classrooms.

Perhaps other parents could help; they should work in collaboration in any case. A "neighborhood watch" on what goes on in schools is much better than sporadic interventions by individual parents. But part of the political action by teachers and parents might be that working parents should be released to spend time in schools, the way they are for jury duty. The fact that parent involvement in schools is given such low priority is just another indication of the way education is being taken over by centralized bureaucratic authorities who think they know best.

Does it matter if students waste a little time in school? What else could they be doing?

The issue is not the waste of time, but the waste of *brains.* And the future depends on the brains of the generation currently in school. A dozen years or more of mindless classroom ritual will not produce individuals who can think for themselves, let alone think on behalf of the rest of the world. Many educators are rightly beginning to realize that it won't do to have children who don't think (even though most of these educators are still programmed to believe that children need to be taught how to think). But the problem is that students rarely have the opportunity to think and to learn in the ways for which their brains are superbly adapted. A climate of drills, tests, and grades suffocates the learning and thinking that is the birthright of every child.

No one today can predict what the future will be like—we are all too immersed in the problems of the present and their solutions. The challenges of the future will have to be met by the people who will live in it. The responsibility of the present generation of adults is to ensure that the brains of the future generation are not destroyed in today's classrooms.

A CHECKLIST FOR PARENTS

Your Child

Is your child interested in school?

> *Good Signs:* Your child is keen to get to school and sometimes to spend extra time there; uses library and school facilities independently; brings home books; telephones friends about school activities.
>
> *Bad Signs:* Your child is apprehensive about school; feigns reasons to avoid school; skips classes; "forgets" to do homework.

Does your child talk about school?

> *Good Signs:* Your child wants to involve you in school activities; is proud of class and school; makes positive comments about the teacher.
>
> *Bad Signs:* Your child talks only negatively of school or not at all; talks of "falling behind" or "keeping up."

What does your child bring home?

> *Good Signs:* Your child brings home materials that interest *you* —stories, maps, models, projects (including ungraded ones), newsletters, collaborative efforts—and homework that your child wants to do because it is interesting.
>
> *Bad Signs:* Your child brings home workbooks and duplicated worksheets with exercises that the teacher will mark right or wrong; repetitive activities; multiple choice exercises or tests.

What does your child like to do?

> *Good Signs:* Your child likes to read, write, figure, and plan; is interested in science and social affairs; plays productively, has a hobby, engages in imaginative pastimes, and hates to miss school; watches television selectively and critically.

Bad Signs: Your child indiscriminately watches television; is bored; doesn't read; gives indications of frustration—is rude, or commits acts of vandalism.

Your Child's Classroom

What kinds of materials are in the room?

Good Signs: The classroom is full of books (not all in class sets), magazines, models, specimens, maps and charts, art materials, musical equipment, games—for casual daily use and reflecting the interests of both the children and the teacher. There is an up-to-date notice board of messages, reminders, and community events.

Bad Signs: The classroom is bare of all materials except what the children happen to be working on at the time. There are unchanging wall displays; a predominance of workbooks and duplicated materials; a teacher's desk that displays only workbooks and class records.

Are there computer facilities?

Good Signs: The teacher understands and uses the technology creatively. Children help each other on the computer.

Bad Signs: Computers are used for drills. Computers are used only for "computer literacy" courses. Children's work is marked by computers.

Your Child's Teacher

Does the teacher encourage visitors in the classroom?

Good Sign: Parents and other visitors participate in the life of the classroom.

Bad Sign: The teacher has no time for visitors, or believes they disrupt the classroom.

How does the teacher talk to the children?

Good Signs: The teacher finds time to talk informally to children individually or in small groups. The teacher and children share interests.
Bad Sign: The teacher's conversation with children is mainly questions.

How does the teacher maintain "order" in the classroom?

Good Signs: There are always interesting activities for individuals and self-selected groups. Children are encouraged to help each other.
Bad Signs: Children are allocated to permanent groups. Groups have discriminatory labels (like "bluebirds" and "blackbirds"); have fixed amounts of work to do. Children can say "where they are" in their work.

How does the teacher talk to you?

Good Signs: The teacher wants to hear your observations about your child and the school; talks of children's achievements and interests; can talk intelligently about how children learn.
Bad Signs: The teacher refers continually to records; discusses whether your child is "keeping up" or "falling behind"; evaluates your child on the basis of test scores; says your child has "needs" or "problems" if your child is bored, anxious, or confused.

Your Child's School

How do you feel on entering the school?

Good Signs: You feel welcome and comfortable. You meet children and adults who seem cheerful and busy. You could be visiting a clubhouse or popular museum.

Bad Signs: You feel isolated and unsure. There is an unnatural quiet and absence of people. You could be visiting a hospital—or a jail.

Are visitors made welcome in the school?

Good Signs: Parents are invited to school regularly and have open invitations to drop in casually. Staff and students have a warm helpful attitude to visitors.

Bad Signs: Parents are received formally in the school—they are isolated in an outside office until they can be seen by a teacher or principal.

Are libraries and workshops generally open for student use?

Good Sign: Parent volunteers are encouraged to help out in these and other school facilities.

Bad Sign: Children only use the library during "library period."

Do teachers and parents collaborate?

Good Sign: Parents are invited to school professional days, or to hear presentations at staff meetings.

Bad Sign: School staff regard parents as outsiders.

Do teachers collaborate with each other?

Good Signs: Teachers are aware of what goes on in each other's classrooms. Your child feels a continuity from one year to another.

Bad Sign: Teachers can only refer to written records to trace your child's progress through the school.

Not all of the good signs listed here will be found even in better classrooms and schools, and bad signs, which are not always the fault of teachers, sometimes cannot be easily changed. School board regulations, union restrictions, or local conditions, for example, may severely constrain the involvement of parents and other volunteers in school activites during and outside the school day. But whatever the reason for the good and bad signs, they indicate the kind of classroom and school your child is in.

NOTES, SOURCES, AND REFERENCES

Chapter 1   Meet the R-bbit

Page 1. **Textbook sales.** Publishers make more money from selling textbooks than from any other kind of sales. Of total book publishing sales of $6 billion in 1980, $1.5 billion was accounted for by textbooks from elementary to college level, compared with $1 billion for trade books—fiction and nonfiction —purchased by the general public. Ten publishers shared 75 percent of the sales of college textbooks, with 40 percent going to the four largest publishers: Prentice Hall, McGraw-Hill, CBS Publishing Group (which includes Holt, Rinehart and Winston Educational Publishing), and Scott, Foresman. The same four publishers accounted for 32 percent of textbook sales to elementary and high schools, with another 21 percent going to the next four publishers, over 75 percent being controlled by just twenty companies. Data from: L. Coser, C. Kadushin, and W. Powell, *Books: The Culture and Commerce of Publishing* (New York: Basic Books, 1982).

Page 12. **Illiteracy.** Estimating illiteracy is technically difficult and emotionally arousing. As noted in Chapter 4, the National Commission on Excellence in Education [*A Nation at Risk: The Imperative for Educational Reform* (Washington, DC: U.S. Department of Education, 1983)] reported that 23 million U.S. adults were functionally illiterate. Educator-critic Jonathan Kozol [*Illiterate America* (Garden City, NY: Anchor/Doubleday 1985)] estimates there are 60 million illiterate adults in the United States. More cautiously, the 1985 report of the Commission on Reading notes that American students were below the international average on most tests in a fifteen-nation survey of reading performance in 1973 and were never first or second on any test. Disproportionate numbers of Americans were among the poorest readers in a 1984 comparison of students in the United States, Taiwan, and Japan. [From Richard C. Anderson, Elfrieda H. Hiebert, Judith A. Scott and Ian A.G. Wilkinson, *Becoming a Nation of Readers: The Report of the Commission on Reading* (Champaign, IL: Center for the Study of Reading, University of Illinois, 1985.)]

Chapter 2   The Learners' Clubs

Page 18. **Child language development.** A multitude of texts exists. See, for example; Moshe Anisfeld. *Language Development From Birth to Three* (Hillsdale, NJ: Erlbaum, 1984); Roger Brown, *A First Language: The Early Stages*

(Cambridge, MA: Harvard University Press, 1973); Herbert H. and Eve V. Clark, *Psychology and Language* (New York: Harcourt Brace Jovanovich, 1977).

Page 19. **Children's vocabulary growth.** See George A. Miller, *Spontaneous Apprentices: Children and Language* (New York: Seabury, 1977); Mary K. Smith, "Measurement of the Size of General English Vocabulary Through the Elementary Grades and High School," *Genetic Psychology Monographs* 24 (1941) pp. 311–345. William E. Nagy, Patricia A. Herman, and Richard C. Anderson, "Learning Words From Context," *Reading Research Quarterly* 20, 2 (1985): 233–53.

Page 22. **Chomsky-Skinner controversy.** Noam Chomsky, *Syntactic Structures* (The Hague: Mouton, 1957); B. F. Skinner, *Verbal Behavior* (New York: Appleton, 1957); Noam Chomsky, "Review of *Verbal Learning* (by B. F. Skinner)," *Language* 35, (1959): 26–58.

Page 24. George A. Miller, "Some Psychological Studies of Grammar," *American Psychologist* 17 (1962): 748–62.

Page 27. Michael A.K. Halliday, *Explorations in the Functions of Language* (London: Arnold, 1973).

Page 31. **Victoria Symposium.** Hillel Goelman, Antoinette A. Oberg, and Frank Smith (eds.), *Awakening to Literacy* (Exeter, NH: Heinemann Educational Books, 1984).

Page 33. Frank Smith, "Learning to Read by Reading," *Language Arts* 53, 3 (March 1976), 297–99.

Page 33. Glenda L. Bissex, *Gnys at Wrk: A Child Learns to Read and Write* (Cambridge, MA: Harvard University Press, 1980).

Page 37. **Literacy Club.** See Frank Smith, *Joining the Literacy Club* (Victoria, BC: Abel Press, 1984, PO Box 6162, Station C, Victoria, B.C.: Canada, V8P 5L5).

Page 37. Miller, *Spontaneous Apprentices, op. cit.*

Page 38. See Margaret Meek, *Learning to Read* (London: Bodley Head, 1982). See also Frank Smith, *Reading Without Nonsense,* 2nd ed. (New York: Teachers College Press, 1985).

Page 38. **Learning to write from authors.** See Frank Smith, "Reading Like a Writer," *Language Arts* 60, 5 (May 1983): 558–67; Frank Smith, *Writing and* *the Writer* (New York: Holt, Rinehart & Winston, 1981). More generally, see Lucy McCormick Calkins, *Lessons from a Child* (Exeter, NH: Heinemann Educational Books, 1983); Donald H. Graves and Virginia Stuart, *Write From the Start* (New York: Dutton, 1985).

Chapter 3   Why Learning Sometimes Fails

Page 43. **Prior knowledge.** See, for example, Judith W. Segal, Susan F. Chipman, and Robert Glaser, (eds.) *Thinking and Learning Skills,* 2 vols. (Hillsdale, NJ: Erlbaum, 1985); Richard C. Anderson, Rand J. Spiro, and W.E. Montague (eds.), *School and the Acquisition of Knowledge* (Hillsdale, NJ: Erlbaum, 1977).

Page 44. George Mandler, "Organization and Memory," in Kenneth W. Spence and Janet T. Spence (eds.), *The Psychology of Learning and Motivation* (New York: Academic Press, 1967).

Page 46. Benjamin S. Bloom, *Human Characteristics and School Learning* (New York: McGraw Hill, 1976).

Page 48. Margaret Mead, *Growing Up in New Guinea* (New York: Morrow, 1976).

Page 49. **IQ.** A huge literature. See, recently, Howard Gardner, *Frames of mind* (New York: Basic Books, 1983). On intelligence and success, see Christopher Jencks *et al., Inequality* (New York: Basic Books, 1972); Christopher Jencks, *Who Gets Ahead? The Determinants of Economic Success in America* (New York: Basic Books, 1979). On schools and predictions of failure, see Patrick Shannon, "Reading Instruction and Social Class," *Language Arts* 62, 6 (Oct. 1985): 604–13.

Page 50. **There are alternative points of view.** For example, Jim Saski and Jade Carter, researchers at the University of Alabama, argue that the emphasis of reading programs for mildly handicapped adolescents should change from a process of acquiring skills to a focus on comprehending what is read— "Serious questions regarding the effectiveness of continuing to teach initial reading skills to adolescents has been raised by regular and special educators alike. . . ." Jim Saski and Jade Carter. "Effective Reading Instruction for Mildly Handicapped Adolescents," *Teaching Exceptional Children* (Spring 1984, *16,* 3): 177–82.

Page 51. Richard Wanderman. Personal communication to the author.

Page 54. Carolyn Burke, "Parenting, Teaching, and Learning as a Collaborative Venture," *Language Arts* (Dec. 1985): 62, 8 836–43.

Page 55. Valerie Polakow, "Whose Stories Should We Tell? A Call to Action," *Language Arts* 62, 8 (Dec. 1985), pp. 826–835.

Page 55. Barbara Eckhoff, "How Reading Affects Children's Writing," *Language Arts* 60, 5 (May 1983): 607–16.

Page 55. Graves and Stuart, *op. cit.*

Page 56. Susan Ohanian, "When the Reading Experts Gather, What's Their Real Agenda?" *Learning* (April/May 1983): 32–38.

Page 57. Richard Feynman, "Judging Books by Their Covers," *Outlook* (Boulder, CO: Mountain View Publishing, 2929 6th St. 56 (1985): 31–43, extracted from *Surely You're Joking, Mr. Feynman!* (New York: Norton, 1985).

Page 57. Virginia Makins, "The Monday Report." *The Times Educational Supplement* (London) 2 May 1980.

Chapter 4   How Not to Create an Expert

Page 64. Nonsense learning. The nonsense syllable was devised by pioneer German experimental psychologist Hermann Ebbinghaus in the late 1870s. He had been influenced by British associationist philosophers, particularly their theory that frequency of repetition was the essential condition for establishing mental connections. The nonsense syllable was invented, "it would seem, out of nothing at all in the way of ancestry," according to historian of psychology Edwin G. Boring in his *A History of Experimental Psychology* (New York: Appleton-Century-Crofts, 1957).

Page 67. B. F. Skinner, *The Technology of Teaching* (New York: Appleton-Century-Crofts, 1968).

Page 67. Daniel Kleppner and Norman Ramsey, *Quick Calculus* (New York: Wiley, 1965).

Page 69. National Commission on Excellence in Education, *op cit.*

Page 70. Kozol, *op. cit.*

Page 71. Roger W. Shuy, "A Holistic View of Language," *Research in the Teaching of English* 15, 2 (May 1981): 101–11.

Page 71. Richard Skemp, *The Psychology of Learning Mathematics* (Baltimore: Penguin, 1972).

Page 72. Victor F. Weisskopf, "The Real Window of Vulnerability," *Outlook* 56 (1985): 25–30.

Page 74. Benjamin S. Bloom, *et al.* (eds.), *Taxonomy of Educational Objectives*, Handbook I: *Cognitive Domain* (New York: McKay, 1956).

Page 76. **Learning hierarchies.** See also Robert M. Gagné, *The Conditions of Learning* (New York: Holt, Rinehart & Winston, 1965).

Page 76. **Chicago and Mastery Learning.** E.R. Shipp, "New Theory on Reading Goes Awry," *The New York Times* (October 8, 1985). See also Bloom, *Human Characteristics and School Learning, op. cit.*

Page 77. Daniel U. Levine, *et al., Improving Student Achievement Through Mastery Learning Programs* (San Francisco: Jossey-Boss, 1985).

Page 78. **Chicago and Mastery Learning.** See p. 76 reference, above.

Chapter 5   The Nonsense Industry

Page 86. 8ational Center of Educational Research and Development, *Educational Research and Development in the United States* (Washington, DC: Department of Health, Education and Welfare, 1969).

Page 87. Thomas S. Popkewitz, *Paradigm and Ideology in Educational Research* (London: Falmer, 1984).

Page 88. **Education's moon.** James E. Allen, Jr.'s speech was reprinted in *Language Arts* 60, 1 (Jan. 1983): 100–01.

Page 89. Siegfried Engelmann and Elaine C. Bruner, *DISTAR Reading* (Teacher's Guide) (Chicago: SRA (A subsidiary of IBM), 1969). The manual tells the teacher, "Don't improvise on materials. . . . Don't introduce variations of the instructions. Don't wander off into other tasks. Don't present additional exercises. . . . And above all, don't become involved in lengthy explanations. Resist the impulse to 'tell' the children. Chances are they won't have the faintest idea what you are talking about; you will unfortunately demonstrate that you cannot be relied on to clarify, that you only confuse." The instructions also tell the teacher not to let the children see words that have not been taught in DISTAR.

Page 91. **Subskills.** For example, David LaBerge and S. Jay Samuels, "Towards a Theory of Automatic Information Processing in Reading," *Cognitive Psychology* 6 (1974): 293–323; David LaBerge and S. Jay Samuels (eds.), *Basic Processes in Reading: Perception and Comprehension* (Hillsdale, NJ: Erlbaum, 1977).

Page 93. **Phonics.** For a detailed analysis of why "phonics" doesn't work as a system for teaching reading, see Frank Smith, *Reading Without Nonsense,* Chapter 4, 2nd ed. (New York: Teachers College Press, 1985), and Frank Smith, *Understanding Reading* 3rd ed. (Hillsdale, NJ: Erlbaum, 1986), Chapter 6.

Page 94. Dr. Seuss, *The Cat in the Hat* (New York: Random House, 1957).

Page 95. **Textbook sales.** See Page 94 note, above.

Page 102. William Strong, *Sentence Combining: A Composing Book,* 2nd ed. (New York: Random House, 1981).

Page 108. Rudolf Flesch, *Why Johnny Can't Read* (New York: Harper & Row, 1955) and *Why Johnny Still Can't Read* (New York: Harper & Row, 1981).

Page 109. Caleb Gattegno, "The Problem of Reading Is Solved," *Harvard Educational Review* 40 (May 1970): 283–86.

Page 110. **Interview with Gattegno.** Maryann Marrapodi, "Reading Your Way Into Mathematics: Caleb Gattegno," *Computer Classroom News* (May/June 1982): 21–22, 72–73.

Page 110. **Interview with Martin.** Ron Brandt, "A Conversation with John Henry Martin," *Educational Leadership* (October 1981, *39,* 1): 60–64.

Page 114. **Spinnaker philosophy.** Quoted in "Small-Business Computing," *Popular Computing* (April 1985): 43.

Page 127. **Direct instruction.** See Wesley C. Becker *et al. Teaching* (2 vols.) (Chicago, IL: S.R.A., 1985).

Chapter 6   *The Tyranny of Testing*

Page 130. W. James Popham, *Modern Educational Measurement* (Englewood Cliffs, NJ: Prentice-Hall 1981)

Page 130. Graves and Stuart, *op. cit.*

Page 133. Germaine Greer, *Sex and Destiny: The Politics of Human Fertility* (New York: Harper & Row, 1984).

Page 134. Walter Karp, "Why Johnny Can't Think," *Harpers* (June 1985 270 1621,): 69–73.

Page 134. John Goodlad, *A Place Called School* (New York: Basic Books, 1984).

Page 134. Linda Darling-Hammond, cited in Beatrice Gross and Ronald Gross (eds.), *The Great School Debate: Which Way for American Education?* (New York: Simon and Schuster, 1985).

Page 135. Carlow, Personal communication.

Page 138. Fillion, Personal communication.

Page 138. Susan Ohanian, "How Today's Reading Software Can Zap Kids' Desire to Read," *Classroom Computer Learning,* (November/December 1984): 26–31.

Page 139. Richard Paul, National Assessment, and Peter Kneedley cited in Lucia Solorzano, "Think! Now Schools Are Teaching How." *U.S. News and World Report,* 14 January 1985.

Page 140. Butler, Sydney. "How Not to Test for Skills." *The B.C. Teacher* (January/February 1981): 97–111.

Page 142. Patrick Shannon, *op. cit.*

Page 146. Ann Adams cited by Shirlee Morris at 1983 International Reading Association meeting, see p. 152 note, below.

Page 152. Harry F. Walcott, *Teachers vs. Technocrats: An Educational Innovation in Anthropological Perspective* (Eugene, OR: University of Oregon Center for Educational Policy and Management, 1977).

Page 155. Kenneth Goodman, Roger Farr, and Jack Cassidy, in *Minimum Competency Standards: Three Points of View* (Newark, DE: International Reading Association, no date).

Page 156. Leo D. Leonard and Robert T. Utz, *Building Skills for Competency-Based Teaching* (New York: Harper & Row, 1974).

Page 158. Patrick Shannon, "Mastery Learning in Reading and the Control of Teachers and Students," *Language Arts* 61, 5 (Sept. 1984): 484–93.

Page 160. George F. Madeus and Vincent Greaney, "The Irish Experience in Competency Testing: Implications for American Education," *American Journal of Education* 93, 2 (Feb. 1985): 268–94.

Page 160. National Commission on Excellence in Education, *op cit.*

Page 161. Beverly Cole and James Vasquez cited in "Renegotiating Society's Contract With the Public Schools," *Carnegie Quarterly 29/30* (Fall 1984/Winter 1985): 1–6.

Page 162. Hawaii Department of Education, *Na Lono Kula* 17, 2 (Oct. 1985).

Page 162. **British Columbia.** Report in *The Times-Colonist* (Victoria, BC), 19 September 1984.

Page 164. Nanette Whitbread, "Managing Consensus in the Curriculum," *Forum* 27, 3 (Summer 1985): 68–70.

Page 165. Larry Mikulecky, "Job Literacy: The Relationship Between School Preparation and Workplace Actuality," *Reading Research Quarterly 17*, 3 (1982): 400–19.

Page 167. R. Darrell Bock, Robert Mislevy, and Charles Woodson, "The Next Stage in Educational Assessment," *Educational Researcher 11*, (March 1982): 4–15.

Page 167. **Testing conference.** Partially reported in *ETS Developments* (Princeton, NJ: Educational Testing Service, Fall 1985).

Chapter 7 *Good Teaching: The Practical Alternative*

Page 174. Jim Sullivan cited by Judith W. Solsken, "Authors of Their Own Learning," *Language Arts 62,* 5 (Sept. 1985): 491–99.

Page 175. Jeannette Veatch, *How to Teach Reading With Children's Books* (New York: Richard C. Owen, 1985).

Page 176. Shirlee Morris, presentation to 1983 International Reading Association convention, Anaheim, CA.

Page 177. **Reinhard and Domke.** Report in *The Times-Colonist* (Victoria, B.C.), 16 April 1985.

Page 177. Ann S. Bayer, "No Remedial Reading Classes," *California English* (March 1977, *13,* 2,): 16–17.

Page 178. Lucy McCormick Calkins, "When Children Want to Punctuate: Basic Skills Belong in Context," *Language Arts* 57, 5 (May 1980), 567–77.

Page 178. Moira McKenzie, "Classroom Contexts for Language and Literacy," in Angela Jagger and M. Trika Smith-Burke (eds.), *Observing the Language Learner* (Urbana, IL: National Council of Teachers of English, 1985).

Page 180. John Willinsky, "To Publish and Publish and Publish," *Language Arts* 62, 6 (Oct. 1985): 619–23.

Page 185. Rita S. Brause and John S. Mayher, "Learning Through Teaching: Language at Home and at School," *Language Arts* 62, 8 (Dec. 1985): 870–75.

Page 188. Frank Smith and Kenneth S. Goodman, "On the Psycholinguistic Method of Teaching Reading," *Elementary School Journal 71,* 4 (Jan. 1971): 171–81.

Page 189. **"Whole language."** See, for example, Orin Cochrane, Donna Cochrane, Sharen Scalena, and Ethel Buchanan, *Reading, Writing and Caring* (Winnipeg: CEL Group/New York: Richard C. Owen, 1984); Kenneth S. Goodman, *What's Whole in Whole Language?* (Portsmouth, NH: Heinemann Educational Books, 1986); Judith Newman, *Whole Language* (Portsmouth, NH: Heinemann Educational Books, 1986).

Page 189. Sharon J. Rich, "Restoring Power to Teachers: The Impact of 'whole language.' " *Language Arts 62,* (Nov. 1985): 7, 717–24.

Page 190. Cochrane *et al., op. cit.*

Page 192. Donald H. Graves, *Writing: Teachers and Children at Work* (Exeter, NH: Heinemann Educational Books, 1983).

Page 192. Mary-Ellen Giacobbe and Donald Graves cited in Anthony Brandt, "Writing Readiness," *Psychology Today* (March 1982, *16*, 3,): 55–59.

Page 193. Calkins, *Lessons from a Child, op. cit.*

Page 193. Nancie Atwell, "How We Learned to Write," *Learning* (March 1985): 51–53.

Chapter 8 The Promise and Threat of Computers

Page 206. Neil Postman, *Amusing Ourselves to Death: Public Discourse in the Age of Show Business* (Elisabeth Sifton/Viking, 1985).

Page 215. **November.** Reported in Dan Watt, "Computing in the Real World," *Popular Computing* (July 1985): 41–42.

Page 224. Stephan L. Chorover, "Cautions on Computers in Education," *BYTE* (June 1984) *9*, 6,): 223–26.

Page 226. **ELIZA.** Joseph Weizenbaum, *Computer Power and Human Reason: From Judgment to Calculation* (San Francisco: Freeman, 1979).

Page 227. Seymour Papert, *Mindstorms: Children, Computers, and Powerful Ideas* (New York: Basic Books, 1980).

Page 228. John Davy, "Mindstorms in the Lamplight," *Teachers College Record 85,* 4 (Summer 1984): 549–58.

Page 228. Robert J. Sardello, "The Technological Threat to Education," *Teachers College Record 85,* 4 (Summer 1984), pp. 631–39.

Page 229. Sally N. Standiford, Kathleen Jaycox, and Anne Auten, *Computers in the English Classroom* (Urbana, IL: National Council of Teachers of English, 1983).

Chapter 9   Protecting Children and Schools

Page 241. Victor Weisskopf, *op. cit.*

Page 242. **Cognitive dissonance.** Leon Festinger, *A Theory of Cognitive Dissonance* (Evanston, IL: Row, Peterson, 1957).

Page 250. David Winkler, "The School's View of Parents," in Cedric Cullingford (editor), *Parents, Teachers and Schools* (London: Royce, 1985).

Page 255. Adams, cited by Morris, *loc. cit.*

INDEX